Hoofprint of the Ox

"PLEASURE WAITING FOR YOU."

—CHAIN REACTION—

"CONCATENATE
THIS
HAGIOGRAPHY

TO
OBLITERATE

OBSCURITY."

A. "EXPRESS INEFFABLE."
'OR'
"THE INEFFABLE NEEDS EXPRESSION."

Hoofprint of the Ox

Principles of the Chan Buddhist Path
as Taught by a Modern Chinese Master

Master Sheng-yen
WITH **Dan Stevenson**

Q. "THE INSIGHT INTO NO-SELF AND THE EMPTINESS OF PHENOMENA THAT IS THE HALLMARK OF GENUINE "PRAJNA" (PAGE 21) is still MISSING" ?

"LIKE A RIVER WITHOUT A RAFT."

OXFORD
UNIVERSITY PRESS

NEEDS TO BE DERIVED.

OXFORD

UNIVERSITY PRESS

Oxford New York

Auckland Bangkok Buenos Aires
Cape Town Chennai Dar es Salaam Delhi Hong Kong Istanbul
Karachi Kolkata Kuala Lumpur Madrid Melbourne Mexico City
Mumbai Nairobi São Paulo Shanghai Singapore Taipei
Tokyo Toronto

and an associated company in Berlin

First published by Oxford University Press, Inc., 2001
198 Madison Avenue, New York, New York 10016
www.oup.com

First issued as an Oxford University Press paperback, 2002

Oxford is a registered trademark of Oxford University Press

Library of Congress Cataloging-in-Publication Data
Chang, Sheng-yen.
Hoofprint of the ox: principles of the Chan Buddhist path
as taught by a modern Chinese Master/
Master Sheng-yen with Dan Stevenson.
p. cm.
ISBN 0-19-513693-4 (cloth); 0-19-515248-4 (pbk.)
1. Zen Buddhism.
2. Zen meditations.
I. Title: Principles of the Chan Buddhist path
as taught by a modern Chinese Master.
II. Stevenson, Dan.
III. Title
BQ9268.3 .L825 2000
294.3'927—dc21 00-027699

1 3 5 7 9 8 6 4 2

Printed in the United States of America

Contents

Preface

DAN STEVENSON

Ven. Sheng-yen is a master in the Caodong (J. Sōtō) and Linji (J. Rinzai) lineages of the Chan (Zen) school, who for twenty-five years now has been guiding students from Taiwan, the United States, and Europe in the practice of Chan Buddhism. *Hoofprint of the Ox* provides a systematic introduction—in Sheng-yen's own words—to the principles that inform his particular style of Chan training.

When I met master Sheng-yen some years ago, I recollect hearing a story that he told about a man with a precious sword who, while riding down a river, accidentally dropped his sword overboard. He marked the spot on the gunwale from where the sword fell, and when the boat finally put in to shore far down river, he spent the rest of the day fruitlessly scouring the waters beneath the boat in search of his lost treasure. The tale, in many ways, is a fitting summation of Sheng-yen's views on Chan practice. Born during the period following the collapse of the Qing imperial system, Sheng-yen has witnessed firsthand the effects of colonial encounter with the West, the devastation of the Second World War, the Communist Revolution, and the ongoing struggle to bring forth a new and revitalized China. All of this has left an indelible imprint on both his person and his teaching. While he remains deeply rooted in his traditional monastic culture, its norms are mitigated by a keen sense of the limitation of that culture gained through his own experience with Buddhist practice and his years of instructing contemporary Chinese and Western students. Not one to mark gunwales, his teaching is unabashedly forward-looking in its selective adaptation of the past.

Of course, the very idea of a Chinese Chan master in this day and age may come as a surprise to many Western readers, if not spark outright suspicion. Prevailing views of Chan history—most of them advanced by everyone *but* the Chinese—hold that genuine Chan practice all but disappeared from China centuries ago, the victim of an irreversible "vulgarization" of Buddhism that began with the fall of the Tang Dynasty (906 C.E.). To this way of thinking, the fact that Sheng-yen's Chan differs from the way we imagine Chan to have looked a thousand years ago will just be further proof of a tradition in decline. And yet, today, Sheng-yen is arguably one of the most sought-after monks in the Chinese saṅgha, his meditation sessions drawing hundreds of applicants and his public Dharma-lectures not infrequently filling entire concert halls. Nor is he an atypical case. In the generation before him, the Chan masters Xuyun (1840–1959) and Laiguo (d. 1953) and Chan institutions such as the Jinshan, Nanhua, and Gaomin monasteries were hailed as models of Chan tradition fully equivalent to anything from the distant past. Whatever comparisons we might choose to draw with earlier periods, one could never conclude that this religious world was not vital to those who participated in it.

Like their counterparts in Japan, Korea, and Vietnam, Chinese teachers and their institutions see themselves as heirs to legacies rooted in the "golden age" of Tang Dynasty Buddhism. Like their counterparts in Japan, Korea, and Vietnam, they also debate questions of tradition and change, authenticity and falsehood, just as Chan Buddhists have always debated these questions. Where some would locate the vitality of Chan in its resistance to change—in its preservation of certain traditional forms of institution and practice—Sheng-yen and others like him find that vitality in change itself. As Sheng-yen himself is wont to remark, "If we must look for a defining feature of Chinese Chan, perhaps it is to be found in the fact that Chan in China has always changed."

As we begin, after years of understudy, to reevaluate some of our prejudgments about Buddhist culture in later China, we are once again giving events of the modern period the scrutiny that they deserve. Holmes Welch charted the course for this project in his monumental studies of the Buddhist revival that gripped China during the early twentieth century. Over the past two decades, Buddhism has seen an unprecedented surge in popularity in industrialized Taiwan.[1] In 1981 I attended public lecture series on the Buddhist sūtras that routinely drew two hundred to three hundred people a night. Today they draw thousands if not tens of thousands. Associations such as the Tz'u-chi Compassion Relief Foundation, founded by the Taiwanese nun Zhengyan, administer Buddhist hospitals and disburse funds and volunteers to assist with a host of social crises. Numerous other organizations (Sheng-yen's Dharma Drum Mountain included) sponsor everything from Buddhist seminaries to environmental projects, hold Chan and Buddha-mindfulness retreats for laity, and bring numerous teachings that were once restricted to the monastery to the public. Much of this activity can be traced to the progressive vision of clergy and laity who were active in the earlier Republican Period revival. As the testimony of a man who comes out of this legacy and who is a leading voice in the Chinese saṅgha today, master Sheng-yen's *Hoofprint of the Ox* provides a timely window on what promises to be a remarkable episode in Chinese Buddhist history.

But such documentary value not withstanding, it would be disingenuous to present *Hoofprint of the Ox* as nothing more than cultural artifact. In the final analysis, it is an unabashedly normative work—a book on Chan practice addressed to an English-speaking public with a personal interest in Buddhism. To the extent that this audience is also primarily Western, *Hoofprint* is more than a passive report of Sheng-yen's personal convictions. It situates those convictions in responsive relation to certain expectations about Chan practice current among Western students, with specific points to be made. Two problems come up as a frequent refrain of criticism in his lectures: one is the notion that Chan practices devolve within an intuitive domain that is unilaterally exclusive of words and conceptual structure; the other, the related idea that Chan practice constitutes itself independently of classical Buddhist teaching. Both are issues that have personal poignancy for Sheng-yen and many of his clerical contemporaries, especially in the retrospective light of their frustrations as young monks in mainland China. But for Westerners who, as a whole, are newcomers to Chan and Buddhism, they take on a special significance. Of this we should say a few words.

As many readers will already be aware, Chan is a Buddhist tradition that is found throughout East Asia (it is known as "Zen" in Japan, "Thiền" in Vietnam, and "Sŏn" in Korea), the distinctive form of which first took shape in China some fifteen hundred years ago. Like most schools of Mahāyāna Buddhism in East Asia, it affirms that every being is intrinsically endowed with the perfect illumination that Śākyamuni himself actualized when he became the Buddha or "enlightened one." Known as the "Buddha-nature," this power of illumination does not have to be acquired, reinstalled, or even rekindled. It is naturally so, and it has always been naturally so. Again, like most any Buddhist tradition, Chan purports to provide a "raft" to reach this "other shore" of enlightenment, a "finger" to point the direction of this "moon" of illumination. But where Chan begs to differ from other traditions is in its claim to stick one's face directly in the moon and the mud of the other shore, rather than encourage preoccupation with the raft and finger. As the saying goes, Chan "refuses to take its stance in words and written texts." It purports to be "a method that involves no-method," which foreswears reliance on discursive thought ("no-thought," *wunian*), stands "apart from doctrinal formulations," and aspires to "point directly and uncompromisingly to the original nature of the mind." The Chan master Mazu Daoyi (709–788) frequently insisted that "the everyday mind is itself the Way or Dao."[2] Linji Yixuan (d. 867) urged his students to "simply be ordinary persons, with nothing to do."[3]

This all sounds quite natural, quite appealing in its unconditional affirmation of our spiritual self-worth. For those disenchanted with the religious status quo, there even seems a promise of lost wisdom without the burdensome restraints of "organized religion." And yet, one of the first lessons learned when one begins to look at Chan is that we are *anything* but "natural." Whatever illumination we may possess by way of native endowment is distorted beyond recognition by timeless habits of craving, aversion, and deluded thinking—what Buddhists refer to as the afflictions of the three poisons. Where there is light, beings see darkness; where there is peace and joy, they experience a world of conflict and suffering, all due to the obstacles imposed by lifetimes of bad deeds (karma) and bad thinking. No matter how self-affirming the idea of Buddha-nature may seem to be at first blush, this problem of affliction does not go away. For Buddha-nature to manifest requires nothing short of a thoroughgoing revolution in the mental habits through which we process our daily lives. Such a transformation, in turn, entails direction, commitment, a lifetime of persistence and discipline, and—last but not least—structure. It is no secret that when Mazu claimed "the every day mind to be the Dao or Way" his words were directed to a monastic community whose lives were regulated by the most intensive of regimens. In the traditional Chan enclaves of China, Vietnam, Japan, and Korea, structure confronts one at every turn: one finds it in the routines of meditation, in the layout and procedures of the Chan hall, in the protocols of master and student, in the morning and evening services before the Buddha altar, in the moral precepts that one accepts as a Chan practitioner, even in the highly stylized language, imagery, literature—yes, *literature*—and in the antics of Chan-style *gong'an* (J. *kōan*) display. This is the stuff of the historical Chan path, at least as master Sheng-yen sees it. It is also the point of departure for the teachings set forth in *Hoofprint of the Ox*.

Since at least the Song Dynasty (960–1279) Buddhists throughout East Asia have been in the habit of speaking of two basic streams within Buddhist tradition, one being the *chan* legacy of "meditative insight," the other the *jiao* legacy of "doctrinal learning." (The "esoteric" or *mijiao* tradition is something else altogether.) Both claim to originate with the Buddha. When the Buddha attained supreme enlightenment, he is said to have scrutinized the capacities of sentient beings and devised the appropriate systems of doctrine and practice—the dharma—necessary to guide others to the enlightenment that he himself had realized. This body of teachings (typified by such formulas as the Four Noble Truths or the Mahāyāna ideal of the bodhisattva) was conveyed through his sermons, which were subsequently collected and codified in the form of the Buddhist sūtras. *Jiao*, or the "doctrinal" stream, upholds a concept of tradition that privileges the received word of the Buddhist sūtras as the authoritative arbiter of claims regarding the original mind and intent of the Buddha. *Chan*, by contrast, locates authoritative tradition not in the spoken word of the Buddha, but in the living wisdom of enlightenment that generated the spoken doctrine and to which that doctrine itself ultimately points.

As the term *chan* itself suggests, the latter conceit describes the position of the Chan or Zen school, while *jiao* is associated with such orders as Tiantai, Huayan, or Pure Land, all of which look centrally to the scriptural legacy. According to Chan claims, the Buddha did not confine himself to a concept of authoritative tradition construed solely in the form of his received word. He established alongside of it a second, "wordless" transmission that centered on the "mind-Dharma" of his living enlightenment. Chan holds that the "flame" of that mind-Dharma has been passed, generation to generation, down to the present day through a continuous line of enlightened Chan "patriarchs" (*zu*) or "masters" (*shi*). Known as the "mind-to-mind transmission," the enlightenment of each succeeding generation of masters is alleged to have been duly tested and "sanctioned" (C. *yinke*; J. *inka*) by the preceding one, in a line that extends directly back to the original sanction that the Buddha bestowed on his disciple Mahākāśyapa, the first Chan patriarch. By definition, a "Chan master" (*chanshi*) is one who is not *only* credited with an enlightenment akin to that of the Buddha, but who has been duly *acknowledged* as such in a formal act—indeed, a *ritualized* act—of Dharma "sanction." This "Dharma-transmission" is the core element around which Chan takes shape as tradition and institution.

Chan being largely new to the West, most of us are not only unfamiliar with its idiom, but the very fact of our attraction to it, as transparent and innocent as it might seem, is bound to be loaded with expectations and agendas that are not altogether commensurate with it. This makes the Chan student and Chan discourse in the United States much different creatures from their counterparts in China, Vietnam, Korea, and Japan. Particularly with its intuitivist emphasis on "wordless" practice and "mind-to-mind" transmission, Chan is susceptible to host of strange, unstated assumptions that might be smuggled in under the name of spiritual growth. As many American groups learned during the Chan-master meltdowns of the early 1980s, when left undisclosed and undiscussed, these assumptions can be destructive to all involved.

One concern of master Sheng-yen is the misunderstanding that arises from representations of Chan as a practice or direct experience that "does not depend on words and texts." Many years ago, when I was acting as interpreter for one of his talks in New York City, Sheng-yen chose to lecture on Chan practice and its relation to Buddhist concepts of prajñā ("liberating insight") and śūnyatā ("emptiness"), a fairly frequent topic in those days. When the time for questions came, a sharp-looking fellow stood up, stared him in the eye, and said cagily, "This is a wonderful menu. Now, where is the meal!" There was a tense silence in the room—all eyes fixed on the master. Without the slightest flinch he calmly said, "Come on a Chan retreat sometime."

The student didn't get the meal that he expected. More than likely he wasn't looking for a meal at all. Since then I have seen this kind of thing at countless talks and classes on Chan-people pounding the floor, grunting and shouting, speaking in poetic paradoxes, glaring in silence like Bodhidharma, often doing everything but saying what was really on their minds. When the topic of practice comes up, one will often hear, "Just get on with it!" or "We just do our practice here; we don't talk about it. What does Zen have to do with talk? What does

Zen have to do with thinking, or with the study of Buddhist doctrine?" True
enough, just as in the classic Buddhist formulation of the eightfold path, Chan
practice does require one to put oneself completely and unreservedly into the
method. At some point you have to stop second-guessing and just let the method
do its work. And yet, when pressed on the issue, few are able to tell you just what
this "practice" involves, let alone where it is headed, what it is going to do for
you, and how it purports to get there. When practice itself begins to produce
effects, the problem becomes even more serious. So why all these elusive antics
with Chan? Why such *dogmatic* resistance to intellect and to constative speech,
especially when the antics of "pure Chan practice" are clearly as contrived and
ideologically ramified as the most formulaic of religious doctrines?

One will find this uncompromising attitude among East Asian Buddhists as
well, as Sheng-yen's story will show. But in East Asia Chan "wordlessness" tends
to be constituted within a much more nuanced environment of institution, learning, and practice than the rhetoric of books on Chan has led us to expect. For
example, the *jiao* schools of "doctrinal learning" and the Chan school of "meditative insight" both point the way to recovery of the original Buddha-nature.
Both traditions likewise emphasize the need for committed practice and personal
enlightenment. It is a very common (and unfortunate) mistake to think that the
so-called doctrinal traditions concern themselves solely with dead-letter learning,
and that Chan is the only school that involves actual meditative practice and experience. Both traditions practice; they simply differ in their respective approaches
to practice and their ways of sanctioning religious authority.

To that extent, one also finds the two streams to be closely involved with one
another historically. Chan monasteries had libraries that contained a wide range
of Buddhist and non-Buddhist works, and the historical record shows that Chan
practitioners not only read them, but that the more illustrious masters were
extremely well versed in them. Doctrinal formulations of Tiantai and Huayan,
the major Mahāyāna sūtras and treatises, the vinaya codes, the general Buddhist
hagiographic and historical record—all routinely find their way into the sermons of Chan masters. Even the tropes of such quintessential Chan formulas
as Linji's dispositions of guest and host, the five ranks of the Caodong school,
and the ten oxherding diagrams have been shown to resonate closely with mainstream Chinese formulations of the bodhisattva path.

All things considered, Chan "mastery" is anything but an innocent chopping
of wood and carrying of water. As master Sheng-yen will often point out, for
all its emphasis on being a "wordless" teaching Chan boasts by far the largest
literary corpus of any of the Buddhist schools, the *jiao* schools included. Moreover, it is through this literature—a highly manicured genre, in its own right—
that Chan practitioners imbibe the rich color and texture of Chan enlightened
encounter. As the stuff that Chan students lecture on, pour over, meditate on,
and rehearse in the course of Chan training, this material becomes the idiom

through which the whole idea of Chan enlightenment takes shape and gets acted out as communicative norm. Transcendent experience or not, the entire project of Zen practice is embedded in webs of signification and expectation that are as routinized as any exercise in abhidharmic analysis, Tiantai exegesis, or Tibetan debate.

In Chinese Buddhist parlance—the Chan school, included—persons who either reject or are not conversant in this generalized idiom of Buddhist learning and practice are often referred to as "darkly enlightened" or "sightless ascetics," meaning that they may have some experience in the practice but that they are unequipped to assess the legitimacy of their own spiritual status, let alone guide others. Chan "wordlessness" is not a license to be indiscriminate about either meditative technique or meditative experience. It does not affirm all practice as good, or all meditative experience as positive. In fact some are downright bad; and without deference to the well-trodden ways of tradition or a genuinely competent teacher to check their every turn, the prospects of the ignorant are considered by most Chinese Buddhists to be little better than demon bait.

Another misconception commonly encountered in Western circles is the notion that there is an absolute form or essence to Chan tradition, and that a particular master or line—Chinese, Korean, Vietnamese, or Japanese—might speak authoritatively for the whole. This problem of reification—which usually amounts to promotion of one's own line—is not unrelated to the previous problem of wordlessness, in that the very idea of Chan transcendence and "wordless enlightenment" has a way of reflexively mystifying everything that it touches, whether the behavior of the master or the specific culture in which it is couched. There is perhaps no person who did more to bring Chan to the West than the Japanese Zen proselyte Daisetsu Suzuki. Suzuki wrote volumes on the Chinese masters of the "golden age" of Chan in the Tang (618–907) and Song (960–1279) Dynasties, the period when Chan tradition was introduced to Japan. However, he took a dim view of Chan in later Chinese history, arguing that it was a corrupted tradition deprived of its original form and spirit. On a cursory visit to China in 1924, Suzuki pronounced that "Japanese Zen travelers in China deplore the fact that there is no more Zen in China as it used to prevail in the Tang and Sung."[4]

Of course, these observations of change and decline are by no means wholly unjustified. Chan certainly did change after the Song Period, just as it changed in the Tang Period (618–907), the Five Dynasties Period (907–960), and the Song Period itself, and just as it varied from lineage to lineage or region to region! Like religions everywhere, including Suzuki's own post–Meiji brand of Rinzai Zen, Chan in China has by no means escaped the ravages of social and political turmoil, as the impact of such recent events as the Taiping uprising of the mid-1800s, the Republican Revolution of 1912, and the Cultural Revolution of the

1960s will eloquently testify. Their monastic economies and traditions disrupted, and faced (like Chinese everywhere) with the pressures of colonial incursion and modernity, Buddhists of this period were thrown headlong into change. Looking for Tang Dynasty Chan under these circumstances would be ludicrous, indeed. Then again, Suzuki never visited such exemplary centers of Chan training as the Jinshan and Gaomin monasteries. Nor did he meet the likes of Xuyun and Laiguo.[5] Neither did Suzuki acknowledge the existence of Sŏn in Korea or Thiên in Vietnam; nor did he mention the Sōtō school in Japan, of whose teaching he is known to have been particularly disapproving. Even if he had, they likely would not have measured up to his particular post-Hakuin brand of Rinzai Zen (itself a creation of the eighteenth century).

But bashing Suzuki for his biases is not very fair, for he is by no means the only one to make such representations. Koreans gripe when Chinese don't jump to their overtures of "dharma combat"; Japanese gripe about Koreans and Vietnamese who stray from their vision of the original Zen. Chinese, Vietnamese, and Koreans, alike, grumble about the rigid formalism of the Japanese Zen robots. In point of fact, this kind of thing has been going on in Buddhist/Chan history for centuries. During the Tang Period, partisans of the Southern School of Chan dismissed the Northern School as gradualists. Chan master Linji Yixuan, founder of the Rinzai line, ridiculed phony Chan masters who put on airs and clung to "the worthless contrivances of old."[6] Then we have the American Channists, the newcomers on the block. If they aren't simply aping or trumpeting the magnificence of their teachers and lineage, then as the self-appointed engineers of Chan history, they are ready to shed the Chan "essence" of its cultural encrustations and make it fit for the new millennium. I remember reading several years ago about an American Zen teacher who ventured that, as moderns who understood historical processes and lived in an era of enhanced communication, American practitioners could engineer an authentically "American" Buddhism without the centuries of adaptation that Buddhism required to reach "maturity" in China. Chan "wordlessness" meets American industry!

How do these considerations affect *Hoofprint of the Ox?* To begin with, *Hoofprint of the Ox* talks openly and systematically about Chan practice. As Sheng-yen would see it, this kind of disclosure has little likelihood of obstructing Chan practice, since most of us are so thoroughly text-bound to begin with, even in our dogmatic Chan silence. Better yet, it may offer direction to persons who otherwise have no idea where their practice is taking them. At the same time, the teachings set forth in this book are the particular construct of a particular Chinese Chan master, forged at the unique juncture of teacher, student, and received tradition. Their "finger" may, after all, point to ineffable mysteries that transcend time and place, but as a system of instruction conceived in dialogue with historical circumstance, it has no illusions about its own temporality. Its representations do not intend to speak universally for Chan through all of Chan history and in all of its local forms. They hope merely to prove a useful primer to persons with an interest in Chan today.

꒕ The title, *Hoofprint of the Ox*, is taken from the Ten Oxherding Pictures, the well-known set of diagrams that have been used by Buddhists in East Asia since at least the twelfth century to chart progress on the Chan path. The oxherd can be said to represent the Chan practitioner—the subjective entity who sets out to tame the defiled mind and appropriate the Buddha-nature through Chan practice. The ox represents the mind that is the object of cultivation. On the one hand this mind may be taken to mean the enlightened mind of Buddha-nature itself. But since the character of the ox changes over the course of the diagrams— eventually disappearing from the diagrams altogether, along with the oxherd—it is more appropriate to regard the ox as the objectification of mind and Buddha-nature that informs different stages of Chan practice. To this extent it could also be read as the defiled mind of the vexations, which the practitioner simultaneously identifies and transforms in the course of Chan practice.

In the opening frames of the oxherding diagrams, the oxherder sets out to locate and harness the ox to serve as his or her vehicle on the Chan path. The first real taste of Chan comes when oxherd glimpses this "ox" of Buddha-nature for the first time *(jianxing;* J. *kenshō).* At this juncture, the practitioner acquires firsthand experience of the relationship between the awakened and defiled mind, and along with it comes the right view and right mindfulness that are the true foundation for the Chan path. Prior to that point, spiritual direction is unclear, and Chan practice itself is tenuous, leaving the oxherd to stumble along with only the confusing prints of the ox's hooves as the guide. What are the hoof-prints? The hoofprints of the ox are the teachings of received text and oral tradition that initially set the Chan student on his or her way. They are the "traces" of generations of Chan practice, but not the living experience that produced. They are the track, but not the ox; the finger that points to the moon, but not the moon itself. They are not the marrow of Chan if by "marrow" we mean the sort of profound transformation of body and mind that can only come through sustained Chan practice. But without explanation in a language that we can understand, no one would ever know of this "marrow" of Chan, much less think to seek it. So the hoofprints are the special words that give Chan wordlessness its special space. The Chan patriarch Bodhidharma begins his famous sixth-century treatise on the *Two Entrances and Four Practices* with the words, "Entrance by [knowledge of noumenal] principle *(li)* means to awaken to the cardinal import of our school by relying on the received teachings *(jiao)*."[7] A millennium and a half later, *Hoofprint* purports to follow its example.

꒕ With the exception of this preface and the biography of master Sheng-yen that follows in the Introduction, the contents of this book originate from teachings that Sheng-yen personally devised and delivered on behalf of his Chan students. The majority of its chapters are taken from classes on meditation, retreat talks, and lecture series for senior students held at the Chan Meditation Center in New York during the late 1970s and 1980s, their contents transcribed from recordings and reworked for clarity and smoothness. Some chapters are the product of a single lecture. Other chapters, such as the sections on *huatou* ("critical phrase") and silent illumination practice or the chapter on the Ten Oxherding Pictures, have been assembled from multiple presentations. Occasionally materials have been adapted from essays that were published by Sheng-yen in Chinese.[8] Clearly, *Hoofprint of the Ox* does not take its stance in the studied orality of the Chan *yulu* or "recorded sayings" genre. It is a systematically crafted work, the selection of its materials and their arrangement into chapters having been guided by the desire to illumine a specific, overarching scheme of the Chan path and practice.

The principles of that scheme were first sketched out by Sheng-yen in his aforementioned *Chan de tiyan* (Experiencing the Heart of Chan), published in Taiwan in 1980. However, by then the rubric had already been applied in meditation classes and Chan retreats for several years. The two decades that follow have seen various shifts in emphasis and approach, but the overall principles and structure of practice have remained largely unchanged. Thus, one could say that *Hoofprint of the Ox* describes on paper a scheme of practice that has served as a core curriculum in Sheng-yen's Chan centers for well over two decades now. The logic of that structure, as reflected in the chapters of *Hoofprint of the Ox*, can be summarized as follows.

Apart from the Preface and Introduction ("A Vow for the Times"), *Hoofprint of the Ox* comprises eleven chapters, which are in turn divided into three major parts. Chapter One, entitled "Chan and 'Emptiness,'" sets Chan aspirations in relation to the cardinal Buddhist teaching of insight (prajñā) into the emptiness or groundlessness (śūnyatā) of mind and objects—the enlightening wisdom that liberates one from affliction and manifests the intrinsic condition of Buddhanature. Chapter Two, on "Meditation and the Principles for Training Body and Mind," discusses the rudiments of bodily posture and meditative concentration that enable liberative insight to be developed properly and safely. As the first of the book's three major parts, Chapters One and Two provide a synoptic orientation to the path that finds application in the specific techniques of the chapters that follow.

Part Two comprises chapters on the traditional Buddhist path of the Three Disciplines: precepts, samādhi, and wisdom (Chapters Three through Five). It outlines classic Indian Buddhist procedures (as described in the sūtras and commentaries) for developing meditative calm (S. *śamatha;* C. *zhi*) and contemplation (S. *vipaśyanā;* C. *guan*), the "two wings of the bird" that, together, enable the practitioner to arouse and deepen liberative insight. Referred to by Chinese Buddhists as the "graduated" approach to practice, this path proceeds sequentially—and to some measure, recurrently—through three phases of emphasis.

It begins with (1) cultivation of moral purity (*sila*), which is achieved through internalization of the Buddhist renunciatory precepts. It then proceeds to (2) develop meditative tranquillity (samādhi) through the practice of one or more of the Five Methods for Stilling or Calming the Mind, and concludes with the development of (3) enlightening insight (prajñā) through cultivation of the Four Stations of Mindfulness. Established on a firm foundation of moral restraint, the techniques of meditative calming and contemplation work in concert with one another to extricate the deep-seated roots of craving, hatred, and delusion that keep beings bound to the wheel of suffering.

Part Three, which consists of Chapters Six through Eleven, shifts the focus from the "graduated" schemes of the classical Buddhist path to the "sudden" and "unmediated" approach of the Chan or Zen path. It may also justifiably be called the heart of the book. Why, then, is it preceded by such a lengthy discussion of the "graduated" system of the three disciplines? Chan may rhetorically promote itself as "the method of no-method," but when push comes to shove this language has always been grounded within the highly structured regimen of the Chan monastery and meditation hall, the routines of which in many ways embody the classic principles of moral purity, samādhi, and wisdom or insight. Without this context there simply is no effective Chan practice. Where the Chan approach differs from the more classical forms of practice is in its realigning of priorities. Rather than set up the three disciplines as discrete "step-like" procedures, Chan puts the last step first, uncompromisingly pressing the practitioner to the wall of emptiness and insight right from the start. Wisdom remains the absolute priority at all times.

In keeping with this shift in orientation, Part Three opens with an introductory overview of "Chan and the Sudden Path to Enlightenment" (Chapter Six) and follows with the two chapters on "The Use of *Gong'an* and *Huatou*" (Chapter Seven) and "The Practice of 'Silent Illumination'" (Chapter Eight). The latter two chapters, together, describe the heart of Chan meditative technique as taught by master Sheng-yen. The more generalized setting of Chan practice—the contextual restraints and routines that are the equivalent of the first or first and second members of the three disciplines—is outlined in Chapter Nine, on "Prerequisites for Chan Practice." The two final chapters on "What It Means to be a Chan Master" (Chapter Ten) and "The Ten Oxherding Pictures" (Chapter Eleven) bring matters to a close by taking up the question of Chan "enlightenment" and the related role of the "Chan master" and "transmission of the Chan dharma."

Acknowledgments

As a product of the interaction between master Sheng-yen and his students, every person who has taken part in the presentation of these teachings has, in some form, contributed to this book. Without the tireless efforts of those who created and administered his Chan Meditation Center, neither Sheng-yen's instruction nor this book would have come to be. But the transformation from lecture to book is an involved process that calls for special acknowledgments. Master Sheng-yen and Ven. Guo-gu provided indispensable "encouragement" to forge ahead at times when circumstances gave me every reason to set things aside. Ernest Heau has made a substantial contribution through his insightful review of successive drafts; and without the careful copy-editing and prompting of Chris Marano, *Hoofprint* would be far less polished than it is at present. To them all, master Sheng-yen and I both owe heartfelt gratitude.

Of course, special thanks must go to those who served as interpreters for master Sheng-yen's lectures, among whom Wang Ming-yee has by far shouldered the greatest burden. Ming-yee was there from the very beginning, struggling with the peculiarities and densities of Buddhist vocabulary when Sheng-yen first started teaching at the Temple of Enlightenment in 1976. Until recently, he served as interpreter at most of the weekly lectures, interviews, and Chan retreats. The impeccability of his English translation notwithstanding, Ming-yee was himself a spectacle to behold. For Sheng-yen could lecture non-stop for a full ten minutes, and Ming-yee, like Ānanda himself, would give a perfect rendering from memory, without missing a beat. It is to his tireless and humble commitment that this book is dedicated.

Introduction to Master Sheng-yen

A Vow for the Times: Sheng-yen and His Mission to "Realize Human Potential" Through "Conjoined Pursuit of Learning and Practice"

DAN STEVENSON

> The Buddhist teachings are very diverse and befitting to all. Those who are unable to integrate them and organize them systematically will make the mistake of seizing on only parts of them. In so doing, they will lose or abandon the whole. This style of practice has brought Buddhism to its present narrowness and poverty.
> —Ven. Yinshun, *Chengfo zhi dao* (The Way to Buddhahood)

Chan master Sheng-yen (Shengyan, according to Pinyin romanization) is an expatriate monk from mainland China who has been teaching in Taiwan and the United States for over two decades now. To Buddhists of the Chinese diaspora he needs no introduction. He is author of numerous academic and popular works that are read widely by Chinese Buddhists; his Dharma Drum Mountain is one of the three largest Buddhist organizations in Taiwan; and he is a regular guest of communities in Singapore, Malaysia, and Hong Kong—and, more recently, mainland China—who are bent on seeking his guidance as a Chan master and Buddhist scholar. In Western countries he is less well known, partly for his lack of exposure but more likely for the misguided assumption in American and European circles that Zen (or "Chan" as it is properly known to Chinese) disappeared from China ages ago.

By his own admission, master Sheng-yen and his teaching are very much the product of his era, an era that he characterizes as one of tremendous challenge and tremendous need for change. Much of the inspiration for his own values he attributes to the legacy of such progressive clergy as Taixu (1890–1947) and his disciple Yinshun. However, more conservative figures such as the Chan masters Xuyun (d. 1950) and Laiguo, the Vinaya master Hongyi (1880–1942), the Pure Land reformer Yinguang, and the Tiantai masters Dixian (1857–1931) and Tanxu (1875–1963) have been equally influential. All of them were, in one way or another, renowned for their commitment to the revitalization of the modern saṅgha.[1]

Caught in the transition between two worlds, religious innovation did not come to these individuals as a casual desire for change. It came as brutal necessity, forced on them by a world turned upside down by colonial incursion, modern technology, war, and revolution. The tumultuous changes that took place in China between the collapse of the old Qing Dynasty imperial order in 1911 and the communist revolution of 1949 were simultaneously foreboding and exhilarating. On the one hand there was the fear of losing all that was familiar. The profound social and economic upheaval that came with these events shattered the equilibrium to which the Buddhist saṅgha had been accustomed. Shorn of their traditional bases of support, monastic institutions were hard pressed to seek out new means to maintain their facilities, let alone return the tradition to any semblance of its former prosperity. On the other hand time and modernization beckoned the more progressive Buddhists with the prospect that one might create the world anew, that a Buddhist tradition shackled by centuries of feudalistic oppression might realize its true potential in a new and shining age.

As with many Chinese Buddhists of his generation, Sheng-yen speaks frequently of the importance of having a "vow" or "mission" (yuan) in life. Along with its more traditional connotations as the bodhisattva "vow of compassion," the word "vow" carries for Sheng-yen a socially proactive sense. The world is not simply to be accommodated as a place to work out one's salvation, but, in the hope of a brighter future for all—in the hope of forging a "pure land among humankind"—Buddhists must actively reach out and shape the world around them. Sheng-yen's discovery and pursuit of that "vow" is the subject of the pages that follow.[2] As he himself would insist, it is not a tale that centers on him alone. It arises from a larger sense of historical destiny thrust on him by China's wrenching entry into the modern era; but it takes its specific shape from a multitude of persons who intersected with Sheng-yen's life and exerted a model influence on his outlook. To that extent, it is a testimony to a collective spirit of renewal that, in the wake of the tumultuous events of the first half of the twentiethcentury, has sparked a remarkable resurgence of Buddhism in contemporary Chinese communities.

Sheng-yen was born in 1930, the youngest of six children in a family of impoverished farmers who eked out a living in the countryside outside Shanghai. Repeated flooding of the Yangzi River and a lack of funds to rent land to

"IDEAL SENTIMENT."

farm sent most of the older family members off in search of work as laborers. Plagued by ill health and too young to be on his own, Sheng-yen remained at home with his mother. Periodically he was enrolled in a local grammar school, but circumstances being difficult, his education was sporadic and brought him only as far as the fourth grade. When he was age 13, the family chanced to learn of an abbot from Guangjiao Monastery on nearby Mount Lang who was looking for a tonsure disciple. By mutual consent of Sheng-yen and his parents, Sheng-yen accepted the offer and was enrolled as a postulate at Langshan. His mentor, the monk Langhui, had once studied at the Jiang'nan Buddhist Academy on Mount Jiuhua in Anhui, which meant that he tended to be more forward-looking than some of the other monks at Langshan. But even then, Sheng-yen remembers his Langshan training as a fairly traditional one, with little attention given to education in Buddhist doctrine and practice beyond the usual emphasis on practical routines and memorization of litanies used in Buddhist services. (The popular breviary known as *Chanmen risong* [Daily Recitations for Chan Monks] was the main text of focus.) KARMA.

The latter proved especially difficult for Sheng-yen to master. No matter how he tried, he could not retain its contents. Disconcerted by Sheng-yen's lack of progress, Langhui concluded that his karmic obstacles were heavy and that he should undertake special prostrations to Bodhisattva Guanyin in order to alleviate them. Since most of the day was taken up with his regular duties, Sheng-yen set time aside to perform five hundred prostrations to Guanyin before the other monks arose in the morning and after they went to sleep at night. For half a year he kept up this practice. Then, one day while bowing, he felt a soothing elixir pour down from the heavens and suffuse through his body. "I was overcome with a very refreshing and comfortable feeling," he relates in *Getting the Buddha Mind*, "as if the whole world had changed. My mind became very clear and very bright. Memorization was no longer a problem, and I began to learn very quickly. To this day I believe that Guanyin gave me assistance. Most important, there arose in me a deep sense of responsibility towards the Dharma."[3] The experience also fostered a personal faith in Guanyin that would later play an important role at various junctures in Sheng-yen's life, from his quest for sponsors to support his six years of solitary retreat in Taiwan, to difficulties he faced during his studies in Japan and his recent founding of Dharma Drum Mountain outside Taipei. To persons faced with crisis he often commends the efficacy *(ling)* of calling on Bodhisattva Guanyin.[4]

In 1946, following the end of hostilities with Japan, Guangjiao Monastery dispatched Sheng-yen and several other young novices to their subtemple in Shanghai (Dasheng Monastery) for the purpose of raising money from funeral ceremonies *(foshi)*. For the better part of the next two years, the 16-year-old Sheng-yen was contracted out day after day to do *jingchan* or "rites of repentance and scriptural recitation" for paying laity. Usually this involved performance of the colorful Ceremony for Release of the Flaming Mouth Hungry Ghost *(fang*

NATURE'S MAGIC.

yenkou). In his autobiography, *Guicheng* (The Return), Sheng-yen recalls this period with special bitterness. He had already been a Buddhist novice for several years, but his family was too poor to afford the Buddhist robes that Langshan required them to supply at the time of his novitiate ordination. As a result, Sheng-yen continued to wear his tattered lay-clothing, over which he would put the ceremonial red-patched robes. Day after day, from morning to night, the young monks of Dasheng Monastery were dispatched to do funeral services at the homes of laity. Often they would be forced to run back and forth between as many as two or three different performances that were taking place concurrently at different locations. They were never taught the meaning of the litanies that they chanted; and there was no time for any other form of study or practice. In the meantime, money came into the temple as remuneration for its work, but no one bothered to think of providing monks such as Sheng-yen with suitable robes and equipment. To this day, he regards this kind of *foshi* or "Buddhist rite for the dead" as one of the most despicable degradations of the Buddhist monastic ideal and forbids his monasteries in Taiwan to engage in it as a means of financial support.[5]

The same year that Sheng-yen took up residence at Dasheng Monastery, students of Taixu founded a new Buddhist academy at Jing'an Monastery in Shanghai. Through the auspices of a former Langshan monk who was an instructor there, Sheng-yen was allowed to take the entrance test and enroll as a regular student. The curriculum at the seminary was deliberately eclectic—modeled on the nonsectarian vision of Taixu, who in turn looked for inspiration to the Ming Dynasty master Ouyi Zhixu (1599–1655). Most of the lecturers were in one way or another connected with Taixu personally, including the Vens. Nanting, Daoyuan, and Renjun. (Renjun later ended up at the Temple of Enlightenment in the Bronx, where Sheng-yen first took up residence when he came to the United States in 1975.) Although life there was very hard and the education had its faults, Sheng-yen remembers the students being greatly encouraged by their exposure to Buddhist history and the teachings of Huayan, Tiantai, Consciousness Only (S. Vijñānavāda), Madhyamaka, Pure Land, Vinaya, and Chan. It was truly something that many of them had never encountered before.

Practice was also an important part of the Jing'an curriculum; and along with seated meditation, rites of repentance (*chanhui*) were a major component. However, the ritual performances at Jing'an Monastery were different from those at Dasheng Monastery. For in the spirit of Taixu's reformist vision, this time they were done with an emphasis on self-cultivation rather than contractual service to donors or the dead. Still, the training proved for Sheng-yen to be less than ideal. In *Getting the Buddha Mind* he recalls:

> We meditated, but did not have a very clear idea of the correct method of practice. Thus it was difficult to gain any real strength from it. We supposed

that it would take years to achieve benefits. I recalled that even Śākyamuni Buddha practiced for six years. I also recalled that master Hsü-yün [Xuyun], who left home at the age of twenty, was still practicing at fifty, although the world had not yet heard of him.

People who had deep meditation experiences, or who had been certified as enlightened, never explained their experience. When they talked among themselves, their language was strange, and its meaning elusive. There were a few older students who had spent several years in meditation halls. When I asked them about practice they would say, "Oh, it's easy. Just sit there. Once your legs stop hurting it's fine." Sometimes a monk would be given a *kung-an* (J. *kōan*) on which to meditate, but on the whole there was no systematic meditation training.

Once at the seminary I participated in a Chan retreat. I would just sit in meditation until I heard the incense board signalling walking meditation. No one told me what to do or gave me any instruction. We had a saying that one had to sit until "the bottom falls out of the barrel of pitch." Only then could he get to see the master.

Sometimes while sitting, I thought, "What should I be doing? Should I be reciting the Buddha's name? Should I be doing something else? What really is meditation?" I kept asking myself these questions until I became a big ball of doubt. However, while at the seminary my doubts never got resolved.[6]

With the impending communist takeover of China in 1949, the Buddhist saṅgha in Shanghai fell into disarray. Prominent clergy who had the proper connections fled to Taiwan (many of them to escape communist reprisals), while the elderly and the younger monks were left to fend for themselves. At that time recruitment posters for a new army on Taiwan began to appear in Shanghai, and at the urging of senior monks Sheng-yen and many of comrades renounced their clerical status and enlisted. That spring Sheng-yen arrived in Taiwan. For the next ten years, until 1960, he served in the military, where he gradually worked his way up through the ranks, acquiring additional education along the way.

Throughout his years of military service, Buddhism remained constantly on Sheng-yen's mind. He kept in touch with many of his monastic colleagues and mentors, and he frequently contributed articles to Buddhist magazines. He also found himself increasingly preoccupied with questions of Buddhist doctrine and practice, as well as a nostalgia for the monastic life. Looking back on his state of mind of that period, he describes himself as an exceedingly troubled or "problem person":

My doubts, still unresolved, caused all kinds of questions to come up. There were many contradictions in the Buddhist teachings that I could not resolve. This was very disturbing, since I had deep faith in the Buddha's teachings and believed that the sūtras could not be wrong. I was burdened by such questions as "What is enlightenment?" "What is Buddhahood?" Questions like these were very numerous in my mind, and I desperately needed to know the answers.

The underlying doubt was always there. When I was working it would disappear, but when I practiced, this suffocating doubt would often return. This situation persisted for years, until I was twenty-eight, when I met my first real master.[7]

A key turning point came in 1958, when Sheng-yen chanced to meet Chan master Lingyuan (1902–88), a dharma-heir of the renowned Xuyun (1840–1959). Himself a most enigmatic and imposing man, Lingyuan was visiting the Fojiao tang in Gaoxiong when Sheng-yen paid a call there. That evening they were assigned to share the same sleeping platform. As Sheng-yen (still a layman) prepared himself for bed, Lingyuan "thrust out his great belly" and seated himself in meditation. Resolved that he, too, should meditate rather than sleep, Sheng-yen sat down next to him. His mind was seething with questions. Master Sheng-yen describes the event as follows:

> I was still burdened with my questions and desperate to have them settled. He seemed to be quite at ease, with no problems in the world, so I decided to approach him.
>
> He listened patiently as I spoke of my many doubts and problems. In reply he would ask, "Anymore?" I continued like this for two or three hours, but he never answered any of my questions. He just said, "Anymore? Anything else?" I was extremely agitated and anxious for answers. Suddenly, with a sigh, he struck the wooden edge of the platform loudly with his hand and said, "So many questions! Drop it and let's go to sleep!"
>
> These words struck me like lightning. My body poured sweat; I felt like I had been instantly cured of a bad cold. I felt a great weight being suddenly lifted from me. It was a very comfortable and soothing feeling. We just sat there, not speaking a word. I was extremely happy. It was one of the most pleasant nights of my life. The next day I continued to experience great happiness. The whole world was fresh, as though I was seeing it for the first time.
>
> At this time I realized two important points necessary for practice. The first has to do with causes and conditions. Certain things not entirely under your control—your karma, the karma of others, environmental factors—must come together in a way that favors making progress in this lifetime. To make great progress in practice you must have this karmic affinity—the proper conditions must exist.
>
> Second, one must have effective methods of practicing under the guidance of a qualified master. From the time I left home I spent fifteen years in my practice. I thought this was much too long. In the past when I asked my teachers for guidance, they would just say, "Work hard. What else is there to talk about?" But now I realized that there were two requirements—working hard on a good method and having a good master.[8]

Master Sheng-yen's encounter with Lingyuan precipitated a final decision to return to the monastic life. Sheng-yen kept in touch with Lingyuan and later received transmission of the Linji dharma from him. However, that same year he met the monk who would become his main teacher—Chan master Dongchu (1907–77) from the Wenhuaguan and Nongchan Monastery in Beitou. During the New Year of 1959 and 1960, Dongchu gave Sheng-yen the ten novitiate precepts, and the following year sent him to be reordained as a full monk at the national ordination sponsored annually by the Buddhist Association of the Republic of China.

By all accounts, Dongchu himself was a most remarkable man. He was a student of Taixu, as well as dharma-heir in both the Caodong and Linji lines of Chan through transmission from master Zhiguang (1889–1963), the former abbot of Dinghui Monastery at Jiaoshan in Kiangsu province. Zhiguang himself had studied at the Jetavana academy of Yang Wenhui, a former teacher of Taixu. Thus, along with a traditional Chan training, Dongchu was thoroughly steeped in the spirit of Buddhist reform.[9] However, at the time when Sheng-yen first met him, he was attracted by Dongchu's unusual bearing and manner of speaking. He knew little about his personal background.

When Dongchu passed away in Taiwan in December of 1977, Sheng-yen was living at the Temple of the Enlightenment in the Bronx. I remember quite well the unusual events that he reported about the night of Dongchu's passing. As part of his daily routine, master Sheng-yen often sat in meditation for several hours before going to sleep. That evening he found himself unable to settle his mind. Over and over he kept returning to thoughts of the Chan lineage. The urge was so strong that, the next morning, he went to the library to search out the more hazy links in the later Caodong transmission. Not long thereafter a call arrived from the monastery in Taiwan, informing him that Dongchu was gone. Master Sheng-yen felt certain that his unusual turn of mind was due to Dongchu's influence. Several years later, when I was living at Dongchu's Nongchan Monastery outside Taipei, I chanced to get the other side of the story from the old nuns there. On the evening that he died, Dongchu bathed, asked for a clean robe, and informed the nuns not to bother to prepare his breakfast. The next morning they found him seated upright in meditation posture, expired—just as we find in medieval Buddhist hagiography!

By all accounts, master Sheng-yen's two years of personal training under Dongchu were deeply formative, but also severe. When recalling the treatment he received from Dongchu, the nuns at Wenhuaguan and Nongchan Monastery could only shudder, shake their heads, and say, "painful, just too painful!" Sheng-yen relates:

> My stay with him turned out to be one of the most difficult periods of my life. He constantly harassed me. It reminded me of the treatment that Milarepa received from his guru Marpa. For example, after telling me to move my things into one room, he would later tell me to move to another room. Then he would tell me to move back again. Once he told me to seal off a door and to open a new one in another wall. I had to haul the bricks from a

distant kiln up to the monastery. We normally used a gas stove, but my master often sent me to gather a special kind of firewood that he liked to brew his tea over. I would constantly be scolded for cutting the wood too small or too large. I had many experiences of this kind.

In my practice it was much the same. When I asked him how to practice he would tell me to meditate. But after a few days he would quote a famous master, saying, "You can't make a mirror by polishing a brick, and you can't become a Buddha by sitting." So he ordered me to do prostrations. Then, after several days, he would say, "This is nothing but a dog eating shit off the ground. Read the sūtras!" After I read for a couple of weeks, he would scold me again, saying that the patriarchs thought the sūtras food only for cleaning sores. He would say, "You're smart. Write an essay!" When I showed him the essay he would tear it up, saying, "These are all stolen ideas." Then he would challenge me to use my own wisdom and say original things.

When I lived with him he forbade me to keep a blanket, because monks were supposed to meditate at night. When tired, we could nap, but we were not to rely on the comfort of a bed or blanket. All of these arbitrary things were his way of training me. Whatever I did was wrong, even if he had just told me to do it. Although it is hard to think of this treatment as compassionate, it really was. If I hadn't been trained with this kind of discipline, I would not have accomplished much. I also realized from him that learning the Buddha Dharma was a very rigorous activity, and that one should be self-reliant in practice.

After two years with Dongchu, I went into solitary retreat in the mountains. When I left I told him that I vowed to practice hard and not fail the Dharma. He answered, "Wrong! What is Buddhism? What is Dharma? The most important thing is not to fail yourself!"

Once master Dongchu told me, "The relationship of a master and disciple is like that of father and son, like teacher and student, but it is also a friendship. The master may guide, criticize, and correct, but the disciple must be responsible for his own practice. The master cannot worry over the disciple like a mother. The master just leads the disciple onto the path. The disciple must walk the path himself."

Finally Dongchu told me that a practitioner must emphasize both wisdom and merit. Practicing alone one can cultivate wisdom and samādhi, but he must remember there are sentient beings needing the nourishment of the Buddha Dharma. He said, "Control yourself. When you can control yourself, you can freely harmonize with the multitudes."[10]

Having completed his tutelage and received dharma-transmission from Dongchu, Sheng-yen began to lay plans for entering solitary retreat in order to deepen his practice. On an earlier occasion, shortly after he was reordained in 1961, he spent some time at Chaoyuan Monastery near Gaoxiong. He found the setting to be most beautiful. Moreover, while in residence there he had a second major experience that left the place printed indelibly in his memory.

As part of their daily routine, the clergy at Chaoyuan Monastery would perform the extended Amitābhā repentance in the morning and the repentance of
Great Compassion (Guanyin's *Dabei chan*) in the afternoon. At night they sat in
meditation. Sheng-yen found the regimen to be very conducive to settling his
body and mind. Menial chores were also a standard part of the daily program,
and at one point Sheng-yen—who has never been physically robust—was
ordered to unpack and move the contents of ten huge crates of books to a sec-
ond-floor library. As he carted the books, case by case, up the stairs, the question "Who is moving these books?" spontaneously arose in his mind. Suddenly
the person moving the books seemed to vanish, with the self that generated the
question disappearing too. When Sheng-yen came to several hours later the
books were on their shelves—all arranged in perfect order.

For entering solitary meditation *(biguan)*, the mountains around Chaoyuan
Monastery seemed the perfect site. The scenery was strikingly beautiful, but the
spot was difficult to reach, so that visitors were infrequent and the surroundings, tranquil. However, being a new ordinand, Sheng-yen lacked the lay support
to build the requisite hut and provide for his needs. Daily he performed
Guanyin's repentance rite of Great Compassion and recited the bodhisattva's
name. Before long one of Zhiguang's lay followers came forward, and with the
additional support of masters Wuyi and Haolin, the necessary arrangements
were quickly realized.

In 1963, at the age of 34, Sheng-yen entered the first of two three-year sessions of solitary retreat. He began the first retreat with an emphasis on ritual
repentance—a practice that he characterizes as "airing the dirty laundry." Upon
arising, he performed the *Dabei chan* or "repentance of Great Compassion."
Through the morning hours he did prostrations. In the afternoon, he set aside
two hours to read through the Buddhist canon, beginning with the *Āgama* sūtras
(a decision he made on the basis of master Yinshun's example). For the remaining hours he returned to the practice of ritual repentance (i.e., the Amitābhā
repentance). At night he sat in meditation. He explained the logic of this program to us some years later. Under the intense pressures of retreat practice, even
the most innocuous aberrance in outlook and motivation can have disastrous
effects. If a person plunges into extended meditation without proper purification
of one's vows and a secure foundation in the moral precepts, obstacles are sure to
arise. Rather than enlightenment, the result is likely to be illness, insanity, and
even death. (Tales to this effect abound among Chinese monks and nuns.)
Sheng-yen describes his life in retreat as follows:

> The first half year of my retreat, I emphasized repentance and prostrations
> in order to undo my heavy karma. First I prostrated through the *Lotus Sūtra;*
> later through the *Avatamsaka Sūtra.* After reading each character, I would recite
> a phrase and then prostrate. For the Lotus the phrase was *"Na-mo fa-hua hui-
> shang fo p'u-sa"* ("Homage to the Buddhas and Bodhisattvas of the Lotus

Assembly"); for the *Avataṃsaka* it was *"Na-mo hua-yen hai-hui fo p'u-sa"* ("Homage
to the Buddhas and Bodhisattvas of the Ocean-like Wisdom of the
Avataṃsaka"). This I did through the whole sūtra. After prostrating for five
hours I would meditate. On other occasions I practiced reciting Amitābhā
Buddha's name.

From the time I started the retreat my mind was very calm and settled,
never restless. I felt very happy, as though having come home. I ate only one
meal a day of leaves from wild potatoes, which I planted myself. I lived in a
hut with a yard. There were walls behind, but the front looked out over a cliff.
Even though I always remained in the courtyard, I never had a feeling of being
closed in.

Eventually I began to prostrate less, spending more time meditating and
reading the sūtras. I also wrote a lot. The six years passed very quickly; I had
little sense of time.[11]

Sheng-yen describes the method that he used during seated meditation as being
quite different from the techniques found in canonical treatises on meditation.
He practiced neither thematic discernment *(guan)* of the mind and body, investigation of Chan sayings *(canchan)*, nor mindful visualization and recollection of
the Buddha *(nianfo, guanfo)*—in fact, he found none of these traditional forms to
be suitable to his situation. Instead he engaged in "pure and simple sitting" *(chun
dazuo)*, a methodless method of "no-thought" *(wunian)*, in which attention is
localized "neither inside, outside, nor in between." In later years he has come to
identify this practice as "possibly akin to the [old] Caodong practice of silent
illumination *(mozhao)*."[12]

Sheng-yen attributes the particular design of his retreat *(biguan)* to the traditional Chinese Buddhist ideal of "conjoined pursuit of meditative practice and
doctrinal learning *(xingjie shuangyun)*" or "conjoined cultivation of samādhi and
wisdom" *(dinghui shuangxiu)*. To this end, he made a point of supplementing his
practice with daily reading of the Buddhist scriptures, gradually working his way
through the most important sūtras and treatises of the Buddhist canon. Of all
the texts that he recited, he feels that he gained the most power and inspiration
from the *Āgama* and *Prajñā-pāramitā* sūtras.

During the second of his two retreats (1966–68), Sheng-yen began to write
extensively. One of the most influential products of this period was his survey
of the Buddhist vinaya and precepts, *Jieluxue gangyao*. Written in a modern discursive and analytic style, the book reflects the growing influence of a new, crit-
ically astute form of Buddhist scholarship that spread through Taiwan Buddhist
circles in the late 1960s. In part, this development is rooted in the progressive
attitudes fostered by such reformist monks as Yinshun, arguably the most influential and original Buddhist thinker in postwar Taiwan.[13] Sheng-yen himself has
always been a great admirer of Yinshun. But in speaking of his own intellectual
development, he gives special credit to the influence of Japanese scholarship, to

which he was introduced by the Chinese authors Yang Baiyi, Zhang Mantao, and his teacher Dongchu.[14]

Keen on the contribution that a Japanese academic training might make to the regeneration of Chinese Buddhism, Dongchu urged Sheng-yen to finish out his solitary meditation and prepare to go to Japan for graduate studies at a Buddhist university. In 1969, at the age of 39, Sheng-yen applied and was accepted into the master's program in Buddhist Studies at Risshō University in Tokyo. At Risshō he worked under Sakamoto Yūkio, one of the most respected scholars of Chinese Buddhism. Within two years he received his master's degree, his thesis being a study of the *Dasheng zhiguan famen* (Approach to the Calming and Contemplation of the Great Vehicle), a controversial treatise attributed to the Tiantai patriarch Nanyue Huisi (515–577). Dongchu had intended for Sheng-yen to return permanently to Taiwan after completing the master's program at Risshō. But impressed with his talent and dedication, Sakamoto Yūkio urged Sheng-yen to enter the university doctoral program, to which Sheng-yen agreed.

Regrettably, Sakamoto passed away shortly after this decision, leaving Sheng-yen without an academic sponsor. "During this time I had financial problems," Sheng-yen relates, "And many times I was ready to return to Taiwan. My advisor used to tell me, 'In clothing and food there is no mind for the Path, but with a mind for the Path there will always be food and clothing.' After hearing this I made daily prostrations to Guanyin. Oddly enough, after a short while, I started to receive annual donations from someone in Switzerland, sufficient to cover my tuition and costs to publish my dissertation. To this day I don't know who the donor was."[15] Under the supervision of Professors Kanekura Enshō and Nomura Yōsho, Sheng-yen wrote his doctoral dissertation on Ouyi Zhixu (1599–1655), the influential Tiantai reformer of the late Ming and early Qing Dynasties. The choice of topics was not an accidental one, for in addition to being grossly understudied, Ouyi Zhixu was particularly admired by reformist monks such as Taixu and Yinshun for his forward-looking eclecticism.

Ever interested in Buddhist practice, Sheng-yen also explored a host of mainstream and nontraditional Japanese Buddhist organizations during his seven years in Japan, including those of such "newly arisen" orders (*shinkō bukkyō*) as the Harada/Yasutani line of Sanbōkyōdan Zen, the Risshō kōseikai, and the Reiyūkai. In the process he undertook the esoteric *shido kegyō* ("four empowering applications") of the Shingon school, and he participated in any number of Zen *sesshin* and training semesters, both at the larger Sōtō and Rinzai training monasteries (*honzan*) and at smaller local temples. He remembers with special gratitude his association with Bantetsugyū Rōshi, a successor to Harada Rōshi renowned for his stern style of Zen:

I attended several winter retreats at his temple in Tōhoku. Being in northern Japan, the temple had a very harsh environment. Moreover, the master seemed inclined to give me an especially hard time and constantly had his assistants beat me. Of the people there I had by far the most education, and he would say, 'You scholars have a lot of selfish attachments and vexations. Your obstructions are heavy.'"[16]

In the end, Bantetsugyū gave Sheng-yen his *inka* or "certification." He also encouraged Sheng-yen's growing inclination to teach Chan in the United States.

At the invitation of Shen Jiazhen and the Chinese Buddhist Association of the United States, in 1976 Sheng-yen came to the United States and began to teach Chan at the Temple of Enlightenment in the Bronx. He remained there until 1978, when Dongchu's death required that he return to Taiwan to take over administration of the Wenhuaguan and the Nongchan Monastery. From 1978 to the present Sheng-yen has annually divided his time between Taiwan and his community in New York, alternating between the two locations every three months. The schedule of activities in the two countries is fairly consistent. There are seven-day Chan retreats, introductory and intermediate meditation classes, regular weekend dharma-gatherings, special classes on Buddhist doctrine, and a bevy of lectures on behalf of surrounding communities. Apart from a greater emphasis on the formalities of Buddhist doctrine and decorum, the sangha in Taiwan sponsors a number of practices that one generally does not see at American Buddhist centers. They include seven-day retreats for mindfulness of the Buddha Amitābha *(nianfo qi)* and rites such as repentance of Great Compassion and the Lotus repentance.

Although master Sheng-yen has, for the past twenty years, divided his time equally between the United States and Taiwan, his life-long project to "regenerate Chinese Buddhism and uplift the Chinese people" has been an object of special concern. In order to locate and educate the human talent necessary to realize this vision, in 1981 Sheng-yen and a handful of other Buddhist clergy established a graduate Institute for Buddhist Studies at the Chinese Cultural University on Huagang. Four years later Sheng-yen received permission from the Ministry of Education to reestablish the institute in Beitou as the independent Chunghua Institute of Buddhist Studies *(Zhonghua foxue yanjiu suo)*. Currently the Chunghua Institute offers a three-year program with a master's degree. Outstanding graduates are provided with support to pursue doctoral studies in Europe, Japan, or the United States, in preparation for returning to Taiwan to take up educational responsibilities.

In 1990 Sheng-yen purchased a large tract of land on a hillside overlooking the seashore to the north of Taipei city. Renamed "Dharma Drum Mountain" (Fagu shan), Sheng-yen envisions the site to be the future home of a combined liberal arts college, graduate institute for Buddhist Studies, international conference center, and center for Chan meditation (including the practice of extended solitary retreat or *biguan*). The institutional plan and its proposed cur-

UPLIFT - HUMANKIND AND REALIZE THE IDEAL OF A PLURALISTIC WORLD AS A SINGLE HOUSEHOLD.

ricula are the idealized embodiment of Sheng-yen's own life experience, reflecting his tribulations as a young monk in mainland China, his training under Dongchu, his solitary meditation in southern Taiwan, and his years of graduate study in Japan.

Whether pursued in the United States or in Taiwan, Sheng-yen's efforts profess to be one and the same "mission" (*yuan*): to use the Buddhist Dharma to uplift humankind and realize the ideal of "a pluralistic world as a single household" (*shijie yijia*). Such harmony, he insists, is not to be found in dogmatic homogenization or elimination of difference. It can only come through a grassroots discovery of commonality within difference and difference within commonality, and the ideal medium for such a project of heartfelt discovery and transformation (*xiuxing*) is the traditional Buddhist formula of "conjoined cultivation of samādhi and wisdom" (*dinghui shuangxiu*) or "practice and study" (*xingjie*).

Wisdom, one could say, means to understand penetratingly both ourselves and the world around us; samādhi (literally, "concentration, settledness, or fixity") means to identify firmly with our most cherished values and truths. Through the open-ended rubric of meditative practice and study, each individual is, in theory, free to discover his or her personal "vow" (*yuan*), without the a priori impositions of nation, race, gender, nation, or sect. Learning enables one to lead reflective lives by enhancing awareness of oneself and the world around one; meditative practice roots that understanding deeply in the heart, so that words and actions become one. In so doing, we find a path through life that intersects responsibly and intelligently with the world around us.

This journey of self-actualization, in Sheng-yen's eyes, is Buddhism's chief contribution to the worldwide project of "humanistic" understanding and communication. One of the key criticisms that Sheng-yen and other Asian thinkers have leveled against Western humanism is its self-centered emphasis on the individual (*renxing* or *rensheng*)—a weakness that, in their eyes, is marked by a lingering Cartesian or Kantian disengagement of the "essential self" from the world. From the Buddhist point of view, the very idea that "self" and all things are "dependently originated" (*pratītyasamutpāda*) means that the personal quest for meaning and fulfillment is intrinsically bound up with that of humankind, society, and the natural environment at large. This is the humanism of the "collective human condition" (*renjian*) as well as the formula for realizing a "Pure land within this very world." To Sheng-yen's way of thinking it is also the quintessential expression of the Mahāyāna bodhisattva way.

— BODHISATTVA PATH —

THROUGH THE OPEN-ENDED RUBRIC OF MEDITATIVE PRACTICE AND STUDY, EACH INDIVIDUAL IS IN THEORY, FREE TO DISCOVER HIS OR HER PERSONAL SELF.

I
Introduction:
Chan and Buddhist
Meditations

I

Chán and "Emptiness":
Chan and the Classical Buddhist Path

The word *chan* (Wade-Giles romanization: *ch'an*), from which Chan Buddhism, or Zen Buddhism, takes its name, is a Chinese transliteration of the Indian Buddhist term dhyāna, meaning "meditative concentration" or "meditative practice." Applied specifically to the Chan or Zen school, it carries the particular sense of the cultivation and experience of enlightenment itself, and not just any sort of meditative experience. Thus Chan Buddhism is often characterized as the school of meditative experience and enlightened insight par excellence, for it claims to embody and transmit the living wisdom that Siddhārtha Gautama achieved when he became the Buddha, or "enlightened one."

As the timeless insight that informed the Buddha's fashioning and preaching of the Buddhist doctrine, this enlightenment can be said to both precede and stand apart from the spoken word of the Buddhist sūtras. Yet, at the same time, it is intimately connected to the sūtras and the spoken dharma, as it is the very subject around which they orbit. Indeed, the scriptures take enlightenment as their foundation and their goal, aspiring to point the way to it, as a finger might point to the moon or a raft might be constructed to help one reach the other shore. The living wisdom to which the Buddha awakened and to which his spoken teachings aspire is the heart of Buddhist tradition in all its forms.

This being the case, Chan is not something utterly distinct from the sūtras, much less antagonistic to them, for it embodies the very insights that the sūtras seek to express, allowing for a profound complementarity between the two: what is stated in words in the Buddhist scriptures will be confirmed in fact in the course of Chan practice, while what is experienced in Chan practice will resonate immediately with what is written in the sūtras.

Today, one hears many American students say that, as practitioners of Zen or Chan, they do not need to learn or think about the Buddhist sūtras and their teachings. Just sitting in *zazen* is the real practice, reading and studying written words is for soulless pedants and academics. In China, Korea, and Japan, where knowledge of the Buddhist teachings was widespread, such a rejection of the written word makes poignant sense. This, however, is a dangerous attitude in a culture that has no native traditions of Buddhist learning of which to speak. For silence, in and of itself, is anything but innocent or neutral, much less free of ignorance. How the more problematic it becomes when it is blissful!

Both Chan/Zen and the sūtras are the wisdom of the Buddha, and between the two there is no real discrepancy. Without the Buddha's word, how would we ever hear about or think to seek the dharma, much less begin to fulfill our vow to help others on the path to enlightenment? If one has already set out on the path of Chan, what is this "enlightenment" that one is seeking? What are the aims of Chan practice? What does it entail and how does it work? If one did start to ask such questions about Chan, one would probably hear a lot of aphorisms, sayings, and stories from previous masters, all of them gleaned from books. If one started to look into this literature, one would soon discover that it is more extensive than any other school of East Asian Buddhism, even the doctrinal ones! Indeed, to be a good priest or Zen master in Japan, one must be trained in this literature through and through. One would also find that the ancient Chan masters and patriarchs were themselves highly literate individuals, whose teachings were deeply imbued with the language of the Buddhist sūtras. Moreover, of all the specialized ideas that one might come across, by far the most common would be liberating insight or wisdom (C. *zhihui*; S. *prajñā*) and its correlate teachings of "emptiness" (C. *kong*; S. *śūnyatā*), "having nothing to obtain" (C. *wu suode*; S. *anupalabdha*), and "having no place to stand or abide" (C. *wu suozhu*; S. *apratiṣṭhā*).

Bodhidharma, the twenty-eighth Indian patriarch and first Chinese patriarch of Chan, once remarked, "The Buddhas expound the Dharma of emptiness in order to eradicate the myriad false views. But should you then cling to emptiness, even the Buddhas will be unable to do anything to help you. When there is arising, it is only emptiness that arises; when there is perishing, it is only emptiness that perishes. In reality, nothing whatsoever arises or perishes."[1]

The sixth Chinese patriarch, Huineng (638–713), once said, "In this teaching of mine, from ancient times up to the present, all have established no-thought (or no-mind) as the main doctrine, non-form as the substance, and non-abiding as the basis. Non-form is to be separated from form even when associated with form. No-thought is not to think even when involved in thought. Non-abiding is the original nature of humankind."[2] The great Chan master, Linji (d. 866/67), said: "I don't have a particle of Dharma to give to anyone.

All I have is cure for sickness, freedom from bondage. You followers of the Way from here and there, try coming to me without depending on anything." Or, "I tell you, there's no Buddha, no Dharma, no practice, no enlightenment. Yet you go off like this on side roads, trying to find something. Blind fools!"[3] Thus, we find throughout Chan history instances where the scriptural teaching of "emptiness" is equated with the heart of Chan practice.

If one looks through the Hīnayāna, Mahāyāna, and Vajrayāna scriptures, one will find that they talk endlessly of the need to realize prajñā or "insight and wisdom." In Hīnayāna teaching, the simple hearing of the Four Noble Truths, and the resolve to seek a solution to the miseries of birth and death (S. saṃsāra), is a kind of prajñā insight. But in its most profound sense, prajñā is nothing short of the living insight—born of meditation—that eliminates the defilements that keep one bound to the cycle of saṃsāra. What that insight discloses is that suffering, in all its forms, is the reified product of false views and topsy-turvy thinking. By awakening deeply to the fact that existence is problematic rather than pleasant, that existence is fleeting rather than stable, and that, as persons, we are not the discrete and enduring "selves" (S. anātman) that we have always thought we were, a world that was formerly experienced as a tangle of conflict (S. duḥkha) is transformed into the ease and illumination of nirvāṇa.

In the Mahāyāna sūtras, prajñā, or insight, continues to carry the same transformative power, but to an even deeper level. Through the "perfection of insight or wisdom" (S. prajñā-pāramitā)—what the sūtras aptly call the "mother of the Buddhas"—the bodhisattva acquires the wisdom that enables one to deliver others from suffering along with oneself. Upon awakening to the fact that every aspect of mental and physical experience is empty of absolute "own-being" (S. svabhāva)—that every individualized moment or object is dependently interconnected with and contingent upon everything else—the bodhisattva sees the unconditioned world of nirvāṇa and conditioned world of saṃsāra as perfectly interfused. In so doing, he or she perfects the wisdom, compassion, and skill-in-means that culminates in the supreme perfect enlightenment of a Buddha. The Heart Sūtra (Mahāprajñāpāramitā-hṛdaya Sūtra) says, "Relying on this perfection of wisdom, the bodhisattva's mind is freed of impediment, and by dint of his freedom from impediment, he is free of fear and departs far from illusory thinking, thereby realizing the highest nirvāṇa. All Buddhas of the three times acquire supreme, perfect enlightenment by relying on this perfection of wisdom (S. prajñā-pāramitā)."

In the Vajrayāna, this insight into "emptiness" (śūnyatā), wherein saṃsāra and nirvāṇa, wisdom and skill-in-means, and enlightenment and afflictions are experienced as identical, is itself the "bliss-void" of the Tantric adept. In the Chan tradition, too, the insight of śūnyatā is the foundation of Chan practice. One could say that Chan enlightenment is itself none other than an awakening to śūnyatā.

BODHISATTVA MIND.

CHAN AND BUDDHIST NOTIONS OF ŚŪNYATĀ OR "EMPTINESS"

The classical Buddhist teaching of "emptiness" and its corollary notions of "there being nothing whatsoever to obtain" and "there being nowhere to stand or dwell" provide an elemental point of connection between Chan practice and the Buddhist sūtras. But what does this concept of śūnyatā or "emptiness" mean, and how is it represented in different Buddhist scriptural sources? How, furthermore, might this Buddhist concept or experience of emptiness stand in relation to experiences of revelation or meditative transport espoused in other religious traditions? In the interest of a better understanding of Chan as a Buddhist tradition, let us look more closely at these questions.

Emptiness as a Conventional, or Mundane, Experience

Notions akin to Buddhist emptiness may be found in a number of areas of conventional discourse. For example, one might have a very powerful dream or nightmare, to the point of breaking out in perspiration or leaping up in confusion; but upon fully waking up, one is suddenly relieved to find that the entire episode never occurred—that it was a dream, never real. Even so, one may still recall vividly the emotional grip of the experience. Then again, while watching a magic show, one may be taken in by the sleight of hand; when seeing heat rising off a road, one may think it water; or one's senses might be confused by the play of light and shadow, as when mistaking a coil of rope for a snake. At that moment the perception is experienced as fully real, bringing with it the full range of associated emotional and physical responses. Although we are taken in by the magic performance, we know that our eyes are deceiving us. On closer inspection, we realize that the perception was an illusion; normality reasserts itself and the responses vanish as swiftly as they arose. All of these are familiar experiences, which we typically refer to as illusions, misperceptions, deceptions, or even hallucinations—instances where we take or experience something to be real that is, in fact, not real.

Rather than appealing to the consistency of sensory habit or conventional experience to distinguish between what is real and what is "empty," or false, philosophical speculation might raise questions about the reality of basic convictions that we hold about existence. Materialists, for example, hold that there is no soul or existence after death, or at least that no such claim can be substantiated. The soul is not eternal, and they act according to this conviction. Life is like a lamp that simply goes out when its fuel is spent. Because it is ephemeral and a play of matter, existence for them is "empty" of ultimate value or grander purpose, as is any system that imposes such a scheme on the world.

Yet another kind of emptiness is experienced in intense religious prayer, devotion, or meditative contemplation. Through spiritual disciplines of this sort,

"REBORN THROUGH INTENSE MEDITATIONS."

people will sometimes experience sudden relief from the burdens and anxieties of everyday existence, as though one was redeemed from a "sinful" or lower form of existence and reborn in spirit to a truer and higher life. The old self and its purposes may suddenly seem false, unreal, empty.

Sometimes these moments are accompanied by deep experiences of ecstatic transport or mystical rapture, wherein one's whole sense of time, space, and person may undergo radical changes. Beneath the surface of ordinary existence, a more fundamental reality or sense of being is discovered. The usual limitations of body, mind, and environment may vanish, to the point of feeling that one partakes of an eternal and divine existence that utterly transcends or subsumes the world at large. One's sense of subjective being may drop away or expand ecstatically, interfusing with the outer world and forming an inseparable unity with the universe. *THE DIVINE REALM OF EXISTENCE.*

One may think that one has experienced God, that one is God, or that one has been appointed as a spokesperson of God. Everyday concerns may suddenly appear sinful, profane, or mundane in contrast to the overwhelming power of the newfound reality, calling one to make a life mission of preaching this truth to others. Often, individuals of this sort become great religious leaders, philosophers, artists, or civic leaders. And indeed, an ordinary person may well consider someone who has had this kind of experience to be blessed, or to be a saint or sage.

Many religious traditions offer detailed taxonomies of the various types and levels of religious transport of this sort. The Buddhist tradition classifies this *class* kind of experience under the rubric of dhyāna, or "states of meditative concentration and absorption." Altogether, four grades of dhyāna are distinguished, with an additional four categorized under "formless samāpatti." They range from coarse to subtle, with the bliss and rapture characteristic of the lower dhyānas progressively giving way to increasingly boundless sensations of space and consciousness in the formless samāpattis.

The distinctions among these different stages of concentration are very technical and involved. What is important to remember about the Buddhist perspective, however, is that these are all considered to be somatically induced experiences still subject to the reifications of deluded existence. The insight into no-self and the "emptiness" of phenomena that is the hallmark of genuine prajñā is still missing. Because these meditative states are shaped and tainted by deluded views, we characterize them as worldly and unenlightened. Whatever novel forms of insight or wisdom they may be held to bring, we likewise refer to as conventional. In order to clearly demarcate this sort of "lower" meditative state from genuine experiences of insight and liberation, the Buddhist tradition refers to the dhyānas and their like as "mundane" (S. laukika), or "possessed of defiling outflows" (S. sāsravas). The meditative experiences associated with genuine insights of emptiness, no-self, and no-mind are designated "supramundane" (S. lokottara) and "undefiled," or "devoid of outflows" (S. anāsrava).

(Pure)
THE INEFFABLE NEEDS EXPRESSION.

Only the best → Bic — crystal fine

The

BENEATH/WITHIN THE MEDIUM OF MIND (ORDINARY MIND) LIES A MORE FUNDAMENTAL AND TRUE EXISTENCE OF MIND AND EXISTENCE—LIFE UNLOCKED THROUGH INTENSE+THOROUGH MEDITATION.

⅄ · Why is it that we refer to such sublime experiences as dhyāna as merely con-   Q.
ventional or mundane? The ordinary, or profane, personality and the coarse
forms of selfish craving associated with it may, indeed, have disappeared, but
deluded views and attachment to the thought or construct of self are still prevalent. Everything that a person does or experiences under the influence of such
states is still structured by the delusions and infatuations of self. The difference
here is that the conventional limitations of body and mind have been dissolved,
and self is now functioning on an extraordinarily expanded and vast scale. Small
self has become a great self, small mind a big mind. All the same, the "universal oneness," "supreme self," "ultimate reality," or "supreme being" that one
experiences or identifies with is still "my" supreme being or self. In sum, it is   A.
because these experiences still orbit around and are colored by the thought of
self that we call them conventional.

The One-sided Emptiness of the Hīnayānist View of No-Self and Nirvāṇa

Where there is ignorance and false view, there is craving and hatred; where there
are the passions of craving and hatred, there is karma-producing action, retribution, and suffering. Only when there is a thoroughgoing penetration of false
views and total letting go of attachment can there be said to be enlightenment,
freedom, and true peace.

If one goes a step further and looks deeply into the experiences described
above, one will find them closely bound to a thought of self and attachment to
self: "I" experience "reality"; "I" know "God"; "I" am "one" with all things. But
if you are "one" or you are "ultimate reality," then where is there room for this
"you"? One could say that the self and its egoistic attachments reach cosmic pro-
portions with the thought that it perceives some ultimate reality or God. If one
were then to investigate the subtle influences of egoistic thinking that pervade
one's moment-to-moment experience, one may find that there really is no fixed
and permanent self.

What we generally regard as self is no more than a chain of momentary
thoughts or impressions—a thought construct, if you will. A "self" is not to be
found anywhere outside this momentary arising and perishing of conscious
thought. Observing the mind's activity like this, one may suddenly experience
the insight that mind itself is wholly shifting, unlocalized, and impermanent; or
that the subjective "self" is just a thought, an "empty" construct to which we
cling needlessly. Rather than the source of all truth and comfort, "self" is the
source of petty craving, fear, frustration, and sorrow. By letting go of the
thought of self and pacifying its negative influences, one experiences a thoroughgoing release from the pain of saṃsāra. This is known as the unconditioned
peace of nirvāṇa and "no-self."

Although, in principle, one at this point may be said to be free from saṃsāra, there may still be a problem, for if one should set up the idea that the and saṃs-āra are wholly "painful" and "false," and cling to the insight of no-self or the emptiness of nirvāṇa as "real," then it becomes a biased emptiness where fear and selfish attachment are still present.

Genuine Emptiness, or Emptiness as Ultimate Reality

The biased attachment to nirvāṇa and the emptiness of self is a problem that Mahāyāna Buddhism, or the Buddhism of the "Great Vehicle," routinely attributes to the Hīnayāna, or the Buddhist teachings of the "Lesser Vehicle." The Mahāyānists hold that Śākyamuni Buddha preached the painfulness (S. duḥkha) of saṃsāra and the goal of extinction in nirvāṇa in order to prepare beings who were deeply attached to conventional existence for the "higher" teaching of the Mahāyāna. Thus, it is regarded as a preparatory expedient to the Mahāyāna. However, failing to recognize this fact, certain persons are said to have clung to the Hīnayāna as the Buddha's final word, thereby fostering an obsessive attachment to "no-self" and to the extinction of nirvāṇa. According to the Mahāyāna view, such individuals still carry the false view and fear that the flux of saṃsāra is real, as a result of which they reify and cling to nirvāṇa and the emptiness of "no-self." Mahāyāna seeks to correct this error by teaching a thoroughgoing emptiness of saṃsāra—an emptiness of both self and the phenomenal flux of sensory activity.

Previously, we described emptiness as the insight that "self" is a false construct or sense of continuity that is projected into the flow of momentary thoughts and impressions. When these impressions and sensory fluctuations are no longer appropriated as self, they become pacified and ultimately cease. With the Mahāyāna view of "emptiness of self" and "emptiness of concomitant objects," we go a step further and realize that the factors that make up this moment-to-moment flow of mental experience themselves have no inherent existence or reality. They arise, combine, transform, and dissipate as a mutually interrelated nexus of causes and conditions. Each constituent factor in the moment-to-moment field of experience is itself contingent upon this network of causes and conditions, and there is absolutely no arising, cessation, or abiding existence of any factor or phenomenon apart from this cause and condition.

As the great Mahāyāna teacher Nāgārjuna once observed, "Nowhere and at no time can an object be found to exist through origination from itself, from another, from both, or from no cause whatsoever."[5] Like the interstices in a net, the entire nexus of cause and condition, with all its individual elements, is "empty" and "void." Thus, in contrast to the simpler idea of "emptiness of 'self' as subjective ego or person" (S. pudgala-nairātmya), the Mahāyāna vehicle advances the notion of "emptiness of 'self-existence' of the dharmas, or psycho-physical constituents, themselves" (S. dharma-nairātmya). With the latter step, saṃsāric existence appears as intrinsically identical with the emptiness of nirvāṇa, since no phenomenon (dharma) exists except by cause and condition. The Hīnayānist is freed from fear of saṃsāra and attachment to nirvāṇa by the simple insight that there is no saṃsāra to renounce or nirvāṇa to apprehend. What appears to be two are, in fact, not-two, but a single middle way. By abiding directly in saṃsāra, one abides simultaneously in nirvāṇa.

While existence is itself understood to be empty and identical with nirvāṇa, Mahāyāna teaching nonetheless continues to distinguish between "ultimate reality" (S. *paramārtha-satya*) as revealed in the light of prajñā and the world of conventional existence in which that ultimate reality is "concealed from view" (S. *samvṛti-satya*). In order to convey the ontological and soteriological importance of this ultimate reality, Mahāyānists have attached a number of other substantivist terms to it, such as "true thusness, or suchness" (S. *tathātā*), "dharma-nature" (S. *dharmatā*), the "unarisen or unoriginated" (S. *anutpattika*), or the "true nature of all dharmas" (S. *sarvadharmabhūtatā*). However, one must always view these expressions in keeping with the actual import of the Mahāyāna teaching of emptiness, wherein the true nature or true character of all things is, in fact, no characteristic, no nature.

Dharma Totally Embodied and the Totally Forgotten:
Emptiness in the Absolute or Highest Sense

It is easy to think that such expressions as "the unconditioned or unarisen nature of dharmas," "suchness," and "genuine emptiness" refer to some metaphysical essence separate from or hidden beneath the phenomenal world with which we are familiar. However, this view is mistaken, for phenomena in and of themselves are empty, non-arising, and non-perishing; and this non-arising and non-perishing "nature" is itself absolutely identical to and not separate from phenomena. In this respect, it is wrong to think that the two extremes of "conventional existence" and "ultimate reality" have discrete reality or "own-being" in and of themselves. Emptiness does not eclipse phenomenal existence; phenomenal existence does not impede or eclipse emptiness. They are interfused and identical, one and the same. It is to express this free and dynamic interfusion that we "negate" the idea of emptiness and say that it is "not empty."

Let us put it another way. In our discussion of "genuine emptiness," we started with the conventional world of reified self and phenomena, then negated them to arrive at the intrinsic emptiness of both self and objects. This we referred to as the fundamental "suchness" of ultimate reality. Now we once again negate the notion that a fundamental "emptiness" or "suchness" might exist apart from phenomena. As such, we turn back and affirm "emptiness" as the "marvelous existence" of phenomena. Emptiness and phenomenal existence, nirvāṇa and saṃsāra, are simultaneously illumined and simultaneously negated. The ultimate "middle way" or "middle truth" that they represent is not a "middle" between extremes, nor a "truth" to be posited in contradistinction to "false-hood." What we have is a single, dynamic, and inconceivable reality—a "non-middle" wherein there are no phenomena and yet all phenomena, no stance and yet all stances. Emptiness and the phenomenal world are totally forgotten and totally interfused in a singularly inconceivable and indescribable way. This is "absolute emptiness" or "emptiness in its highest sense."

But here it seems we are ever relegated to paradox, or an endless dialectic regress of assertion and negation. How, then, is one to express directly this vision of emptiness and identity of opposites? More important, what does it mean to live or embody this vision directly, to escape the limitations of dualistic think-ing and dialectic, and directly know or speak of the inexpressible? When, where, and how does one make the leap from secondary description to primary expe-rience, or from being a prisoner of discriminatory constructs to being their master?

On this point the *Vimalakīrti Sūtra* offers an instructive passage. In the course of the sūtra, the layman Vimalakīrti asks a group of illustrious bodhisattvas to each state his or her way of entering the gate of non-duality. One after another the bodhisattvas relate the dualistic extremes that must be transcended in order to know true emptiness: arising and perishing, darkness and light, nirvāṇa and saṃsāra, existence and emptiness, reality and unreality. Offering what seems to be the last word, the great Bodhisattva Mañjuśrī himself says: "When you can neither speak nor talk of any event, when you neither indicate nor know any 'thing,' when you pass beyond both questions and answers, this is entering the gate of non-duality."

Mañjuśrī then turns to Vimalakīrti himself and asks, "Sir, each of us has spo-ken. Now you yourself tell us how a bodhisattva enters the gate of non-duality."

At that point Vimalakīrti kept silent and did not utter a single word. Mañjuśrī thereupon praised him, saying, "Excellent! Excellent! This is truly entering the gate of non-duality!"[6]

Vimalakīrti's thunderous silence is a most eloquent demonstration of empti-ness in its highest and most inconceivable form; and it is with this living enlight-enment—emptiness not as a proposition but as an embodied experience—that Chan itself is identified. After all the talk about emptiness, one still comes back to things at hand; and it is these everyday activities that constitute the very ground and function of Chan enlightenment. The sixth patriarch, Huineng, stated that seeking enlightenment apart from the phenomenal world is like look-ing for horns on a rabbit. A second-generation spiritual descendant of Huineng, Mazu Daoyi (709–788), frequently asserted that the ordinary, everyday mind is itself the Way, or, that among all phenomena, there is none that is not already liberated. Chan master Linji urged his disciples to "just act ordinary, put on your clothes, eat your rice, pass the time with nothing particular to do."[7] A student once asked master Yunmen Wenyan (864–949), "Please, master, show me a road in?" To which the master replied, "Slurping gruel, eating rice."[8]

METHODS OF PRACTICE ASSOCIATED WITH THE DIFFERENT STAGES
OF MEDITATIVE EXPERIENCE

Although the situation will vary from person to person, there is a logic—or a process—to the way in which these different experiences of emptiness take shape and build on one another. From the time of Śākyamuni Buddha himself, Buddhist meditation masters have charted this process in terms of sequential stages of spiritual progress, carefully specifying the transformations of body and mind (e.g., the defilements that are eliminated and meritorious attributes that are appropriated) that take place with each phase of development. They have also indexed to these schemes various methods of spiritual discipline designed to bring about their realization. Thus, the Buddhist tradition preserves a rich and varied technology for spiritual cultivation that is one of the most complex of its kind.

Different Buddhist systemizations of the path will each have its particular representations and methods, but the basic principles of organization are similar. Stated in the simplest terms possible, those principles describe a process of taking body and mind from a state of confusion and disparity; through a condition of one-pointedness, or unity; to the experience of no-mind, or no-thought. Methods of practice may themselves be functionally classified as: (A) procedures for purifying the mind of basic hindrances and obscurations; (B) methods for concentrating or unifying the mind, with the aim of inducing various states of conventional or mundane meditative absorption; (C) techniques for developing the uniquely Buddhist insight (prajñā) into selflessness that opens the door to true liberation, followed by; (D) Buddhist techniques for extending the insight of no-self to that of genuine emptiness, and finally; (E) emptiness in its absolute or most profound sense.

Simplifying the Mind and Purifying the Mind of Basic Obscurations

2· Virtually any object or repetitive activity can serve as a support for focusing the body and mind. It can be a concrete external object, an internal thought or process, an activity such as verbal recitation, even a physical movement such as walking or standing, although activities that are not too physically exhausting are best. If the individual puts his or her entire physical and mental attention into such an object or activity, wandering and confused thoughts will gradually disappear; one's awareness will become very calm, focused, and pure; and the signs associated with the condition of a simplified and concentrated mind will emerge.

While this sort of discipline need not be overtly religious (certain types of athletic training can produce the same experience of concentration), virtually all religious traditions prize mental concentration and purity as a foundation for the spiritual life, and they offer techniques to assist their development. Purity of mind and heart, utmost sincerity, and wholeheartedness are qualities held by most religions to be instrumental to the higher life of grace and beatitude. The contemplative techniques that assist them may range from devotionally oriented disciplines such as prayer, prostrations, and various forms of penance, recitation of scripture, singing of hymns, continual intoning of names or incantations of deities (mantra), to the more autonomous practices of Indian yoga and Chinese martial arts.

In classical Buddhist tradition there is an extensive collection of methods designed to promote initial purification and calming of the mind, both autonomous and devotional. Typically, these begin with a regularized physical routine, such as sitting in the "lotus" position (the formal posture of meditation), standing or kneeling with palms joined in reverence, or slow-walking. One might then take up a specific forms of mental contemplation, such as observation of the inhalation and exhalation of the breath (S. ānāpāna-smṛti), contemplation of bodily impurity or decay, visual recollection of a given Buddha or bodhisattva (S. buddhānusmṛti), meditation on kindness, compassion, joy, and equanimity (the four brāhmavihāra or apramāṇa), and so forth.

Known in certain Buddhist circles as the "Five Methods for Stilling, or Pacifying, the Mind," the latter meditations have the twofold power to counteract specific emotional imbalances while simultaneously providing a ground for developing mental concentration. For example, concentration on kindness, compassion, joy, and equanimity will alleviate deeply rooted malice and anger; concentration on the breath will eliminate distractedness, or scattered mind; contemplation of a Buddha or bodhisattva will counteract fear and uncertainty. Depending on whether a student's disposition tends toward one or another of these habits, a technique may be assigned accordingly.

As the heart begins to be unburdened of its grosser emotional afflictions and obscurations, body and mind become increasingly easeful and are melded into a pure, unalloyed stream of awareness. The mind will begin to slow down and simplify, becoming clear and open. It will wander less and less, until it reaches a point where it becomes so calm and supple that it stays effortlessly engrossed in the object at hand, as though entertaining its full presence for the first time. Initially, this condition may be quite fleeting, but in time it will occur with more frequency and endure for longer periods, eventually arriving at what we call "access concentration," the condition from which the higher states of mundane dhyāna, or "enstatic absorption," are generated. Thus, in addition to providing a preparatory therapeutic, the Five Methods for Stilling the Mind can seamlessly take the practitioner from the grossest to the most sublime of the mundane states of meditative concentration.

Producing a One-Pointed, or Unified, Mind

Having harmonized body and mind and achieved the preparatory condition of access concentration, if the meditator continues to use any one of these techniques for an extended period of time, he or she will reach "unified mind," or "mental one-pointedness." As the mind enters deeper and deeper into calm and becomes utterly absorbed in and unified with its object, any sense of effortful practice or attention to method may seem to disappear. Eventually, the object of concentration itself, or the awareness of body, mind, and environment, will disappear as well. Absorptions of this sort are genuine experiences of unified mind, equivalent to the mundane concentrations of the four dhyāna and formless samāpattis described earlier.

There are numerous differences in degree to these dhyāna absorptions. Some are shallow, others profound; some coarse, others subtle. The instant that any such experience occurs, it will be so markedly different from our ordinary "dissipated" experience of body, mind, and environment that the practitioner will have no choice but to look upon it as a radically new insight into the nature of self and existence. This sense of transformation is precisely what is meant by the "conventional or mundane emptiness" described in the preceding section. The deeper one progresses in meditative absorption, the more informed one becomes about not only the subtlety and coarseness of different grades of experience, but also the subtlety and coarseness of the meditative technique itself. In this respect, one given method of meditation—such as mindfulness of the breath—can have many different levels of application, which evolve or unfold according to the depth of experience.

Techniques for Developing Insight into No-Self (No-Mind), Genuine Emptiness, and Emptiness in Its Highest Sense

Just as Buddhist tradition draws a firm line between "defiled" (S. sāsrava) and "undefiled" (S. anāsrava) experiences of emptiness, or "mundane" (S. laukika) states of "unified mind" and "supramundane" (S. lokottara) experiences of "no-mind," so it also distinguishes between the different techniques that produce them. Generally speaking, those techniques that are designed especially to concentrate the mind and produce the mundane absorptions of "unified mind" are referred to as techniques of "calming," or "concentration" (S. śamatha; C. zhi). They are qualitatively distinguished from a second class of meditative techniques known as "contemplation" or "discernment" practice (S. vipaśyanā; C. guan), which is held to bring about the uniquely liberating Buddhist insights of "no-self" or the emptiness of person (S. pudgala-nairātmya) and phenomena (S. dharma-nairātmya).

Like the mundane experiences of dhyāna absorption themselves, the Buddhist techniques of "calming" are not necessarily peculiar to the Buddhist tradition, but have equivalents in numerous other religions. In fact, the Buddhist tradition itself holds that Śākyamuni Buddha learned many of these practices from the various non-Buddhist teachers under whom he studied prior to his enlightenment. The techniques of "contemplation," or *vipaśyanā*, on the other hand, are regarded to be the Buddha's exclusive contribution and the sole property of the Buddhist tradition. Having grown directly out of the Buddha's personal experience of enlightenment, they alone can reproduce the unique insights of no-self and emptiness that are at the heart of the Buddhist path to spiritual liberation. In offering these techniques, the Buddhist tradition sets itself apart from all other contemplative traditions.

Hīnayāna and Mahāyāna Buddhist treatises expound a variety of different approaches to *vipaśyanā*, or "contemplation" practice, but for the most part they are extensions of the classic formulation known as the Four Stations or Abodes of Mindful Observation (S. *smṛtyupasthāna*; C. *nianchu*): (1) mindfulness of the body; (2) mindfulness of sensation; (3) mindfulness of the mind, or psyche; (4) mindfulness of dharmas, or the constituent factors of psycho-physical experience. When applied by a mind that has been duly purified and unified by prior practice of meditative concentration (S. *śamatha*), mindful observation of body, sensation, mind, and dharmas will rapidly bring insight (prajñā) into the basic Buddhist truths of suffering (S. *duḥkha*), transitoriness (S. *anitya*), and absence of enduring selfhood (S. *anātman*). With the realization of no-self, the liberating insight into Buddhist emptiness (śūnyatā) begins to emerge.

But when the mind itself is still in a state of turbidity or confusion, it becomes exceedingly difficult to develop a penetrating awareness of these four spheres, much less produce a deeply transformative experience of insight into impermanence or no-self. Thus, it could be said that the unified mind engendered by "calming" practice is a necessary precondition for effective contemplation practice and the realization of emptiness and no-mind. Without the liberating insight of contemplation practice, one's meditation will never pass beyond the experience of mundane dhyāna, and true enlightenment will never appear. Without the power of mental concentration and clarity generated by calming practice, efforts at mindful contemplation will produce only the most meager or fleeting insight.

At the heart of Buddhist contemplation practice, the Four Stations of Mindfulness—especially the fourth station of "mindful observation of the dharmas, or constituent mental factors"—provide the door to the Buddhist insights of no-self, genuine emptiness, and emptiness in its highest sense. The technique is common to both the Hīnayāna and Mahāyāna teaching. But whereas Hīnayāna stops at the "extinction" of saṃsāric suffering that arises with the insight of no-self, Mahāyāna carries this contemplative practice to the deeper levels of the emptiness of phenomena, genuine emptiness and emptiness in its absolute or highest sense. Principally, this is accomplished by extending the fourth station of mindful observation of the dharmas through ever-deepening dialectic refutations of emptiness and existence, until all biased views and attachments are refuted and the perfect, inexpressible middle way stands revealed.

Thus, there is the practice of the Three Gates of Liberation (S. *vimoksa-mukha*), or Three Samādhis of Emptiness, whereby the practitioner sequentially (a) refutes existence in order to realize the emptiness of self; (b) refutes the dharmas to realize the marklessness, or emptiness, of all dharmic attributes; and (c) refutes all notions of existence and emptiness to arrive at utter desirelessness, or unconstructedness. Then again, we also hear of a series of meditations that lead through eighteen different insights of emptiness and their refutation, beginning with insight into the emptiness of subjective selfhood and ending with the emptiness that transcends all notion of arising and perishing, existence and nonexistence.[9]

The Sudden Approach to Enlightenment: Techniques That Offer Direct,
or Immediate, Access to Absolute Emptiness

The path of meditative calming and contemplation that we have described above unfolds in a graduated or sequential fashion. Different disciplines or meditations are equated with different levels of practice, and together they build on and supplement one another, leading one step-by-step from delusion to full enlightenment. First one begins with ordinary existence and the conventional sense of self. Through the practice of meditative calming and concentration, one purifies the mind and begins to experience the expanded self and unified mind of mundane dhyāna. Turning to contemplation practice, one uproots the notion of self and begins to work one's way dialectically through successive levels of emptiness, to arrive finally at the perfect enlightenment of emptiness in its highest sense.

Yet, classic Mahāyāna statements about Buddhahood and absolute emptiness assert unequivocally that the afflictions are, from the outset, identical with enlightenment; samsāra, as it is, is nirvāna. Thus, it is feasible to say that enlightenment might occur immediately, without the need to burden oneself with the illusory task of removing afflictions that do not need to be removed, and appropriating an emptiness that is never appropriated. If, by a simple expansion of horizon, one can open oneself to the inconceivable totality of existence and emptiness just as they are, then the perfect enlightenment of a Buddha is fully at hand.

This is precisely the point on which both Chan and certain forms of Esoteric, or Tantric, Buddhism take their stance. Asserting the intrinsic unity of enlightenment and afflictions, wisdom and skill-in-means, and emptiness and existence, they offer a "speedy" path to Buddhahood for those whose endowments are keen enough to grasp their lightning-like message. Thus, Chan tradition foregoes "dependence on words and texts" or "reliance on provisional expedients," striving instead "to point directly and immediately to the enlightened nature." In lieu of elaborate refutations of existence and emptiness or endless theorizing about the identity of enlightenment and everyday activity, Chan masters, in principle, strive to allow the enlightened function of absolute emptiness itself to serve as both the medium and the method of Chan.

For example, a student once asked the Chan master Caoshan Benji (840–901), "What is it in phenomena that is ultimately real?"

"Phenomena themselves are the real," the master replied.

The student asked, "How would one show this?"

Caoshan responded by simply lifting his tea tray.[10]

A student once asked Chan master Yunmen, "What is the most urgent phrase?"

The master simply said, "Eat!"[11]

On another occasion, someone asked Yunmen, "What does it mean to say that 'form is nothing other than emptiness'?"

Yunmen replied, "The staff is hitting your nose!"[12]

This approach is what Chan tradition calls "direct pointing to the nature of mind," namely, using the moment to yank away the student's blinders and attachments and directly reveal the enlightenment at hand.

Of course, this by no means implies that Chan, as a religious path, is wholly without form or procedure. Quite the contrary, Chan also has its basic institutions, its requisite conditions, and its procedures for practice, which are fully as intensive as the "gradual" approach. This includes distinctive forms of meditation that are designed to facilitate Chan awakening, such as the practice of "silent illumination" (mozhao) or use of gong'an and huatou. In point of fact, it is only within such a highly disciplined setting—or with such a highly focused mind—that the rhetoric of Chan can have its desired impact. Thus, while Chan tradition may be uncompromising in its presentation of enlightenment, its institutional routines embody many of the same techniques and principles of spiritual development found in the "gradual" formulations of the Buddhist path.

The chapters that follow comprise two basic parts. The first section discusses general principles of meditative development, then illustrates how these principles are embodied in the Three Learning, or Disciplines, that traditionally describe the graduated approach to enlightenment: moral purification through observance of the precepts, development of samādhi power through meditative concentration, and development of insight or wisdom through meditative contemplation. The second section turns specifically to the "sudden and direct approach" of the Chan school. It describes basic practices, such as silent illumination and the use of huatou, outlines prerequisites of Chan training, and takes up the question of enlightenment and spiritual progress in Chan.

2

Meditation and the Principles
for Training Body and Mind

Meditation—above all, seated meditation—has always been one of the foundational practices of Buddhism. Śākyamuni Buddha realized supreme enlightenment while seated in meditation beneath the bodhi tree. When he set out to establish the teachings and convey this enlightenment to others, he organized the Buddhist path according to the three basic disciplines of purity in the observance of the precepts, or moral restraints (S. *śīla*); meditative concentration, or samādhi; and wisdom, or prajñā. The two factors of concentration and wisdom are developed primarily through formal meditation practice, with moral restraint as a preparatory basis. The Chinese word *"chan,"* which we use to distinguish the Chan and Zen schools in East Asia, is a transliteration of the Indian word *dhyāna*. *Dhyāna* originally refers to states of meditative calm and absorption produced through the practice of seated meditation. Although *zuochan* (J. *zazen*), or "sitting in meditation," takes on a semantic range in Chan that is different from that of its Indian Buddhist predecessor, the formal practice of sitting quietly with legs folded in the "lotus posture" remains one of the most distinctive features of Chan training. If one were to visit a Chan monastery or center for practice, one would find seated meditation to be one of the most distinctive features of the daily routine.

In this chapter I describe the basic postures for seated meditation; discuss the inner procedures for harmonizing body, breath, and mind as well as developing mental concentration; and explain how this concentration can be extended to activities outside of seated meditation.

Whether we are meditating for one period of sitting, undertaking a week's intensive retreat, or engaging in a lifetime of spiritual practice, the development of meditative concentration and wisdom proceeds by certain uniform principles. In essence, this process entails a movement from the coarse to the subtle, from the external to the internal, from the taming of the body to the taming of the mind, and from a state of activity to a state of quietude. It is not just a discipline of the "mind," but a discipline that encompasses the entire person and all aspects of life. It has both a beginning and an end, as well as a foundation and a culmination. One cannot simply choose to concern oneself with one point and neglect the others, otherwise one's efforts will prove fruitless. *THREE BASIC STAGES.*

The aim of meditation is to develop the mind through three basic stages: first, to collect the scattered and confused mind and focus it to a concentrated mind with few thoughts; next, to purify and further concentrate this simple mind into a highly unified and one-pointed mind; finally, to pass from the unified, or one-pointed, mind to no-mind. For successful Buddhist practice, one must learn to find perfect quietude and concentration while in the midst of activity, as well as activity in the midst of quietude. Proper integration of the body and mind are instrumental to this process. To describe this process of training we distinguish three basic aspects: (1) harmonizing the body; (2) harmonizing the breath; (3) harmonizing the mind.

PRECONDITIONS FOR EFFECTIVE MEDITATION: HARMONIZING THE BODY

Five lay precepts.

Our daily habits and patterns of interaction with the world around us are extremely important, and proper practice of meditation begins here. Behavior and attitudes that lead to tense relations with others will impede even the most basic mental ease. A lifestyle that impairs the health of body and mind is also a serious obstruction. Excessive stress and dissipation can exhaust the body to such a point that meditation will be difficult to develop, and its powers will be insufficient to bring rejuvenation and lasting benefit. It is precisely for the purpose of harmonizing our interactions with the world at large and establishing an environment that is conducive to meditative development that the Buddhist moral precepts are emphasized. Thus, every meditator should at least receive and observe the five lay precepts: (1) not to take life or cause injury to other beings; (2) not to steal or take what has not been properly given; (3) not to engage in sexual relations that are harmful or socially unacceptable; (4) not to lie or deceive; (5) not to indulge in intoxicants. These precepts are the minimum criteria for being a decent human being and the foundation for effective meditation.

Daily routine is also a crucial factor in meditation practice. Meditation must become part of one's everyday life—if not the very center of it—and this condition must be maintained uninterruptedly. For laypersons, it is best to set aside specific times for meditation twice a day—in the morning after getting up and in the evening before going to bed. The noon and midnight hours should be avoided. Moreover, it is best not to meditate any sooner than one hour after eating.

Ideally, as meditators you should try to preserve the calm and concentration of the morning sitting throughout the entire day. As the power of practice begins to grow, you will feel that the calm and clarity of the morning meditation naturally infuses other activities over the course of the day. In time you may feel that every activity is meditation.

There are also techniques of exercise and self-massage that are recommended before and after sitting in meditation. When sitting down to meditate, the aim is to proceed from a condition of activity to a condition of deep stillness, or from a condition of mental and physical coarseness to one of great subtleness. When coming out of meditation, the process is reversed: one moves from stillness to activity, from the subtle to the coarse. These techniques of exercise and self-massage help relax body and mind in preparation for sitting, and help reactivate them after sitting. The latter is especially important, for rushing directly into activity from quiet sitting can exert a dangerous shock to the system. As a rule, there are proper procedures for going about all of the basic activities of walking, standing, lying down, even eating and defecating.

One useful model for understanding meditation is to think of it as a holistic discipline that seeks to bring about the integration of body, breath, and mind. With the harmonizing and progressive calming of these three factors, body, breath, and mind become completely interfused, as though they are one. When this total concentration of body, breath, and mind becomes truly one-pointed, samādhi, or "meditative absorption," is at hand. Wisdom, or prajñā, develops in response to samādhi.

Many Asian traditions of healing and religion employ methods of physical exercise as a supplement to meditative contemplation. In Indian yoga, for example, there are various sequences of movements and postures known as āsana, the particular study of which is known as Hatha yoga. These āsana are used to prepare the body and mind in preparation for deeper methods of samādhi, or meditative concentration. In Chinese Daoism, gymnastic exercises (daoyin) such as Taiji quan and the various martial arts forms are used for much the same effect. The Chinese Buddhist tradition makes use of the martial exercises of the famous Shaolin Monastery.

One could say that such methods of exercise and self-massage are designed to harmonize the body and develop concentration in the midst of activity. They improve the circulation of the blood and the vital energy known as qi, causing them to flow smoothly and profusely so that the tissues and nervous system are rejuvenated. When the vital energy is harmonious, the body becomes vigorous and healthy. As the condition of the body improves, the mind becomes even and concentrated. Although people are not always aware of it, these so-called exercises used in Asian traditions have always had an intimate connection with the practice of religious contemplation. Effective meditative concentration itself can only come with a profoundly healthy body and mind. In fact, it is not uncommon for meditators to discover deep obstructions in their vital energy during the course of their practice, whereupon they may spontaneously initiate subtle and precise exercises to open them.

The system of energy points and meridian lines used in Chinese acupuncture actually originates from the motion of the vital energy as experienced by the ancients through the practice of meditation. Today, many people think that Chinese medicine, acupuncture, and the martial arts are a completely separate world from that of meditation and spiritual discipline. This is not true. In China, we have never made such a distinction between physical health and spiritual well-being. The sense of ease, vitality, and mental clarity that comes with proper exercise is itself the foundation of meditative concentration. Thus, yoga and other techniques for harmonizing the vital energy are powerful assistants to the cultivation of samādhi and spiritual insight. One should not equate them with the shallow machismo so popular in the martial arts movement today.

Seated Meditation

Meditative concentration can be developed on the basis of virtually any physical activity—sitting, standing, walking, lying down, and so forth—so long as it is consistent and enduring. Indeed, in most Asian meditative and yoga traditions, you are deemed a capable meditator only when you can maintain concentration in the midst of any circumstance. Nevertheless, certain postures and activities are more conducive to meditative development than others. For the beginner, a body that is still, at ease, and alert is of paramount importance to calming and focusing the mind.

When the body and motor system are enervated, the mind also becomes active, involving itself with physical movement and interacting with environmental stimuli. When the body is relaxed and still, distractedness disappears and the mind becomes calm and concentrated. Meditation seeks to use a relaxing and stable physical posture to influence the mind.

It is possible to meditate while standing, walking, or engaging in miscellaneous activities, but these postures are relatively stressful and distracting, especially for the beginner. You can also meditate while reclining, although reclining poses the opposite problem—the mind tends to become dull and inattentive.

Of all the postures and activities, the seated position is acknowledged as superior, for it offers the optimum blend of relaxation and alertness. Naturally, there are many forms of sitting. Over the centuries, the Buddhist tradition has developed guidelines for sitting, so that posture and practice can bring the greatest meditative benefit. The most important factor is the alignment of the spine, head, and pelvis. The spine should be erect yet at ease, with the vertebrae neatly supporting one another like a stack of cups. The pelvis should be erect and lifted slightly forward, so that the lower vertebrae in the "stack of cups" balance comfortably on it. The lower back and shoulders should not slump forward; otherwise, pressure will be placed on the diaphragm, causing breathing to become shorter, more erratic, and more labored. With the pelvis and lower back erect and the shoulders and head properly aligned with them, the skeletal frame will effortlessly support the weight of the body, taking pressure off the joints and muscles. As the chest and lower abdomen begin to relax, breathing will become long and deep, allowing the internal organs—particularly the lungs and heart—to function at their most efficient levels. Circulation of the blood and vital energy will open up, the nervous system will relax, and the entire body will be rejuvenated. Until one gets used to the posture, there may be some discomfort; but ultimately, when the posture is correct, the muscles that join the spine and pelvis in the lower abdomen—the point where the "stack of cups" meets the pelvis—should be the only place where one feels tension. All other tensions should gradually dissolve (including the tension in the lower back and abdomen), so that the body comes to feel refreshed and almost weightless.

Seated meditation posture is not intended to force the body into a rigid stillness, but is designed to allow it to relax progressively to the point where it settles into perfect equipoise. When proper sitting posture has been achieved, one will feel quite alert, both mentally and physically. Thus, posture and mental state are closely related. Should the back slacken and begin to slump over, it will most certainly be a sign that the mind is wandering and concentration is bad. If the posture is too forced, it is an indication that the mind is tense and anxious. Through the practice of meditation one will discover just how intertwined body and mind really are. Before long one will begin to learn how to use one to cultivate the other.

A variety of positions for the legs can be used, but the principle behind them is the same: legs and buttocks must provide a stable base that will allow the pelvis to come slightly upward and forward, and bring the lower back and torso into comfortable alignment, as described above. The best and most time-honored posture for sitting is the so-called full-lotus posture (S. *padmāsana*). When Śākyamuni Buddha achieved perfect enlightenment beneath the bodhi tree, he did so seated in the lotus posture. Even today, visual representations of the Buddha nearly always portray him in this form. Hence, one could say that, for Buddhists, the lotus is the sacred posture, par excellence.

In the full-lotus posture, the right foot is placed over the upper thigh of the left leg, and the left foot placed over the thigh of the right. The legs are thereby locked into place, with the two knees and buttocks planted firmly on the ground. It is your preference as to which foot rests on top—left or right. When done correctly, the feet should be tucked snugly into the joint between pelvis and thighs, with the soles pointing upward.

Because of the intertwining of the legs, the full-lotus requires a very flexible body. For most people, it may be difficult at first (if not impossible). Nonetheless, it can be achieved with the help of regular practice and leg exercises. Simply take it a step at a time, starting out with short periods and gradually extending them. The mind can also have an impact on flexibility and posture. As the mind begins to settle down, one will find that the body naturally relaxes and untightens.

If the full-lotus posture is too painful, you may use the half-lotus posture. In the half-lotus, one foot (either left or right) is placed on the thigh of the opposite leg. The other foot rests on the ground and is tucked under the opposite thigh. If this still proves difficult, the raised foot may be placed on the calf of the opposite leg rather than the thigh. Or it may even be placed on the ground.

A popular position among Japanese is the kneeling posture known as *seiza*. In the *seiza* posture, the knees are placed flush with one another and the forelegs are tucked under the buttocks so that the buttocks and torso actually sit on the heels. The toes should be relaxed and kept flat against the floor. A cushion may be placed between the heels and buttocks in order to minimize the pressure of the body's weight.

If your legs are tight or your thighs large, a simple cross-legged posture is all right. But this position is generally not recommended, for it is unstable and tends to throw the weight of the body toward the buttocks, causing the lower back to strain and tire more quickly. The superiority of the full-lotus and half-lotus postures lies in the fact that they allow the pelvis and spine to be aligned with a minimum of effort, and distribute the weight of the upper body evenly between the knees and buttocks.

When sitting in any one of these postures, a firm cushion should be used to raise the buttocks off the ground, as well as a folded blanket or thin mat-like cushion to protect the knees from the hard floor. Also, it is a good idea to drape a towel over the legs to prevent them from becoming chilled. Sitting for a long time with legs exposed to the cold air can lead to joint problems.

The size and type of cushion used for the buttocks is quite important. The best is the round or square meditation cushion stuffed with kapok that is typically used in Buddhist monasteries in East Asia. It should not be too soft or thin. When the meditator is seated, the cushion should be thick and firm enough to raise the buttocks off the floor by several inches. It is essential that this height be adjusted appropriately, for it is what ultimately enables the lower back, abdomen, and torso to come into proper balance and alignment. If the height is too great, the posture will be unstable. If it is too little, the body will feel stressed and tend to slump forward after a while. It is best to experiment in order to find what thickness of cushion works best for you.

Furthermore, never sit directly in the middle of the cushion. The pelvis and buttocks should be perched solidly on the front half of the cushion, so that the upper thighs actually drop down off the edge of the cushion and the lower back and abdomen come upright. If you sit back too far on the cushion, the thighs will become elevated, causing the back to slump. Ultimately, your body should be erect and alert, with shoulders relaxed, spine straight, pelvis gently raised, and your weight centered effortlessly in the lower abdomen.

If sitting on the floor is too difficult, you may meditate using a chair. In this posture, the forelegs should be perpendicular to the floor, with the feet resting flat on the ground and the knees separated by a width of two fists. The buttocks should be perched on the edge of the chair, with thighs free. Otherwise, all the same points of posture apply.

☞ After assuming the proper position for seated meditation, place the hands lightly in the crux of the lap and thighs, palms up, with the back of the left hand resting snugly in the palm and fingers of the right. The thumbs should be elevated and their tips brought together, so that thumbs and palms form an ellipse. The hands should be drawn up snug with the lower abdomen, with the wrists resting in the notch of the thighs and the elbows extended outward to either side. The upper arms should fall comfortably down from the shoulders—neither drawn in too tightly nor pushed out too far. The shoulders should be perfectly relaxed and in an even position with the torso. They should neither slump forward nor be drawn back too forcefully.

The head should be positioned so that the plane of the face is perpendicular to the floor. Buddhist meditation manuals say that when the head is properly positioned, the tip of the nose will be in line with the navel, and the ears in line with the shoulders. The chin should be tucked in slightly, but not so much that it constricts the throat. Breathe in and out through the nose. The mouth should be closed with the teeth slightly parted and the tongue curled gently upward so that its tip touches the edge of the soft palate located between the teeth and the roof of the mouth. This helps to regulate the flow of saliva. The eyes should remain partially open and relaxed, with the gaze directed to an area of the floor approximately two to three feet in front of the meditator. At first there may be a tendency to become preoccupied with focusing on the floor or the wall in front of you, but it is best not to be distracted by this: simply return your attention to your particular method of meditation.

Sometimes, drowsiness will be a problem, especially if one is meditating for long periods of time (as in retreat). When this occurs, I recommend another kneeling posture. Move off the flat cushion onto the hard floor and kneel down with thighs, buttocks, and torso perfectly erect and forelegs extended behind you, so that the entire weight of the body is balanced over the knees. Place the palms of your hands together (in the gesture of prayer or adoration) and hold them in a position extended slightly outward from the breastbone. Focus your mind firmly on the tips of your fingers.

These are the basic physical guidelines for seated meditation. If they are applied correctly, body, breath, and mind will settle down quickly and a feeling of refreshing ease will pervade one's entire body.

Methods for Walking Meditation

Although sitting meditation is deemed the best way to settle a scattered mind and cultivate meditative concentration, one cannot sit all the time. Therefore, Buddhist teachers have developed techniques that allow one to meditate while engaged in other sorts of physical activity as well—walking, standing still, lying down, doing manual labor, and so forth. Among them, Buddhist practitioners most often use walking meditation in conjunction with seated meditation. When engaged in extended meditation retreats, interspersing walking meditation with extended periods of sitting helps to prevent the meditator's legs from becoming stiff or fatigued. It can also be used to counteract drowsiness or collect a scattered mind. In the Chan tradition we distinguish two methods of walking—fast-walking and slow-walking.

Slow-Walking

In slow-walking, the torso should be erect and alert, and the head perpendicular, just as in seated meditation. The entire body should move in perfect unison and concentration—as a single entity. Body and mind should be focused on the ball of the leading foot. The mind should not be allowed to wander upward. Thus, with each step that is taken, your attention and center of gravity should shift with unbroken continuity from one foot to the other, then back again.

The right hand is rolled into a loose fist, and the left hand wrapped gently, yet securely, around it. The two should be extended slightly outward from the body, in a position even with the bottom of the rib cage. The walking pace should be slow and measured, with each step being no more than a half or full foot's length in measure. The eyes should be partially closed and directed at about a 45 degree angle toward the floor in front of the meditator, just as in seated meditation. If space is restricted, slow-walking may be performed by pacing back and forth along a straight line, or in a clockwise fashion (right shoulder toward the center) around the perimeter of the room.

Usually, the specific meditation techniques applied in seated meditation—counting the breath, following the breath, and so on—are not used doing periods of walking meditation. Instead, concentration is placed on the sole of the forward foot. Nevertheless, you may find that certain breathing techniques provide a useful support to your practice. For example, you may coordinate breathing with walking, so that you inhale during one step and exhale during the next step. Or, if moving at a slower pace, you may find it more comfortable to inhale while lifting the foot and exhale as it descends to the floor. If you intend to count the breaths while walking, it is better to count while exhaling, just as in seated meditation. In the end, you must experiment to find the combination of walking and breathing that is most naturally conducive to concentration. Once a particular variation is selected, however, it is best to stick to it for a while and not continue to flit from one to another. Also, it is important not to waffle back and forth between different objects of concentration, such as focusing on the breath one moment, and the balls of your feet the next. This especially becomes a problem when you try to incorporate and become used to all aspects of slow-walking meditation at the same time. In general, focusing awareness on the feet is probably best, since—as the chief instrument of motion—our attention naturally tends to fall to the feet when we walk.

You may think that an activity such as walking would inhibit the experience of samādhi, or meditative absorption, but this is not the case. If you apply yourself wholeheartedly to slow-walking meditation, it is possible to enter the same states of samādhi as in seated meditation, although it may be more difficult to achieve.

Fast-Walking

Another walking exercise that is useful for alleviating leg pain and promoting harmony of body and mind is fast-walking. In Chan meditation halls, this is called "running the incense" (paoxiang). If outdoors or in a large facility, meditators may walk in a straight line. In a meditation hall, where space is limited, walking clockwise in a circle (right shoulder toward the middle of the room) is the accepted procedure. People who are old and weaker may walk in smaller circles in the center of the room, while stronger people may walk around them at a more vigorous clip. The speed should start at a moderate pace and steadily increase as the walking proceeds. Apart from the sensation of walking ever faster, there should be no other thoughts in your mind. Just walk! This is an excellent method for alleviating tensions and focusing the mind when you are tired and sore.

Method for Meditating While Standing

To meditate while standing still, the toes of the feet should be aligned with each other, and the feet themselves separated by a distance equal to about the length of your foot. The outer edges of the feet should be even with the shoulders. The torso is erect, just as in seated and walking meditation, with the whole body perfectly aligned and relaxed from the head through the lower abdomen, right to the soles of the feet. When the posture is correct, you will have the sense of the body's weight being supported by the skeletal frame so that it rests fully on the balls of the feet. The arms and hands should hang loosely at your sides. The knees must not be allowed to lock, otherwise they will feel the brunt of the body's weight and quickly become fatigued. If they are slightly bent, the weight will be directed more effectively to the feet. As with slow-walking, attention should be placed on the point of the feet where the weight of the body centers.

BREATHING'S RHYTHM IS INTIMATELY CONNECTED TO OUR
MENTAL X PHYSICAL CONDITION.

Method for Meditating While Lying Down

When lying down to sleep or rest, it is best to lie on the right side. The legs should be flush, with the knees bent and drawn slightly forward. The left arm is draped along the torso and left thigh, the right forearm extended forward. In this position you will experience fewer dreams, sleep more soundly, digest food better, awaken more refreshed, and will not experience nocturnal sexual emissions.

Lying on the back with face up can be very effective for helping to regain energy when you are fatigued. However, it should be used only for short stretches of time. When resting in this position, relax the entire body, avoiding even the slightest muscle movement.

Meditation in the Midst of Miscellaneous Daily Activities

The Chan school often says that everyday activity—eating, cleaning, defecating, carrying water, chopping wood—is itself Chan. This point is quite profound and not something easily understood by persons who are new to the practice. If supplemented with a regular routine of seated and walking meditation, in time the ability to find meditative power in these activities will deepen. Thus, it should be understood that everyday activity itself becomes increasingly subtle as the practice matures. Like riding a bicycle, one gets only a rough idea from hearing instructions. However, as a rule of thumb, attend to the activity at hand with your entire body and mind. Do not think of the past; do not think of the future. Just do what is called for, using slow and precise movements.

PRECONDITIONS FOR EFFECTIVE MEDITATION: HARMONIZING THE BREATH

Breathing is something that is with us all the time. It is probably the most constant activity that we know, and its rhythm is intimately connected to our mental and physical condition. As a physical sensation, one could say that the sensation of breathing falls midway between the grossness of the physical body and the subtlety of the mind. The cyclic motion of inhaling and exhaling pervades and influences our entire being. It can become quite constricted and rough, like the gross physical body, or so smooth and subtle that it seems immaterial, like the mind. Because the breath is so central to our mental and physical condition, Asian systems of meditation have traditionally placed a strong emphasis on the breath and breathing techniques. Their understanding of the breath and its relationship to our psychological and physiological processes is highly sophisticated. All of them speak of a subtle dimension of the breath known as the vital breath, or vital energy. In Chinese the term is *qi*; in Sanskrit, *prāṇa*; and in Japanese, *ki*.

"BREATH IS THE PRANA WHICH ANIMATES THE
BODY."

PURE — PRANAYAMA — PRANA.

In the conventional sense, breathing refers to the sixteen to eighteen cycles of inhalation and exhalation that normal individuals experience in a given minute. Breath is the air that passes in and out of nose and mouth and animates the body. However, for the experienced meditator, breath and breathing mean something more. The cycle of inhalations and exhalations in meditation will gradually slow, deepen, and extend, becoming very fine and subtle. In fact, if you observe the breath long enough, you will discover that a goodly part of our sense of physical constriction is itself a sensation that comes from shallow and constricted breathing. As breathing becomes deep and harmonious and the body's channels open up, body and breath will seem immaterial, like pure energy, or like the mind itself. This is the sensation of vital energy known as qi, or prāna. The experience of this vital energy entails a kind of subtle or fine breathing that is quite different from our ordinary inhalation and exhalation. This condition will stimulate blood circulation and vitality, which can be experienced as a flood of vital energy (qi) that circulates through the body and passes freely in and out of the pores, nourishing whatever it touches. Most ordinary people are not even aware of this vital energy of qi, much less the possibility of achieving such a subtle form of breathing. But anyone who experiences this in meditation will feel that it is a blessing for which one should truly be thankful.

Forms of Breathing

During meditation, breathing is brought from a condition of coarseness to a condition of subtlety. We distinguish four types of breathing on this continuum: (1) winded breathing, or panting (feng); (2) forced, or constricted, breathing (chuan); (3) vital breath, or energy (qi); (4) subtle, or fine, breathing (xi).

Winded breathing refers to the gasping or labored breathing experienced after strenuous activity. The rate and force of the breath will be like a rushing wind. This is not at all suitable for practicing meditation. Constricted breathing is the irregular and forced breathing that occurs when one feels tense and nervous, or when one is suffering from the aches and pains of illness. The condition of constricted breathing is not suitable for meditation either. If you are physically exhausted or stressed, it is better to lie down and rest for a bit. After regaining a measure of strength and equilibrium, you can then meditate.

Winded and constricted breathing are not normal conditions. The third type of breathing—that of vital breath, or energy (qi)—is the breathing of a healthy person engaged in normal activity. In this state a person will breathe about sixteen to eighteen times per minute. Listening quietly, the sound of the breathing will be audible, but it will be relaxed and natural. This condition is the minimum requirement that a practitioner must meet in order to meditate effectively. It is also the safest rate of breathing for a beginning meditator. However, during the course of meditation practice, breathing may relax and harmonize so that it passes from qi to the fourth condition of subtle breathing, or xi.

CENTER OF GRAVITY.

Subtle, or fine, breathing (*xi*) is the optimum condition for developing meditative concentration. *Xi* itself can be further subdivided into four levels: (a) nasal breathing; (b) abdominal breathing; (c) embryonic, or womb, *(tai)* breathing; (d) turtle breathing.

When sitting in meditation, the mouth is closed and breathing occurs through the nose. At first, while still in the condition of ordinary, or *qi*, breathing, you will be able to hear the sound of your own breath. At the first level of *xi* breathing (nasal breathing), the rate and rhythm stay basically the same, but the breath becomes inaudible and less forced. It is important not to impose an imagined rate and subtlety to your breathing, but instead allow it to change on its own. Breathing should be determined solely by the spontaneous action of the lungs. If you deliberately try to control your breathing, the rate may become unnaturally fast and induce dizziness. Or, it may become unnaturally slow, causing the chest to feel tight. If such symptoms appear, it is a sign that the breathing is forced. Relax and allow it to find its natural equilibrium.

In abdominal breathing, you still breathe through the nostrils, but you will have the keen sensation that the motion of inhalations and exhalations has dropped down and is initiated from the lower abdomen rather than the chest. A beginner who has not experienced abdominal breathing should not intentionally try to press the air into the lower abdominal region. With regular meditation, the breathing action will automatically extend past the diaphragm and descend to what we call the lower *dantian*, or center of gravity and vital energy in the lower abdomen. When this occurs, your body and mind may suddenly feel quite supple, light, and at ease. Breathing will become progressively slower, deeper, and more extended. A natural and spontaneous rhythm of breathing will develop deep in the abdomen. As this rhythm takes hold, you may feel that the breath is gently cycled and suffused throughout the body, opening obstructions and rejuvenating every cell.

When a fetus is in its mother's womb, it does not breathe with its nostrils, but absorbs air through its umbilical connection with the mother's circulatory system. If abdominal breathing is carried to yet a further degree of subtlety, the sensation of inhaling and exhaling air through the nostrils will cease altogether. Body, breath, and mind meld into one indistinguishable substance, and all the pores of the body open up to become a channel for breathing. Regardless of whether such a function actually exists or not, like a fetus in the womb, it seems as though one absorbs breath and vital energy effortlessly from the universe around oneself. This is embryonic, or womb, breathing.

Turtle breathing takes its name from a species of black turtle that is said to have extraordinary powers of endurance and longevity. According to legend, if one were to bury this turtle under the ground, it would still be alive after several years, even without food, water, or air. If your practice of meditation reaches a truly deep level of dhyāna or samādhi, breathing will seem to cease completely, while your physiological system will remain very much alive. At this point, your

INTERNAL WELLSPRING OF VITAL ENERGY

TURTLE BREATHING

meditative state will be situated somewhere between embryonic breathing and turtle breathing. When the true condition of turtle breathing is reached, the psycho-physical body will form its own microcosmic universe, nourished directly by its own internal wellspring of vital breath, or energy. The body will no longer need to take air or vital energy from the outside environment in order to replenish its vitality. Instead, energy wells up from a wholly internal source, naturally suffusing the body and requiring no effort whatsoever.

The levels of coarse and subtle breathing described above represent a natural progression that is commonly experienced by persons who practice meditation over an extended period of time. It is helpful to know about these things so that one can evaluate the effectiveness and progress of one's practice. But such knowledge may prove harmful if you set up unrealistic expectations for yourself, or become overly anxious to attain advanced stages. These stages must develop naturally and without artifice. You must first learn to practice well with nasal breathing. If, in time, abdominal breathing develops, then it is a good start.

PRECONDITIONS FOR EFFECTIVE MEDITATION:
HARMONIZING THE MIND

Once the harmonious concentration of body, breath, and mind has been established, the experience of samādhi and wisdom will be within reach. The Buddhist tradition offers many different techniques to develop samādhi, wisdom, and insight, each of which is designed to counter impediments and develop the mind in its own particular way. Nonetheless, their basic principle is the same: they strive to take the mind from its usual scattered and coarse condition, simplify it and unify it with concentration, and bring it to what we call the insight of "no-mind" (wuxin), or "no-thought" (wunian).

The mind of the ordinary person swings like a pendulum between two sorts of mental condition: scatteredness and drowsiness. When one is energetic and full of vigor, outwardly the mind romps through the sense fields and, inwardly, it boils with thoughts. In such an excited condition, it is not easy to even conceive the thought of calming down, much less actually collecting and settling the mind. This is true for almost everyone. If such excitation were not so important to us, we would not feel bored and dejected when there is nothing to do. Then again, when one's energy is dissipated and exhausted, one may sink into a dull torpor or melancholy. If this condition did not exist, one would not need to sleep after spending the day at hard mental or physical labor.

In the former condition, the mind is characterized by distractedness and confusion; in the latter case, by dullness and torpor. These two mentalities are the great enemies of meditators. Every beginning practitioner must guard against them and learn to bring them under control.

When you are slightly drowsy, there are methods to remedy the situation, such as opening the eyes very wide or concentrating your attention on the spot between the eyebrows. For extreme drowsiness, however, it is best to put down your given method of meditation, close your eyes, and rest for a few moments. Just do not allow yourself to fall into the habit of stopping your meditation and drifting off at the slightest suggestion of drowsiness!

By far, the biggest problem faced by meditators is the condition of a scattered and confused mind, and the majority of the techniques for taming the mind are designed to address this problem. The Buddhist scriptures describe many such practices, each with its own particular content and procedure. However, despite their apparent differences, these methods share the common aim of bringing the scattered mind to a condition of one-pointed concentration and, finally, to the realization of no-mind. For the purpose of conveying to my students some idea of this process, I use a series of seven diagrams, each of which illustrates a particular degree of mental concentration (or lack thereof). These seven diagrams are not meant to describe a set of fixed stages that every person must experience. Meditative development is highly individualized and cannot be so rigidly codified. At best, this scheme is meant to give a basic understanding of the meditative process and some measure by which to determine whether one's practice is correct.

Buddhist teachers will generally assign different techniques of meditation according to the specific emotional disposition and meditative needs of the given student. We will have occasion to discuss some of these methods and their usage later. For the sake of the present illustration, I will discuss the phases of meditative development in relation to the method of counting breaths. Counting breaths is the most elemental practice in a traditional set of techniques known as "recollection, or mindfulness, of breathing" (S. *anāpāna-smṛti*; C. *nianxi*). *Anāpāna-smṛti*, and especially counting breaths, is particularly effective for counteracting a scattered, distracted mind. Thus, it has long been used by Buddhists as a method for beginners, as well as a foundational practice for other meditation methods.

SEVEN PHASES OF MEDITATIVE DEVELOPMENT

1. *The Scattered Mind Prior to Meditation*

Before taking up the method of counting breaths, there is no consistent object on which to focus the mind. Thoughts ceaselessly turn and stir. Attention is fragmented from one instant to the next, as it darts off in countless directions, in pursuit of one object after another. We hanker after sensory data and sensations from our surroundings, reminisce over the past, and anticipate the future. The scattered dots in the diagram represent the random thoughts and sensations of a confused and unfocused mind; the broken dashes, the fragmented stream of one's attention.

2. Initial Efforts to Apply the Method of Meditation

When first taking up the practice of counting breaths, your attention will often wander away from breath and number. Or, many associated thoughts will intrude, such as concerns over how to count the number or how to regard the breath. You are able to sustain the count for short stretches, but usually this is interrupted before long. By repeatedly bringing your attention mind back to the method, the confusion of wandering thoughts gradually is brought under control, and a steady stream of focus begins to develop, enduring for longer and longer stretches of time. The broken line running through the center of the diagram represents the fitful emergence of a steady stream of concentration; that is to say, the mind concentrated on the method. The surrounding marks and dots indicate the continued presence of distractedness and scattered thoughts, but the firm line developing in the center shows that concentration is beginning to assert control.

3. Coarse but Unbroken Application of the Method

By the third level, you are able to maintain uninterrupted concentration and count each number in perfect succession for a span of at least ten minutes. Nevertheless, concentration is coarse and there still exist many subtle wandering and scattered thoughts that impinge on the margins of your attention. Although concentration may ripple and waver momentarily, these thoughts are never powerful enough to cause you completely to lose sight of the number and the method. The solid line through the center represents the uninterrupted flow of concentration over time. The surrounding dots and occasional slashes that intersect the line illustrate the subtle mental static and coarse thoughts that periodically invade your field of awareness.

4. Subtle and Unbroken Application of the Method

Just as before, you are able to maintain concentration on counting breaths without interruption, but at this point, scattered thoughts are now greatly reduced.

Distractions associated with the sensory environment pose almost no problem. Occasionally, wandering thoughts invented by the mind will come into consciousness and then slide away. To you, however, their presence and subsequent rippling effect remain peripheral to the main stream of mindfulness. In this respect, diagram four represents a more subtle stage of concentration than diagram three, and awareness is now quite clear and securely settled on the method. When a wandering thought does arise, you are clearly aware of it, from beginning to end, but the stream of concentration is too deep and strong for these eddies of thought to divert it.

5. Pure but Effortful Concentration on the Method

In the fifth diagram there exists only pure counting of breaths. There are neither scattered distractions from the sensory environment nor internal fantasies of deluded thinking. Nonetheless, there is still a lucid sense of the act or process of meditation itself. There is an awareness of a self that is counting breaths, the breaths that are being counted, and the number that is counted and seized upon as the main object of concentration. Concentration itself is pure and unified, but there is still an effortful and ongoing attention to the method. Though all other extraneous disturbances may have disappeared, the thread of this tripartite complex of thoughts remains and continues without interruption—inhale-exhale-count, inhale-exhale-count. Thus, the single thread of concentration, when investigated more closely, is really a complex weaving of three basic threads, which is represented in the diagram by the three lines together. At this juncture, your mind is highly simplified and concentrated. In fact, you will likely be on the doorstep of samādhi, or "unified mind."

6. The Unified Mind of Samādhi

In the sixth diagram, your mind is so concentrated that the act of meditation itself—both the counting of the number and the presence of the breath—is forgotten. As the mind becomes truly calm and concentrated, the act of effortful meditation itself seems coarse and distracting. Letting go of it, number and breath vanish, and body, breath, and mind meld into a single unity. At this point, you may feel as though spatial distinctions no longer pertain among body, mind, and the world. The opposition between self and other people seems to vanish, and the boundary between the internal and external dissolves. The previous sense of dividedness is replaced by a feeling of pure and harmonious being that is so wondrous as to be indescribable. This is the basic experience of samādhi, or what we variously refer to as "meditative absorption,". "unified mind," and "one-pointedness of mind." However, there are many levels of samādhi, some shallow, some deep. They can range from the simple and relatively shallow experience of purity and oneness described above, to experiences of infinite light and sound, boundless space, limitless consciousness, limitless emptiness, and even the inconceivable experiences of enlightenment described in such Buddhist scriptures as the Avataṃsaka, or Huayan, Sūtra.

Regardless of how sublime the content, such states of meditative absorption are still defiled by the presence of discriminating thought and attachment. This defilement is none other than the subtle sense of "selfhood." At deeper levels of samādhi, the mind becomes so supple and powerful that even the subtlest thought is experienced on an extraordinarily vast scale. Because attachment to self is still operating in samādhi, samādhi actually entails the magnification of self to a cosmic scale. The experiences of limitless consciousness, bliss, being, and other feelings associated with samādhi are actually the projections of what we call the "great or expanded sense of self." Until this particular impediment is removed, enlightenment has not dawned and one is still subject to the bonds of deluded existence. Samādhi experiences of this ilk will be no more than a mundane or worldly samādhi, and the spiritual insights generated from them, a mundane wisdom still tainted by defiling outflows.

7. No-Self, No-Mind

In the seventh diagram there is no line of concentration, no thought, no mark of any kind. Body, mind, and environment have all genuinely disappeared. Time and space are blown apart, and any sense of existence or nonexistence has vanished. You have entered a realm of emptiness and quiescence, a realm that transcends all subjective emotion and point of view. This is the experience of supramudane samādhi and wisdom of "no-mind" that is free of the defiling illusion of self. There is no way to effectively describe it. All words and images are useless; but you will have tasted true freedom and peace.

Just as with the experience of mundane samādhi, you should be aware that there are also many levels of supramundane samādhi and many degrees of insight into no-mind, or no-self. Sometimes the influence of the root illusions and defilements is merely lessened or temporarily suspended. Sometimes it is severed, but only to a partial degree. In all these cases, the insight of emptiness or no-mind will qualitatively be the same, but the intensity and clarity will vary. Imagine, for example, that you are stuck inside an old well, the mouth of which has been boarded over with planks and covered with dirt. A wind comes up and blows some of the dirt off, allowing a flicker of light to shine through the boards before another wind covers them over again. Suppose, then, that someone brushes away the dirt and removes a plank, so that light begins to stream steadily into the well; or that one is finally able to hop out of the well and see the full sun. Then, suppose that one actually becomes the sun itself. All of these experiences of sunlight are qualitatively similar and may be called "illumination," but the difference in degree is vast. The same holds for the experience of emptiness and no-mind. In principle, the first glimpse of no-mind is the same as the enlightenment of a Buddha. One has seen the Buddha Mind, knows its character, and has developed a firm faith that this enlightenment is intrinsic to all beings. But there is still a big difference between this experience and the full and perfect enlightenment of Buddhahood itself, in which this enlightened potential is fully actualized. Indeed, the Buddhist tradition has many different systems for describing enlightenment and its stages, from the four fruits and the concept of arhat in Hīnayāna Buddhism, to the schemes of ten, thirteen, forty-two, or fifty-two stages of the Mahāyāna bodhisattva.

II

The Three Disciplines
in the Graduated Path
of Practice

The Buddhist Precepts and Meditative Development

The *Avataṃsaka Sūtra* says, "The precepts are the foundation of supreme enlightenment."[1] Thus, one could say that the basic spirit of Buddhism is to be found in the solemn dignity of the precepts, or moral restraints, that describe the life of the Buddhist renunciant, and in the importance that followers of the Buddha's teaching attach to their observance. For anyone who becomes a disciple of the Buddha, whether a layperson or one who has formally left the household life as a renunciant, the first great act by which one enters the gate of Buddhism is to receive the precepts. Without this, one is not really sanctioned by the Buddhist tradition, even though one may consider oneself to be a believer and practitioner of Buddhism. One is just an ordinary person who hangs outside the gate.

Because there are differences among Buddhist practitioners themselves, different types and levels of precepts have been distinguished. The most basic division is between that of the householder, or layperson (male, S. *upāsaka;* female, S. *upāsikā*), and the officially ordained renunciant, or "home-leaver" (Buddhist monk, S. *bhikṣu;* Buddhist nun, S. *bhikṣuṇī*). For the householder, or lay practitioner, there are altogether four levels of precepts that may be received:

1. The three refuges *(san guiyi)*
2. The five precepts *(wu jie)*
3. The eight precepts of the monthly *uposatha,*
   or fast-day observance *(ba guan [zhai] jie)*
4. The bodhisattva precepts *(pusajie)*

For the individual who chooses to renounce the household life and embark on the career of a Buddhist monk or nun, there are altogether five levels or types of precepts:

1. The ten precepts of the novice monk (S. *śrāmaṇera*) or novice nun S. *śrāmaṇerikā*
2. The precepts of the intermediate novice nun (S. *śikṣamānā*)
3. The precepts of the full monk, or male renunciant (S. *bhikṣu*)
4. The precepts of the full nun, or female renunciant (S. *bhikṣuṇī*)
5. The bodhisattva precepts

As with the three refuges and five precepts, which the layperson always takes together, the ten novitiate and full renunciatory precepts constitute a defined sequence. Naturally, this sequence must include the three refuges at its beginning, although they are not listed here. First, there are the ten basic precepts of the novice renunciant (novice monk, S. *śrāmaṇera*; novice nun, S. *śrāmaṇerikā*). These are received at the formal ceremony when one first renounces the household life (S. *pravrajya*), and are observed over a subsequent period of probation. The second set includes the precepts for the *śikṣamānā*, an interim probationary status for the female novitiate. Third and fourth are the precepts of a *bhikṣu*, or male renunciant, and *bhikṣuṇī*, or female renunciant. These are taken during the ceremony for full monastic ordination known as *upasampadā*, during which one is admitted to full "adult" status in the monastic saṅgha. Finally, there are the bodhisattva precepts—a set of precepts that, once again, may also be taken by laity.

For all Buddhists, receiving the three refuges is the first and most elemental act on the Buddhist path. In the presence of a duly ordained monk or nun, one pledges to take refuge in the Three Jewels: the Buddha; the Dharma, or Buddhist teaching; and the Saṅgha, or Buddhist assembly. Some people think that the three refuges are simply a profession of faith and should not be considered precepts. In fact, the three refuges also are precepts. One of the characteristics of a Buddhist precept is that it carries a sense of prohibition, or restraint. Restraint is indeed an attribute of the refuges. When one takes refuge in the Buddha, one vows for the rest of one's life not to seek or resort to depraved or demonic spiritual ideals. The Buddha is one's ideal of perfection. In taking refuge in the Dharma, one vows for the rest of one's life to avoid wayward paths and false teachings. The Dharma is the true path. In taking refuge in the saṅgha, one vows for the rest of one's life not to rely on followers of wayward or false paths. As such, taking refuge in the Three Jewels of the Buddha, Dharma, and Saṅgha entails a very basic sense of restraint—commitment to proper spiritual ideals and attitudes, as defined by Buddhist tradition.

The five precepts comprise the vow to (1) refrain from taking life; (2) refrain from theft; (3) refrain from harmful or socially unacceptable sexual involvement; (4) refrain from lying; (5) refrain from intoxicants. The first four deeds specified in this list—taking life, theft, unacceptable or harmful sexual activity, and lying—are considered grave violations in Buddhist tradition. Commission of these actions on the part of monks and nuns constitutes a particularly heinous offense, which in the monastic *vinaya*, or "preceptural codes," is known as *pārājika*, or "expulsion." If a monk or nun is found to have committed such a deed, he or she must be "expelled," or "excommunicated," from the monastic saṅgha. Thus, one can see that these four actions warrant special attention on the part of all Buddhists: they are a foundation of all Buddhist morality, value, and spiritual growth. The fifth deed, indulging in intoxication, is considered an evil only insofar as it beclouds the mind and readily contributes to the other four offenses. Thus, it is less serious than the other four, but of crucial importance nonetheless.

By committing the four cardinal evils of killing, theft, engaging in unacceptable sexual activity, and lying, one is not only doing terrible violence to others, one is also undermining the ground of openness and trust that is the foundation of all spiritual growth. From a karmic point of view, the personal repercussions of such actions are, likewise, devastating, for one thereby engenders much evil karma, which will result in rebirth among the animals, hungry ghosts, or Buddhist purgatorial hells. In these lower, or turbid, realms, mental and spiritual faculties are greatly impaired, and suffering is intense, making it very difficult to generate the karmic causes and conditions necessary to return to higher realms, much less receive the Buddhist teachings. On the one hand, the five precepts forestall the possibility of this sort of painful retribution in lower realms, and help to ensure that we will be born in a condition—preferably that of a human being—where our faculties are keen and our circumstances are conducive to the practice of the Buddhist dharma. On the other hand, they also enable us to foster an environment that is suitable to our collective well-being and spiritual growth.

From a purely humanistic standpoint, the five precepts also describe the basic requirements for a healthy human society. No one would get along with one another if killing, theft, complete sexual license, deceit, and intoxication were condoned. Suspicion and violence would reign, and human relations would fragment into utter self-isolation. The actions prohibited by the five precepts are simply unacceptable if people are to live in peace and harmony. Accordance with these precepts represents the minimum criterion for being considered a decent human being.

Thus, in all respects, the five precepts are the foundation for our individual and collective deliverance from saṃsāra. Without them, the Buddhist dharma, as a tradition, cannot survive, and we as individuals cannot work our way to liberation.

Figuratively speaking, one could say that there are many "paths" that one may take in this world, spiritual and otherwise. If you act like an animal or ghost, you become an animal or ghost. Act like a human and you become a human. Act like a Buddha and you become a Buddha. If you want to become a Buddha, you must walk the path of a Buddha. This is a matter of direction and choice. The five precepts are the gate to the path of Buddhahood and the moral bedrock on which all genuine spiritual progress rests. Hence, together with the three refuges, they are the foundation for both lay and monastic life.

᠅ All other sets of Buddhist precepts are, by and large, elaborations of the basic moral program set forth in the five precepts. The ten precepts of the novice monk and nun, the 250 to 300 precepts of the full monk and nun, all begin with the five precepts, adding to them various stipulations that define in detail the renunciatory lifestyle of the full-time Buddhist cleric. The eight precepts of the monthly *uposatha*, or "lay fast," expand on the five precepts by incorporating additional restraints that usually pertain to the monastic life—namely, (6) the foreswearing of perfumes and cosmetic adornments; (7) the avoidance of song, dance, and other forms of public entertainment; and (8) refraining from taking food after the noon hour. The third of the five lay precepts that prohibits improper sexual relations, in this instance, is also reinterpreted to mean avoidance of any and all forms of sexual activity. Actually, these eight precepts comprise nine of the ten novitiate precepts taken by the *śrāmaṇera* and *śrāmaṇerikā* during the ceremony for renouncing the household life (S. *pravrajya*). However, whereas novice monks and nuns become renunciants by profession and observe these precepts continually, laypersons take them only at specifically appointed times.[2] According to the Buddhist ritual calendar, there are six days in every lunar month, known as the days of the *uposatha* fast, which require special religious observances. They are the two days of the dark moon, the two days of the full moon, and the two days of the half moon. In addition to observing the eight precepts, laypeople on these days will often visit temples, attend lectures or meditations, take part in rites of worship and offering, read or recite scripture, and engage in other forms of meritorious activity. Because they so closely anticipate the monastic life, the eight precepts are literally called the "eight precepts that shut the gate" (*baguan jie*), meaning that, through these observances, one temporarily shuts the door on saṃsāra and the household life and moves toward the liberative path of the renunciant. The *uposatha* observance itself is commonly referred to in China as the "days of purificatory fasting" (*zhairi*), primarily because lay people at this time keep the restraints and the post-noon fast ordinarily observed by the monastic saṅgha. Thus, the eight precepts are also known as "the eight precepts of the purificatory fast that close [the gate of saṃsāra] (*ba guan zhai jie*)."[3]

The five precepts close the gate to the sufferings of the lower destinies and open the way to birth in the upper realms of the human and heavenly beings (S. *deva*; C. *tian*). However, as they stand, they cannot counteract and deliver one from the cycle of birth and death per se. By actively "restraining" sensual lust, the eight *uposatha* precepts can help shut the door to rebirth itself, opening the way to liberation. The precepts of the novice and full renunciant go on to actually define the optimum path for achieving nirvāna and deliverance from the cycle of birth and death, the traditional goal of the Hīnayānist arhat. In similar fashion, the bodhisattva precepts go a step further to set the parameters for the bodhisattva path of the Mahāyāna, the path that leads to the supreme enlightenment of Buddhahood itself.

As Mahāyāna Buddhist practitioners, the purpose of our practice is to attain unsurpassed perfect enlightenment (S. *anuttara-samyak-sambodhi*), or Buddhahood—to emulate the Buddha himself, empowered by our confidence in and understanding of the Three Jewels. To achieve this exceedingly lofty goal, we strive to cultivate wisdom (S. *jñāna*) and accumulate virtue and merit (S. *punya*). Through this twofold practice we are able to bring spiritual benefit to ourselves and to others. This practice is precisely the task of the bodhisattva practitioner as set forth in the bodhisattva precepts—the "three cumulative sets of vows" (*sanjujie*) that we receive in the precept transmission ceremony. Buddhahood is the fruit or result that comes with traveling the path of the bodhisattva as described by the bodhisattva precepts. Just as the renunciatory "restraints" of the *bhikṣu* and *bhikṣunī* set the course for the personal elimination of saṃsāric suffering and the realization of nirvāṇa, so the bodhisattva "restraints," or "precepts," set the course for realization of the inconceivable wisdom, compassion, and expedient powers of a Buddha, a Fully-Enlightened One.

The term "bodhisattva" is formed by conjunction of the two terms "enlightenment" (S. *bodhi*) and "sentient being" (S. *sattva*). Together they convey four basic meanings. First, the bodhisattva is a sentient being (S. *sattva*) that aspires "upwardly" to attain unsurpassed wisdom and enlightenment (S. *bodhi*). Second, he or she aspires to this goal in order—"downwardly"—to bring genuine benefit to all other sentient beings (S. *sattva*), so that they too will attain enlightenment. Third, in the course of striving for enlightenment, each individual bodhisattva awakens to his or her intrinsic Buddha-nature. Fourth, at the same time that the individual bodhisattva so awakens, he or she awakens all of the countless sentient beings to the same intrinsic Buddha-nature that resides in each and every one of them. By considering these four meanings together, one can say that, upwardly, the bodhisattva seeks self-enlightenment, and downwardly, the bodhisattva seeks the enlightenment of all other sentient beings. Moreover, Buddhahood, or enlightenment, is a quality with which all beings are already intrinsically endowed, so ultimately there is nothing for bodhisattvas to either acquire or give, either for themselves or for others! This is the dignity of true compassion.

Without the actual experience of enlightenment, how can bodhisattvas or aspirants in the Mahāyāna tradition rise to the seemingly impossible task of vowing to help all sentient beings to attain enlightenment? If they themselves have not attained enlightenment, how can they truly help others achieve it? Many practitioners, daunted by such questions, place exclusive emphasis on faith in or devotion to the Buddha, while others focus solely on cultivating an experience of insight into emptiness, wishing to escape the travails of life. We can understand such responses because, after all, we are only human. If I do not know how to swim, how am I going to help others learn? One type of person says, "Let the lifeguard do it." The other says, "Let me become an Olympic swimmer first!" In fact, if you want to save others from drowning, you cannot just stay on the shore. Similarly, if you yourself want to learn to swim, the only place to learn is in the water. No matter how you look at it, you simply have to jump in. The bodhisattva path must be practiced in the midst of suffering, in the turmoil of the ocean of cyclic existence. To accomplish the goal of the bodhisattva, we need to develop the strength and skills to keep ourselves as well as others from drowning in this ocean of saṃsāra. We cannot rely wholly on the power of the Buddhas to do it for us; nor can we wait to become fully enlightened. We need—here and now—to develop directional discernment, unshakeable faith and vows, boundless love and compassion, and a penetrating view of the nature of emptiness (śūnyatā). Acquiring these four faculties will eventually enable us to subdue the afflictions of both ourselves and others, and lead us to the highest wisdom of a Buddha—to the consummate view of emptiness that brings correct understanding of the interrelatedness of all beings and all conditions of existence. It is the Bodhisattva Precepts that enable us to ascertain the path and to establish ourselves firmly on it.

In the *Brahmajāla Sūtra (Fanwang jing)*, it says that the bodhisattva precepts are "the original source of all the Buddhas, the root of the bodhisattva, and the foundation of all children of the Buddha in the grand saṅgha." If one does not walk the bodhisattva path, one will never become a Buddha, even if one believes or has faith in the Buddha. If you want to walk the bodhisattva path, you must receive the bodhisattva precepts. Thus, the bodhisattva precepts are the original root-cause that enables all the Buddhas to realize their Buddhahood.

One will notice that the bodhisattva precepts can be received in common by both the laity and the members of the monastic saṅgha. In China, they traditionally have been received by monks and nuns concurrently with the full renunciatory precepts. At the same time, one could say that the bodhisattva precepts and the role or status of the bodhisattva also stand outside of the usual sevenfold saṅgha of layman, laywoman, novice monk, novice nun, intermediary novice nun, full monk, and full nun. That is to say, the role of the bodhisattva need not be defined by any particular social or institutional form. According to Buddhist lore, even non-human beings may receive them.

In terms of content, the bodhisattva precepts are distinguished according to the "three cumulative sets of pure vows" *(sanju jingjie):*

1. To observe or keep all of the precepts of purity, without exception
2. To cultivate all the wholesome or good dharmas, without exception
3. To deliver all sentient beings, without exception

As represented in the Buddhist sūtras, the monastic precepts of the Hīnayāna—as restraints against action—contribute actively to the elimination of evil deeds, but can only contribute passively to cultivation of good deeds. That is to say, they will prohibit one from taking life, but they do not actively require one to save beings. The bodhisattva precepts, on the other hand, both actively restrain evil and compel one to undertake good deeds. One could say that they simultaneously encompass the restraints of the monastic vinaya, the positive qualities of enlightenment, the liberation that the practitioner is personally enjoined to develop by way of Buddhist practice, and the deliverance of other sentient beings. In fact, the three cumulative groups of the bodhisattva precepts themselves correspond directly to the "four all-encompassing vows" (si hongshi yuan) of the bodhisattva that we, as clergy and laity, recite daily in our services:

1. Sentient beings without limit I vow to deliver
2. Afflictions without end I vow to sever
3. Approaches to Dharma without number I vow to master
4. The unexcelled enlightenment of a Buddha I vow to attain[4]

Within recent generations in China, the bodhisattva precepts have been uniformly based on the system of ten major and forty-eight minor precepts found in the Fanwang jing, or Brahmajāla Sūtra. Because the precepts of this scripture are primarily directed toward helping other beings achieve salvation, it is thought that their observance does not require any special distinction in religious status. Therefore, they traditionally have been open equally to layperson and renunciant. Lately in Taiwan, however, renunciants and laypersons are divided when bodhisattva precept ordination is given. Only those individuals leaving home as renunciants receive the precepts of the Brahmajāla Sūtra, while laypersons receive only the six major and twenty-eight minor precepts of the Upāsaka Precept Sūtra (Youposhejie jing). Again, this distinction derives largely from reading the Brahmajāla precept against sexual license as an injunction to monastic chastity and celibacy. In actuality, this program needs further discussion, for the Upāsaka Precept Sūtra states quite clearly that the six major and twenty-eight minor precepts are the "foundation" of the bodhisattva precepts, but are not necessarily equivalent to the bodhisattva precepts themselves.[5]

It is said that, in principle, the bodhisattva precepts do not distinguish between householder and renunciant. Both are equal when it comes to the bodhisattva path. But, even though Buddhist teachings may speak of equality or sameness, it is sameness with respect to essential Buddha-nature, not sameness in terms of phenomenal cause and condition. It does not automatically obliterate all distinction between old and young, honorable and lowly, before and after. The Buddha says that all people can become Buddhas, because every person fundamentally possesses the enlightened nature of a Buddha. But, without having actualized this intrinsic Buddhahood—without fully knowing that they are Buddhas—sentient beings are still sentient beings. They are not yet Buddhas. Thus, with regard to the Buddhist precepts, there are distinctions in level and stage that must be observed, such as the three refuges, five precepts, ten precepts, and so on.

The three refuges are the foundation. The bodhisattva precepts and the renunciatory precepts of the bhikṣu and bhikṣunī are what we call the "complete, or full, precepts" (jujie). A person who receives the three refuges cannot thereby automatically be said to fulfill the moral demands of the bodhisattva and bhikṣu precepts. What is more, there is no bhikṣu or bodhisattva who will not have first received the three refuges. Thus, one can see that the three refuges are merely a preliminary expedient that leads one to the gate of Buddhist practice. The renunciatory and bodhisattva precepts describe the conditions for actually entering the gate and walking the path.

All the Buddhas of the past, present, and future are said to attain Buddhahood as humans among human beings. When they do so, they all display the demeanor of a bhikṣu, or renunciant. Hence, any person who decides to take the three refuges should strive to go on to receive the five precepts. Likewise, a person who has received the five precepts should go a step further and take the bodhisattva precepts. Having received the bodhisattva precepts, if he or she is able to make the resolution to leave home as a renunciant, the merit will be incalculable. But, if one is incapable of completely severing worldly entanglements and leaving the household, one should still keep the eight observances of the uposatha fast in order to open a road out of the prison of cyclic birth and death. One must, above all, never think that the work of the Buddhist path is completed by a simple profession of faith in the Buddha or refuge in the Three Jewels.

When one receives the refuges and precepts, it is very important that one undergo the proper ceremony for transmission of the precepts. This may take two forms. Ordinarily, one begins by fostering a serious and thorough determination to commit oneself fully to the precepts. Then, one formally recites the vows and receives confirmation of the precepts in the presence of a preceptor and witnesses from the monastic saṅgha. This is necessary to sow or instill the causal "seed" or "essence" of the vows in one's mind-stream. If the necessary monastic preceptors and witnesses are not available, one may prostrate and repent before an image of a Buddha or great bodhisattva, until one experiences an auspicious sign. Such signs may include visions of radiant light and flowers, or the vision of a Buddha or bodhisattva appearing and granting one the precepts. When this occurs, it is a sign that one is confirmed in the precepts.

However, receiving the precepts is just the beginning. After obtaining them, one must go on to study and embody them. Among the four great vows recited daily by Chan Buddhists in China, the third can be rendered as, "Dharma-gates beyond reckoning I vow to study." What is a "Dharma-gate" and what does its study entail? A "Dharma-gate" is an approach or access to the Dharma, or Buddha's teaching. To study a Dharma-gate is to study whatever the Buddhas have studied, practice whatever the Buddhas have practiced, and eventually realize whatever the Buddhas have realized. The Buddhist precept codes themselves constitute a broad and vast dharma-gate that teaches people how to learn what the Buddhas have learned, practice what the Buddhas have practiced, and realize what the Buddhas have realized.

Most people familiar with Buddhism will have heard that the main function of the precepts lies in their preventing wrong and putting a stop to evil. They may also be aware that the precepts bear a resemblance to the legal codes that establish norms and juridical procedures for secular societies. Precepts are prohibitional, prohibiting Buddhist followers from engaging in evil, much as laws do. They also provide formal steps for dealing with offenses. People may also have heard that the Buddhist precepts are limited in number, ranging from three, at the very least, to the three-hundred-odd vows of the bhikṣuṇī, or female, renunciant. Being limited and essentially prohibitional, how could the precepts ever be an access or "gate" to the dharma at large?

The fact is, while the Buddhist precepts certainly do prohibit doing specific evils, they equally prohibit apathy or resistance to doing good. Thus, observing the precepts carries two senses. On the one hand, there is "observance that entails abstinence or restraint." These are the precepts that are fulfilled by refraining from doing what must *not* be done. If one engages in an action that is prohibited by law, then it is infraction of the precepts. On the other hand, there is also "observance that entails action or engagement." These are precepts that specify actions that *should* be done. If one does not do what is required, it is also considered an infraction of the precepts.

Generally speaking, most people only know of the negative, or prohibitive, aspect of the Buddhist precepts—that aspect that is designed to put a stop to evil. They are not aware that there is also a positive side to the precepts, a side that requires one to "undertake to cultivate all that is good." If one looks at the precepts in terms of their relationship to the totality of Buddhist virtues, one will realize that such apparently prescriptive systems as the five precepts contain within them the most profoundly positive spiritual and ethical ideals. One of the oldest and most venerable statements of the Buddhist path says:

> To refrain from engaging in any evil,
> To undertake to cultivate all that is good,
> And to pursue the purification of one's own mind.
> This is the teaching of all the Buddhas.
> —from the *Dhammapada*

The five precepts are the simplest among the Buddhist precepts. At the same time, they are referred to as the "root, or foundational, precepts" (*genben jie*), because they are also the foundation of all the other Buddhist precepts. The eight *uposatha* precepts, the ten novitiate precepts, the precepts of the full bhikṣu and bhikṣuṇī, and the precepts of the bodhisattva are all simply an expansion of the five basic precepts. All of them recognize the five precepts as basic to the Buddhist path and look upon their infraction as cardinal sins. Thus, of all the precepts, the five precepts are the most important. If one does not study the five precepts and bring oneself fully into accord with their ethical implications, all other precepts will elude one's grasp. If one is pure in one's observance of the spirit of the five precepts, all other precepts can be kept quite easily.

At first glance, observance of the five precepts will seem a quite common and simple matter. Only after researching and reflecting on their contents thoroughly, will one realize that they are not as trivial a matter as one might think. Great master Hongyi (1880–1942), one of the most illustrious monks of the modern era, was especially renowned for his study and observance of the Buddhist vinaya, or moral codes. Not only did he feel that he was not bhikṣu material, but he considered himself unequal to the demands of a novice monk and even lacking in observance of the five precepts of a layman! Just think! If such a sternly observant monk as Hongyi would not dare to consider himself pure in the five precepts, who among us could ever do so?

You should realize that master Hongyi's motives for assessing himself in this way definitely did not come from the guilt of having actually broken the precepts. It came from his appreciation of just how difficult it is to fulfill the true spirit of the precepts once one understands their total import. Any person who wishes to receive the precepts should keep this point in mind and not allow himself or herself to become too proud, thinking that he or she is already a pure follower of the Buddha. After receiving the precepts, one must study the precepts thoroughly, otherwise one will never appreciate their sublime nature. Even then, the real purpose of receiving and studying the precepts is to embody them. If one receives but does not study the precepts, one is arrogant and ignorant. If one studies but does not strive to embody them, it is like talking about a meal or counting jewels that are not one's own. One is then even more ignorant and arrogant. There is no benefit whatsoever.

Why do we need precepts? There is a common saying that "though the sword is sharp, it does not behead the blameless." In theory, the laws of nations are of no use to a citizenry that, by nature, is harmonious and restrained. But, for the security and benefit of those who are, by nature, law-abiding, it is still necessary that there be laws, for there is no guarantee that society and its members will be free of individuals who would violate others. Laws act as a warning not to overstep certain bounds. They set down norms of proper behavior for society at large, and they provide the means for taking action against those who would harm society, thereby protecting it.

The Buddhist tradition has precepts for much the same reason. During the first few years after the Buddha attained enlightenment and began to teach, there really were no precepts of which to speak. The disciples who came to him during this early period all left home as renunciants with the best of intentions. Their karmic capacities were high, such that two or three lines of explanation from the Buddha were sufficient to cause them, then and there, to become enlightened and realize sagehood. Since the majority of the Buddha's followers were already quite pure, the early saṅgha had no use for explicit regulations to keep them in line. But, during the fifth year into the Buddha's preaching career, there occurred an incident in which a bhikṣu gave in to sexual relations at the urging of his former wife and another woman. Allegedly, it is from this event that the first precept codes came into existence. As the saṅgha grew, precepts and rules for monastic procedure were expanded bit by bit, all in an effort to protect the purity and solemn respectability of the saṅgha, as well as to ensure that monks and nuns would not lose the essential spirit of the renunciatory life.

If the monastic and lay saṅgha, as a whole, will keep the precepts, the Buddhist tradition and humankind at large will surely flourish. But if the saṅgha has no precepts to serve as a blueprint to unify and guide it, not only will the condition of the Buddhist teaching decline, the tradition itself may well vanish like smoke. For this reason, the Buddha on his deathbed made a point of stressing for the generations of disciples to come that they should take the precepts themselves as their teacher or master. Just like a great nation, even if its original founder dies, so long as the constitution is preserved intact and everyone continues to observe it, a new leader can be selected time and time again, and the political integrity of the country will not be shaken. So long as Buddhists keep the vinaya precepts intact, the Buddhist saṅgha, both collectively and individually, will be able to endure as long as the world itself. Thus, one of the most important roles of the precepts is to preserve the Buddhist tradition from age to age.

The state of the saṅgha aside, however, in their ultimate sense the real contribution of the precepts lies in their power to sever the karmic causes and conditions that keep one bound to the cycle of birth and death. It is said in the sūtras, "If you want to know the past, it is what you are experiencing here in this present life. If you want to know the future, it is what you are doing right now in this present life." If we do not create causes for continued birth and death, we will leave no trace, even if we remain in the midst of birth and death and give no conscious thought to seeking release. Therefore, the creation of the vinaya precepts was not a case of the Buddha dispensing some sort of absolutely binding commandment to his disciples. In reality, it was just a path for the spiritual liberation of his disciples and a counteragent to the possible corruption of the saṅgha at large.

In summation, we can say that the vinaya precepts perform two main functions. First, the precepts provide a foundation for Buddhist practice by closing the door to the unwholesome paths that will lead to painful karmic retribution, and by fostering the purity of mind and deed that will lead to liberation. Second, they ensure order and high standards of purity within the Buddhist community, thereby enabling it to flourish and function as an inspirational model for society. The relevance that the precepts have for maintaining collective order and discipline within a religious community is easy to understand. But, for many people, the implicit connection between the precepts and meditation may be more difficult to understand. "The aim of meditation," they may think, "is to enlighten and liberate us, to make us spontaneous and free. Precepts are restrictive and confining. Isn't this going in the opposite direction?"

Indeed, one can say that enlightenment does represent spontaneity and untrammeled freedom—a world where things are perfect just as they are. What is more, Buddhist tradition teaches that we already have this enlightenment within us and all around us. There is nothing we need add or remove from either ourselves or the world. But there is a vast difference between knowing this in theory and living it in truth. It is easy to talk about being spontaneous and free, but most of us do not have a clue as to what spontaneity and freedom really are. Precisely because we are so complex and out of control, we need discipline to restrain and simplify our lives to the point where we can uproot the habits of greed, hatred, and delusion that inhibit true freedom. The five precepts free us from anxiety and provide the stability and emotional space for meditative practice by helping to straighten out our lives and create positive relationships with the people around us. Properly nourished, this sense of spaciousness and ease develops directly into meditative clarity and calm. For the Buddhist monk or nun, the experience is even more profound, since all attachments are severed. As it says in the Sāmañña-phala Sutta, "Endowed with this body of moral restraints, so worthy of esteem, one experiences within oneself a sense of ease without alloy."

Another important function that the precepts serve is to safeguard the meditator. Without precepts, one's practice will be like a leaky bucket. Every day, the purifying waters of meditation are poured in, until one begins to feel strong and full of vigor. Unless one is firmly grounded in the precepts, this vigor may spill out in all sorts of destructive ways, bringing harm to oneself as well as to others. If lust, anger, and foolishness increase, it is simply not Buddhism that one is practicing.

4

The Five Methods for Stilling the Mind

Buddhist literature contains many different techniques for developing samādhi and wisdom. The Hīnayāna, Mahāyāna, and Vajrayāna teachings all have their respective systemizations. One of the most classic formulations of the meditative path is the scheme of the Five Methods for Stilling the Mind and the Four Stations of Mindfulness. When called upon to summarize Indian Mahāyāna and Hīnayāna teachings on meditation, Chinese Buddhist masters have often used these two formulations to provide an overview of the Buddhist meditative path. Together, they provide a good introduction to the basic principles that inform Buddhist meditation in all its different forms.

Simply stated, the Five Methods for Stilling the Mind (wu tingxin) represent five different techniques that are designed to purify the mind of emotional turbulence and foster meditative calm (S. śamatha), eventually leading to the experience of samādhi, or meditative concentration. The word for meditative calming in Chinese is zhi, which literally means "to halt" or "to fix in place." Thus, the five methods seek to halt the wandering mind and fix it in the one-pointedness of samādhi.

Meditative calming (S. śamatha; C. zhi), in turn, serves as a basis for meditative contemplation (S. vipaśyanā). In Chinese, vipaśyanā is rendered as guan, which means "to discern or observe." As the mind is purified and unified by samādhi, it becomes very deep, powerful, and clear. This clarity is then directed to the practice of contemplation or meditative discernment (S. vipaśyanā; C. guan) proper. The Four Stations of Mindfulness (S. catur-smṛtyupasthāna; C. si nianchu) are essentially methods of contemplation. Through contemplation of the four stations of body, sensation, mind, and mental factors (dharmas), one uproots the basic afflictions of craving, hatred, and delusion, thereby realizing emptiness and achieving liberation from birth and death.

Often, meditative calming and contemplation are likened to two wings of a bird or two wheels of a cart. When both wings and both wheels work together, a bird can fly and a cart can move. Meditative calming enables contemplation to reach and remove the root afflictions; by removing the afflictions, contemplation, in turn, deepens meditative calm. Thus, the two work together to lead one along the path to enlightenment. As techniques of meditative calming, the Five Methods for Stilling the Mind can produce the experience of "unified mind," or samādhi, described in diagram six of the seven stages of mental concentration. As techniques of contemplation, the Four Stations of Mindfulness can eradicate attachment to the illusion of self, bringing about the experience of "no-mind" described in diagram seven (as described at the end of Chapter Two). Thus, the Five Methods for Stilling the Mind serve as preliminary expedients to the Four Stations of Mindfulness, which are primarily techniques for developing wisdom or insight (prajñā).

Different Buddhist texts sometimes give different versions of the Five Methods for Stilling the Mind. In the Abhidharma treatises, two techniques are most frequently mentioned—the practice of mindful recollection of the breath (S. ānāpāna-smṛti) and meditation on impurity or decay (S. aśubha-bhāvanā). To these, meditation on the four boundless mentalities (S. apramāṇa-citta), meditation on cause and condition (S. pratītyasamutpāda), and the contemplation of dharmic categories (S. dhātu) are usually added, bringing the number of methods to five. Many Buddhist sources, especially those of the Mahāyāna, describe variant formulations of the Five Methods for Stilling the Mind that give special importance to mindful recollection of the Buddha (S. buddhānusmṛti, C. nianfo) as a technique for purifying the mind and developing samādhi. Thus, it is not unusual to find versions of the Five Methods for Stilling the Mind that replace the contemplation of dharmic categories with Buddha-mindfulness.

Treatises on meditation often cite mental distraction and dullness as the most basic impediment to the development of samādhi. Subjected to a slightly more detailed analysis, they are expanded into a set of five basic obstacles known as the five types of mental "covering," or "obscuration" (S. nivaraṇa): (1) lust; (2) hatred or anger; (3) stupidity; (4) excitability or distractedness; and (5) torpor. They are called "coverings," or "obscurations," because they color the mind's activity and conceal its intrinsic potential for samādhi and wisdom. For the most part, ordinary persons who have yet to take up meditative practice will be plagued by one or more of these emotional excesses. The successful pursuit of samādhi depends on concurrently removing these obscurations and concentrating the mind. This is the function of the Five Methods for Stilling the Mind. Each method is designed to target one of these coverings: meditation on impurity counteracts lust; the four boundless mentalities counteract anger and hatred; meditation on conditioned origination counteracts delusion and stupidity; meditation on the breath counteracts distractedness; and meditation on dharmic categories counteracts torpor. Similar to meditation on dharmic categories, mindfulness of the Buddha counteracts both spiritual torpor and fear. Thus, the five methods fulfill the dual function of acting as a cathartic for the obscurations, while, at the same time, providing a basis for bringing the mind to one-pointed concentration.

MEDITATION ON THE BREATH

꩜ Contemplation or mindfulness of the breath, or *ānāpāna-smṛti* (C. *nianxi*), is one of the most popular forms of Buddhist meditation. Buddhist teachers of all persuasions—Indian Hīnayāna and Mahāyāna masters of the past, Southeast Asian Theravādins, Chan, Pure Land, Tiantai, and Esoteric Buddhists in East Asia— have long valued it as one of the most effective means for helping beginners to develop mental concentration. Among the Five Methods for Stilling the Mind, mindfulness of the breath is distinguished as a counteragent for excessive distractedness. Since a scattered mind is a problem that plagues nearly every beginning meditator, this technique is particularly suitable as a foundational practice for almost everyone.

However, simply because mindfulness of the breath is good for novices, one should not think that it is a shallow practice. As a technique, mindfulness of the breath is multifarious and capable of evolving into a variety of subsidiary forms, depending on the capacity or level of the individual's practice. In effect, it comprises an entire path unto itself, ranging from shallow to deep. For example, in China, mindfulness of the breath is often taught in the form of the "six marvelous gates" *(liu miaomen)*, which distinguishes six basic levels and techniques of meditation: (1) counting the breath; (2) following the breath; (3) calming, or concentration *(zhi)*; (4) contemplating, or discerning *(guan)*; (5) reverting; and (6) purification. One can see that both meditative calming *(zhi)* and contemplation *(guan)* are contained in this scheme. What is more, the last stage—that of purification—is associated with the manifestation of wisdom, or enlightenment. For our purposes, we will distinguish three basic methods of mindfulness of the breath: counting the breath, following the breath, and concentration *(zhi)* on specific energy spots—or centers—in the body known in Chinese as *dantian*, or "cinnabar fields." These three methods correspond roughly to the first three of the six marvelous gates.

Counting the Breath

Counting the breath is one of the simplest forms of meditation and is the method often used for controlling the scattered mind of the beginner. In doing this method, you should place your full attention on the cycle of the breath—

inhalation and exhalation. Every time you exhale, count each exhale in sequence, beginning with 1 and proceeding in sequence up to 10. When the count reaches 10 (i.e., ten exhalations), return again to 1. This cycle of counting from 1 to 10 is repeated over and over throughout the entire period of meditation.

It is important that one be consistent in coordinating the counting of the number with the exhalation only. When inhaling, simply try to remain gently aware of the inhalation, and allow this awareness to carry on unbroken to the next exhalation. When exhaling, count the next number. If, in the process of counting from 1 to 10, the mind becomes distracted and you forget the number, you must immediately return to 1 and begin the cycle over. The reason we count on the exhalation is that exhaling is naturally relaxing, and its span lasts longer than the inhalation. This facilitates the development of concentration. Should beginners count inhalations, it is quite easy for breathing and counting both to become forced. This, in turn, can cause constriction in the chest. If you are able to practice very well, and your breathing is very light, perhaps nearly imperceptible, then the practice may be varied in certain ways to suit your needs. Otherwise, it is best to stick to the practice of counting on the exhalation.

There are several problems that beginners commonly experience when they first take up this practice. For example, when counting the number, it is relatively easy to be free of distracting thoughts. But between exhalations and inhalations, or while inhaling, often the mind will wander. Simply remain aware of the inhalation and try to refrain from allowing the mind to wander away. Another common problem that beginners often experience is headaches, dizziness, and constricted breathing. These almost always arise because the meditator is trying to force the practice and is not being natural. The breathing should be relaxed and natural. You should allow the body to follow the course most natural to it, and the counting should be adapted to this natural process. Be careful not to try to force the rate of breathing to follow an artificial rhythm of counting. Moreover, one should also refrain from tensing the body and breathing in an effort to chase off wandering thoughts.

Another problem frequently encountered by beginners is the tendency for the counting to become mechanical or dream-like. They should strive to maintain a fresh and clear sense of awareness at all times. If this problem appears, they can vary the count in order to revive interest. For example, one can count backwards from 10 to 1, or count cycles of 20 by odd or even numbers.

Following the Breath

Following the breath is somewhat more difficult than counting the breath, and requires more skill in concentration before it can be practiced effectively. There are many variations to this practice. The technique that I teach (which I feel is safest) is to place the attention on the tip of the nose—the nostrils. When both inhaling and exhaling, simply remain aware of the breath as it passes in and out of the nostrils. Do not force or restrict the breath in any way, but breathe naturally and just watch. Often this technique will be taken up after one has practiced counting the breath to the point where the counting of the number interferes with developing more subtle concentration on the breathing itself. Thus, this technique can be seen as a natural progression from counting the breath.

Three basic stages are distinguished in the practice of following the breath. In the first stage, simply place your concentration on the nostrils and remain gently aware of the inhalation and exhalation. Do not try to control your breathing; breathe naturally and just observe. Above all, do not intentionally try to make the breath descend to the lower abdomen or to any other place in the body. Simply allow the body to breathe as it will.

Sometimes, when concentrating hard, your mental focus may tend to shift to the forehead. If this happens, more blood will rush to the head, causing headaches, dizziness, or a sense that the head is expanding. When such sensations appear, it is best temporarily to forego the method of following the breath and, instead, to place your concentration gently on the sole of the uppermost foot in the full-lotus or half-lotus posture. If concentration is strong, you will soon be able to establish mindfulness of both feet. Try to locate the soft part that is in the middle of the sole, slightly toward the ball of the foot. Concentration established on this spot will relieve pressure in the head. During each inhalation, you may feel a sensation develop at this spot on the foot. Initially there will be only a vague, subtle feeling, but later you will sense that this feeling rises and falls distinctly with the respiration. Sometimes it may feel warm, sometimes comfortably cool. It is an interesting fact that when a person is ill or in poor condition, this spot on the foot will feel tender or sore. Meditation upon this spot can be used to help cure illness.

If the body feels uncomfortably warm, you can focus concentration on the inhalation, because air coming into the body is cooler, and concentration upon it will cool the body. The reverse applies for the exhalation. The air is warm and thus, when you are cold, you may focus attention on it in order to warm the body.

Over a period of time, breathing will naturally deepen and drop to the lower abdomen. This represents the second stage. As the breath descends to the lower abdomen, an undulating motion of breathing begins to develop in that area. This is something that appears spontaneously and feels totally natural. It is dangerous to try to induce this process intentionally. By forcibly breathing into the abdomen, the stomach may feel bloated and uncomfortable; and in the case of women, it can lead to menstrual complications. It is a common tendency to try to press the air down when concentrating, because meditators by so doing feel they can eliminate a fair amount of distracting thoughts. The safest approach is to allow the body to relax and breathe as it will, and to maintain attention on the nose. At least initially, you should not allow your attention to wander with the breathing to other parts of the body.

[handwritten: Polluted ampersand Pure.]

In the third stage, breathing is not merely located at the nostrils or in the lower abdomen. Rather, you will sense that the flow of breath has extended to the fingers and toes. The sense develops that the air is entering directly through all pores and circulating throughout the body to every cell. It will feel as though the entire body is inhaling and exhaling. Upon every exhalation, you will feel that polluted air and obstructions are being expelled; and upon every inhalation, it will seem as though purity and freshness are entering your system. If this level of concentration is nourished, you will naturally come to feel very relaxed and comfortable. After this condition of great relaxation, it will be possible to enter samādhi.

[handwritten left margin: PORES]

[handwritten: CHAKRAS.]

Concentration on the Dantian—*the Energy Centers of the Body*

In the human body there are various energy centers, concentration upon which can produce powerful sensations or experiences. We have already mentioned the benefits of concentration upon the soles of the feet. In the Chinese tradition, we often speak of the three *dantian*—"cinnabar, or elixir, fields." The upper *dan-tian* is located approximately between the two eyebrows. The middle one is above the diaphragm, roughly between the two nipples. The lower *dantian* is just below the navel. Various subdivisions of these spots may also be made.

Depending upon different situations, a person may concentrate on a different *dantian*. In the beginning, when it is difficult to concentrate, or if you are drowsy, you may concentrate on the upper *dantian*. However, it is best not to practice in this manner for too long, otherwise unpleasant sensations may arise. Since it is difficult to watch this point, it may help to visualize a cool light radiating from this upper *dantian*. As practice continues, you may feel that the entire head or body becomes nothing but radiant light.

If you feel tired and weak, or if it becomes difficult to concentrate on breathing, you may observe the middle *dantian*. Think of it not as a part of the body, but as a moon. In the beginning, visualize it as if it were a small moon far away and deep inside the chest. As practice continues, the moon becomes larger and larger, until it fills the entire chest and body. Eventually, it may grow to include the entire world, so that meditator and environment are one moon. This light or moon should not be perceived as something exterior into which you are seeking to merge; rather, the light or moon should come from within. Eventually, every bodily sensation other than this pure light will drop off and only the moon's radiance will remain.

[handwritten left margin: VISUALIZE MOON CHAKRA .]

When meditating on the lower *dantian*, the practice is different for men and women. Men should watch a point three-fingers' width below the navel. They should not focus their attention lower than this, for it may cause a sexual response. Such a phenomenon may not occur right away, but as practice develops and health improves, it can happen. Women should not meditate on any point too far below the navel, nor should they practice this concentration upon the lower *dantian* for an extended length of time, otherwise it may interfere with their menstrual cycle. However, if a person is practicing only for one or two hours a day, it will not be long enough to cause a problem.

When using this third method, naturally the abdomen will relax and breathing will tend to drop quickly to the lower abdomen. This can have many good effects on the body and personality. For people who tend to be overly nervous or flippant, or for those who are insecure or overly shy, this method can bring positive changes in emotional disposition. If your practice is effective, especially when concentrating on the lower *dantian*, various phenomena will occur. First, there will be a sensation of soothing warmth that will come from the *dantian* and spread to other parts of the body. This sensation may spread up through the chest to the mouth, or it may go back through the rectum, then proceed up along the spine to the head and back down through the chest. Then again, the sensation of warmth may simply radiate from the *dantian* directly to all parts of the body. This warmth is not like ordinary heat, but has a rich and nourishing feeling. At this stage, you will feel tension and discomfort in the body begin to dissolve. Eventually, only a profound sense of comfort and relaxation will remain. You may even forget about your body entirely. Nevertheless, the sense of comfort and pleasure will remain.

This is the highest level of experience that one can actually reach by concentrating on the *dantian* itself. It is a level prior to the experience of samādhi proper. For deep samādhi to develop, the technique must proceed to a more subtle level. Thus, meditation on the breath and the *dantian* are good practices for establishing a foundation for Chan or other forms of insight meditation. To bring the Buddhist path to fulfillment, however, one needs the rest of the six marvelous gates or another form of meditation, such as the Four Stations of Mindfulness.

REGARDING BODY AS SELF Ū A DELUSION!

MEDITATION ON IMPURITY

The method of meditating on impurity (S. aśubha-bhāvanā, C. *bujing guan*) mainly entails concentrating on bodily impurities or on the process of decomposition of the physical body. Many of our vexations arise from taking the body to be the center of our existence and regarding it as self. Far from being a conscious attitude, this sort of posture on existence is at once deeply instinctive and subconscious. It is not difficult to see how many such responses or impulses associated with the body serve as protective instincts that ensure our individual and collective survival. Reaction to pain, the sexual drive, hunger, and aggression are all handy examples. Just as with other sentient animals, from the start these instinctual attitudes set up certain patterns of interaction between ourselves and the world. By going a step further and developing these instincts into the conscious world of self and personality—my body is cold, I am hungry, I want comfort, I need sex, and so forth—we project a very concrete sense of self into all of our actions. Not only do we cater to the immediate urges of the body, we often deliberately plan our entire existence around them. We become concerned with appearance, acceptability, style, and fashion, and we lay preparations for acquiring wealth, security, and stable environment for self. On the basis of the physical body itself, we also begin to seek embodiment and stability in terms of environment.

Meditating upon the impurity of the body means to deeply experience the body as impermanent and impure. Through experiences such as these, people can reduce the craving that builds up around the body and can eventually liberate themselves from the strong sense of self associated with it.

There are two basic approaches to contemplating the impurity of the body. One is to contemplate another person's body as impure; the other is to contemplate one's own body as impure. There are also variations in the manner or type of impurity to be contemplated. One may, for example, contemplate the natural filthiness of the internal organs of the body and the body's external secretions. The most common method, however, is to meditate upon the process of physical decomposition.

It is difficult to imagine effectively the process by which your own body decays. Hence, it is easiest to use the corpse of another person. While seated in the standard posture of meditation, you would spend all of your time intently concentrating on and reviewing the corpse placed before you. As days pass, it gradually changes. First it begins to ripen and change color, yellow to blue-black. It swells through exposure to sun and the elements, and, eventually, the skin bursts and peels. By this time, flies will have been attracted to the corpse and will cover it entirely. The stench of rotting flesh will be nearly unbearable, far greater than that of any small dead animal. After flies have laid their eggs, maggots will appear. They will move in a writhing mass, first in and around the orifices, then covering the entire body. As they will grow fat on the carrion, you will most likely not feel like eating, due to this repulsive sight and the overpowering smell. Furthermore, it will be increasingly impossible to deny the fact that you will eventually undergo the very same decay.

Once the worms have finished their work, most of the flesh will be gone. There will be nothing left but a heap of filthy bones, held together with ligaments and tendons and stained with remnants of rotting flesh. The bones will not appear like the neatly arranged skeletons in a museum. They will be scattered and twisted in a terrible and ugly way. With the passage of rain and weather, the tendons and remaining flesh will be washed away, leaving gleaming white bones. Eventually the bones themselves will begin to break up and disappear. Smaller pieces will be carried away by animals or ground up. Only the bigger pieces will be left lying in a disordered heap, with the skull in one place, the leg bones somewhere else.

Once the meditator has been through this process, the images will be firmly engraved on his or her mind. Because meditation on the decomposition of the corpse is carried out with intense meditative concentration, as concentration deepens the meditator will be able to recreate and rehearse the entire process of decay through mental visualization, as though one were watching a movie. Henceforth, whenever one sits down to practice meditation—regardless of whether it is night or day, in the presence of a corpse or not—one will reproduce with great vividness the entire process. The more one does this, the deeper will grow the sense that one's own body is destined to undergo this decay as well. A profound sense of detachment will develop, and feelings of sexual desire, vanity, and material craving will lessen.

Persons with an overabundance of these sorts of attachments can enhance this particular corrective power by exaggerating and lingering upon the feelings of disgust that arise from the images of decay. Eventually, they will come to think less of their own bodies and persons, and will become truly compassionate and considerate of others. They will also be more appreciative of life itself, and will strive to make the noblest use of the limited time that they have.

But how, one might ask, does this practice contribute to the development of samādhi itself? At first glance, this process of visualization, with its many diverse and complex images, would hardly seem to contribute to one-pointedness of mind. It is different from more familiar methods such as counting the breath, in which the mind is fixed on one activity or one spot.

Actually, even though the visionary content of the meditation changes, it does so in a very continuous and thematic progression. In this respect, it is nothing like the ordinary scattered mind that tends to flit randomly from this object to that object. This thematic process of visualization can enable a person to enter samādhi very quickly. In the final phase of decay, as the meditator concentrates intently on the glistening white bones, he or she will come to see only the white color. With deepening mental calm and clarity, the whiteness itself will turn to cool and radiant white light. Eventually, the practitioner will feel the world itself disappear and perceive nothing but this light radiating out in all directions.

At yet a more subtle stage of meditative development, the sense of being in the midst of radiant light may also disappear, taking with it both the sense of self and that of the environment. Thus, through the meditation on decomposition, it is possible to experience samādhi and, depending on one's karmic capacity, even liberation from birth and death.

Naturally it is quite rare to come across a corpse in this day and age, much less have the opportunity to sit down and meditate on it daily. In ancient times, when corpses were a more common sight, or when (in some countries) it was the custom to leave the dead to rot on charnel grounds, it was easier. Such a practice in most developed countries would likely be illegal, and if you were to haul off a corpse and meditate on it day after day, people would probably think you were insane and have you institutionalized. Nevertheless, by way of visualization, it is still possible to do this meditation without meditating on an actual corpse. Moreover, you can mentally apply this visualization to yourself. Basically, the process is the same as described above, but rather than meditating on the body of another, you visualize your own body—as a corpse—going through the process of decay. You should not dwell on the question of how you die, or what it feels like to die. Simply start with the process of decomposition. First visualize the head; then work down very gradually over the entire body, allowing the image to become very sharp and clear. When sitting, contemplate the body in the sitting position; when reclining, in the reclining posture. Repeatedly going over the body from head to foot, imagine that your body begins to ripen and change color. Then move on progressively to the other phases of decay—swelling, peeling skin, oozing liquids and stench, and so forth—until the bones fall apart and slump over in a pile. Then imagine that a great downpour of rain comes and washes the bones clean. They become gleaming white—cool and pure—until they turn to pure radiant light. Just as in the other practice, this light grows and expands, until eventually the sense of light, self, and environment all disappear.

It is very difficult to develop a truly vivid sense of impurity, disgust, and impermanence, much less convince yourself that this fate will inevitably come to you one day. To encourage this sense, it helps to reflect on the disgusting features or impurities that already plague our bodies while alive. We may ordinarily think of our bodies as youthful and pure, but the nose is filled with mucus and the ears with wax, the pores ooze sweat and oil, the body continually expels urine and feces, and, without constant cleaning, it reeks and suffers all sorts of discomfort. You may imagine that a part of your body has become paralyzed or immobile, that it slowly begins to atrophy and rot. Then you can expand this sensation to other parts of the body, thereby coming to appreciate what it means to suffer debilitating illness. However, you must be careful not to go too far and imagine that the heart stops or the other internal organs cease to function, for it could have actual adverse physical effects. The aim is to passively watch this decay just as if it were happening to another, just as if your body were, after all, not really your own.

MINDFUL RECOLLECTION OF THE BUDDHA

Although the term "mindful recollection of the Buddha" (S. *buddhānusmṛti*; C. *nianfo*), or "Buddha-mindfulness" for short, refers to meditation on the Buddha, actually it includes meditation on the great bodhisattvas as well. As one of the foundational practices of Mahāyāna Buddhism, it is a widespread and venerable practice, found everywhere throughout Tibet and East Asia. It is a rich practice, with many different levels and dimensions to it.

In its most basic form, two approaches to Buddha-mindfulness are distinguished. The first involves concentration on intoning a Buddha's or bodhisattva's name. In China, often the name of Amitābhā Buddha *(Amituo fo)* or Bodhisattva Avalokiteśvara *(Guanyin pusa)* is used. The second approach is to meditate on the image of a particular Buddha or bodhisattva. This latter practice can be further divided into two aspects: (I) mental visualization of the Buddha's magnificent physical form and spiritual merits, known as the body of form (S. rūpa-kāya, C. *seshen*), or manifestation body (S. nirmāṇa-kāya, C. *huashen* or *yingshen*); (2) contemplation of the Buddha as the embodiment of the essence of Dharma itself (S. dharma-kāya, C. *fashen*). This may be done collectively (where, for example, the entire form of the Buddha is reviewed systematically from the crown of the head to the feet), or according to specific attributes. In the latter case, the practitioner focuses on just one feature or spiritual attribute. Finally, since Buddha-mindfulness entails meditation on the sacred image of the Buddha and, to some extent, seeks to invoke the Buddha's profound salvific power, Buddha-mindfulness is often set within an extended ritual framework. This may involve such religious devotions as the offering of incense, prostrations, circumambulation, singing of praises, confession, and the making of vows.

Persons who have seen Buddhist painting and sculpture may wonder what Buddhists do with all these strange images. Some images carry flaming swords or have dozens of arms that grasp fearsome weapons. Some have blue or red skin, wear elaborate crowns and jewelry, and have splendorous halos. Others are serene and unprepossessing, with their hands poised in very delicate but unusual gestures. Most have human form, but they are very stylized and seem to show no distinctive human personality whatsoever. What are these images? People who have been to Asia or have seen films of East Asian Buddhism may have witnessed ceremonies of offering, reverence, and worship performed by Buddhist monks and laypeople before these deities. Do Buddhists revere or worship these images and icons as living gods, as idols from which they plead for good fortune, mercy, or redemption?

Such naive ideas about Buddhist devotion are not uncommon among Westerners. Actually, these images are symbolic and not really "living gods" or "graven idols" at all. One could say that they use the medium of the visual image to express subtle aspects of the enlightened mind. How could such an omnipotent being as the Buddha Amitābhā or the great bodhisattvas Avalokiteśvara (Guanyin) and Mañjuśrī—beings intent on delivering all sentient beings from suffering—ever be limited by an image or the need for religious offerings? They are as inconceivable and omnipresent as enlightened Buddha-nature itself. The images and rituals that we traditionally associate with them are not essential to them. They are a function of their compassion, for it is through this imagery that their world of enlightenment touches our lives and arouses our hearts. This is really the function of mindfulness and worship of the Buddhas. It is to inspire our own spiritual imagination, and help us begin to identify in a living way with the qualities of the supreme enlightenment of Buddhahood.

Traditionally, it is said that the glorified body of a Buddha possesses thirty-two major auspicious marks and eighty minor excellent qualities.[1] These are idealized attributes—aspects of physique and bearing that suggest great nobility of person. To every one of these features there is a spiritual significance, from the fleshy topknot on the crown of the head, the curled white hair between the eyebrows, and the long ear lobes, downward to the golden hue of the skin and the eight-spoked wheels on the soles of the feet. When one mentally recollects them, it is important not only to visualize them clearly, but also to be clear about their significance.

This idea that the visual form of a Buddha is ultimately expressive of the Buddha's spiritual stature naturally suggests that, to truly know the Buddha, we must appreciate his spiritual virtues. Mahāyāna Buddhist scripture often characterizes the meritorious powers of the Buddha as inconceivable, inestimable, infinite. Thus, in terms of his enlightened wisdom and compassion, the Buddha's salvific presence and powers range far beyond the limited images and concepts that are used to represent his manifest body of form. Mahāyāna scholastic treatises define the Buddha by such spiritual attributes as the "ten powers," "four fearlessnesses," "eighteen unique qualities," "great compassion," "great skill-in-means," and "great wisdom." Finally, if we are to single out the one elemental factor that is the wellspring of all other powers and attributes of the Buddha, there is the Buddha's unchanging and inconceivable body of Dharma-essence (S. dharma-kā ya). This body of dharma-essence is none other than the enlightened Buddha-nature that is intrinsically present in all things. As unenlightened beings, we are unaware of it; but for a Buddha it is the essence of his very being. He is a Buddha precisely because he has fully awakened to and has actualized this enlightened nature. For this reason, many Mahāyāna texts also refer to the Dharma-body as the "true body or essence" (zhenshen) of the Buddha.

For the purposes of our present discussion of Buddha-mindfulness, we will discuss the spiritual merits of a Buddha from four general perspectives: (1) a Buddha's great wisdom; (2) his great compassion; (3) his great vows; and (4) his great practice or deeds. Actually, these four enlightened qualities are symbolized by the four great bodhisattvas: Mañjuśrī, Avalokiteśvara (Guanyin), Kṣitigarbharāja (Dizang), and Samantabhadra, respectively.

Intoning, or Reciting, the Name of the Buddha

The technique of reciting the name or names of Buddhas and bodhisattvas is as old as the practice of Buddha-mindfulness itself. From earliest times, this practice of vocally intoning the name—often accompanied by prostrations—has been combined with mental visualization as a single practice. In fact, the term nianfo—the Chinese translation of the Indian word for "Buddha-mindfulness" (S. buddhānusmṛti)—is still routinely used to refer to both "recitation of the Buddha's name" and "recollection of the Buddha's form." However, ever since the spread of Pure Land Buddhism in China, recitation of the name has been the more dominant form of practice. Pure Land Buddhism worships the Buddha

Amitābhā (Amituo fo), who is said to preside over a marvelous spiritual paradise known as the Land of Highest Bliss (Sukhāvatī), located far across the universe to the west. According to the Pure Land sūtras, Amitābhā has made a great compassionate vow to save anyone who devotedly meditates on him and calls his name. Through this practice, one will not only remove aeons of karmic obstacles and generate vast spiritual merit, but, at the time of death, Amitābhā will appear and lead one to rebirth in his Pure Land. From there, one will quickly achieve the enlightenment of a great bodhisattva and Buddha.

Chan Buddhism does not sanction the idea of seeking rebirth in the Pure Land or relying on the power of the Buddha for one's salvation. In Chan, the emphasis is on not being attached to anything. The goal is to use meditation to actualize directly the enlightened Buddha-nature that is within us all. Nonetheless, Chan Buddhists do often practice Buddha-mindfulness and meditation on Amitābhā Buddha or Bodhisattva Avalokiteśvara (Guanyin); but the emphasis is really on the Buddha as being identical with the dharma-body and our intrinsic Buddha-nature, rather than on rebirth in the western Pure Land. Thus, in Chan circles there is a saying that "Amitābhā is our original nature, and the Pure Land is none other than the mind" (benxing mituo, weixin jingtu). Buddha-mindfulness, or nianfo practice, is directed toward the realization of our Buddha-nature within. In fact, when recitation of Amitābhā's name is used by Chan practitioners, often it is turned into a Chan-style huatou by adding the question, "Who is it that is reciting the Buddha's name?" Moreover, many great Chinese Pure Land masters, such as the twentieth-century monk, Yinguang, were highly respected for their accomplishments by Chan practitioners as well.

Recitation of the Buddha's name may be performed alone or in the company of others. Although it may be recited silently, it is best for one's concentration to recite it aloud. When alone, attention should be focused on the sound of one's own voice. If practicing in the company of others, one should listen to the sound of their chanting as well, so that one can harmonize one's voice with the collective recitation.

When doing this practice, there is no need to concern oneself with trying to visualize the Buddha. Simply place full attention on the recitation. Some people recite the two syllables namo before the name of the given Buddha or bodhisattva, as in namo Amituo fo or namo Dabei Guanshiyin pusa. In effect this means "Homage to Amitābhā Buddha" or "Homage to the Greatly Compassionate Bodhisattva Guanyin." One may also repeat the deity's name, stringing together the syllables Amituo fo or Guanyin pusa in a continuous, even rhythm, listening intently to the sound as each syllable is spoken. It is essential that these three components of mouth, ears, and mind be unified. If the mind wanders from the sound, one is no longer reciting the Buddha's name. Furthermore, it is a good idea to learn how to invoke the Buddha's name properly, otherwise it may not sound right, or it may be too hurried or too slow. It is important to chant in a very measured, concentrated, and solemn manner, putting one's entire being into the recitation so that one may achieve a state of "single-minded concentration without confusion" (yixin buluan).

When reciting, every word must be clear in one's mind. Also, just as with other meditations that we have described, it is essential to be calm and relaxed. One should not become overanxious or frustrated if it is difficult to remain focused on the sound. Above all, one should not be distracted by thoughts of having to evoke some special attitude of devotion or seek some special spiritual feeling. Overanxiousness can lead to headaches, anxiety, and so forth, so it is best not to force things. All one need do is recite the name and let the method do the work. When the mind wanders, simply bring it back and do not worry over it any further. Eventually, concentration will deepen, to the point where one may enter samādhi.

Another problem that can arise with reciting the Buddha's name is the tendency for the practice to become mechanical. Some people place emphasis on how many times they repeat the name, and do not pay attention to the quality of the recitation. They feel satisfied if they simply repeat the name, say, ten thousand times. This is useless. Because they have so many scattered thoughts, they will never reach "single-minded concentration without confusion" (yixin buluan) or experience real spiritual benefit with this kind of practice.

In the event that one becomes tired or chanting becomes too taxing, one may recite silently rather than chant aloud. Because this is a more subtle form of practice, it is easier for the mind to wander. Hence, if one is a beginner, it is still best to chant aloud.

As the act of concentration seems to be the most essential element in the practice, one may well wonder whether a person might just as effectively recite the name of a dog. Actually, it is natural for our minds to be drawn to and become involved with the object whose name we are invoking. The difference here is that if we intone a Buddha's name, our minds will be drawn to the qualities of purity and perfection that are associated with a Buddha. The religious inspiration that comes from this can help to further one's practice in many ways. Moreover, since recitation of the name (nianfo) can invoke the compassionate presence of the Buddha or bodhisattva to whom it is directed, it is also capable of enlisting the Buddha's power to help us remove karmic obstacles and experience samādhi.

Because of its constancy of focus as well as its devotional richness, recitation of the Buddha's name is an easy and effective method for developing samādhi. For those who find themselves exhausted from intensive meditation practice, or unable to calm their minds with such techniques as counting the breath, this method provides a good way to settle the mind. Even when plagued with stray thoughts or a scattered mind, many people feel very good both during and after this practice. During extended periods of Buddha-recitation, they find themselves less vexed by discomfort. Often, they will experience auspicious dreams that encourage them and inspire greater faith in the practice. When it is over, they feel happy and uplifted. It is perhaps for this reason that those who follow the Pure Land teachings have been known for their particularly strong faith and determination.

Mental Recollection of the Form and Spiritual Merits of the Buddha

The method of meditating upon the magnificent appearance of a Buddha is more difficult than that of the practice of reciting the Buddha's name. Reasons for this are several. On the one hand, it is a more mentally involved practice. Like the meditation on decomposition of a corpse, Buddha-mindfulness requires that one simultaneously visualize and contemplate the significance of the thirty-two major and eighty minor marks of the Buddha's body, proceeding sequentially from the crown of his head to the soles of his feet. Because of the complexity, it takes great time and effort to establish a keen mental image of the Buddha.

Furthermore, since we do not have access to a living Buddha, we have no real way of appreciating the immediacy of a Buddha's qualities. Should we meet a Buddha personally, surely he would make a very deep and vivid impression upon us. Later, we could recall and reflect on this experience, and it might be inspirational and beneficial to us. In fact, in some Tantric or Esoteric Buddhist practices, students are urged to use the living memory of their guru or teacher to personalize and animate the image of the deity, but this is not a widespread practice in Mahāyāna Buddhism. Hence, even though today we may have descriptions of the thirty-two major and eighty minor marks of a Buddha, as well as statues and paintings, these remain somewhat abstract and lifeless for most of us. We are like blind men trying to understand color: it can be explained, but we still cannot appreciate the actual experience. Thus, it takes great effort, time, and imagination to make this form of Buddha-mindfulness come to life.

Contemplating a Buddha's spiritual merits or his dharma-body is even more difficult. For most people, these qualities will be no more than hazy ideas. Once I told a student that he must act with more compassion, but the student answered that he did not really know what compassion was. Then I told him to act with faith in the Buddhadharma, but he replied that he did not know what faith was. Finally I told him to act with faith in me, and to this he agreed, but only to a certain degree. The same kind of problems can arise with trying to appreciate the spiritual merits of a Buddha. Because we have no tangible sense of what the Buddha's enlightenment entails, we can only rely on the vague musings of our imagination. For this reason, it really takes prior experience in meditation practice to effectively contemplate the Buddha's spiritual merits and dharma-body. There is no way, for example, that a beginning meditator is going to know what is meant by the saying, "Amitābha Buddha is one's original nature; the Pure Land is nothing more than mind."

As mentioned above, we can summarize a Buddha's merits under four broad descriptions: vast wisdom, vast compassion, vast vows, and vast practice, or deed. What do we mean by wisdom? The Bodhisattva Mañjuśrī is the personification of wisdom. Wisdom here means the insight of no-self, no sentient being, no phenomena. What about great compassion? Avalokiteśvara (Guanyin)is the personification of great compassion; she (or he) responds to and delivers all beings in distress. Great vows are symbolized by the dedication of the Bodhisattva Kṣitigarbha-rāja (Dizang) to save all sentient beings in the hells and other lower destinies. Great practice is the idea that one will do whatever should be done, no matter how demanding. In a sense, Mahāyāna Buddhist practice is the unceasing effort to accomplish the impossible. It entails great dedication and great suffering. Through this experience, karmic obstructions are removed and beings are spiritually matured. The Bodhisattva Samantabhadra is a personification of great practice, or great deeds. The famous Tibetan yogin, Milarepa, can also be considered an exemplar of great practice.

When contemplating the Buddha's form and merits, however, there is a right way to do it and a wrong way to do it. Basically, it is a matter of attitude. The wrong way to do it is with a strongly self-centered or spiritually materialistic mind. The worst attitude is to call the Buddha's name out of the hope of receiving some sort of lowly personal benefit. Why would a Buddha respond to someone who wants no more than to indulge her or his greed, anger, and delusion? It is essential in Buddhist practice that one's motives and attitude be in harmony with the basic values of the Buddhist teachings. Even when someone shows all the obvious signs of being spiritually conscientious, it may be no more than a disguise for the most prideful and base selfishness. Priding oneself on the strengths or accomplishments of one's practice as well as lamenting one's inability to measure up to the practice are both egotistical attitudes. They are riddled with self-centeredness. The proper way to practice Buddha-mindfulness is to try to nourish the spiritual qualities that the Buddha represents. Thus, the difference between right and wrong attitudes is that, on the one hand, you are trying to appropriate these values in your personal terms and in a self-centered way; and, on the other hand, you are trying try to let go of petty self-centeredness and allow these values to help transform you into something more genuine. Actually, the majority of students are of the first sort because they are overanxious to have a great accomplishment. If they persist in indulging this kind of greedy attitude, they will never change, regardless of the form of practice they adopt.

MEDITATION ON THE FOUR BOUNDLESS MENTALITIES

The four boundless mentalities (S. apramāṇa-citta, C. wuliangxin), which are also known as the four brāhmavihāra, or "abodes of Brahma," consist of the four mental states of (1) loving-kindness; (2) compassion; (3) joy; and (4) equanimity. They are referred to as boundless mentalities for two reasons. First, unlike such techniques as meditation on impurity and the breath, meditation on the boundless mentalities employs abstract mental attitudes as its object rather than a concrete physical object or sensation. Second, having no specific point of origin or focus, the four mentalities can easily be made to expand and fill all of space.

In Hīnayāna and Mahāyāna teachings alike, meditation on the four boundless mentalities is said to be particularly beneficial as an antidote for hate and anger. Moreover, in the Mahāyāna tradition, compassion (karuṇā) for the suffering experienced by other sentient beings is also considered one of the most cardinal virtues of the bodhisattva and an essential aspect of enlightenment itself. Thus, while compassion is simply listed as one of four boundless mentalities, it is really the most central. In fact, it can be said that the four boundless mentalities together comprise a single thematic contemplation designed to generate deep and genuine compassion. In Mahāyāna Buddhist scripture and treatises on meditation, one frequently finds them used in this manner.

What is the feeling of compassion and how is it related to the other three qualities of loving-kindness, joy, and equanimity? When a creature is in pain, one feels drawn to that creature, empathizing with its suffering and wishing to bring it happiness through alleviating its suffering. This is an aspect of compassion, but compassion is not limited to the feeling of empathy alone. It involves loving-kindness—the desire to take positive action to bring happiness to others—as well as the ability to selflessly celebrate the happiness of others. Relatively speaking, there are two sorts of happiness. There is the conventional notion of happiness, which is happiness that derives from fulfillment of limited everyday ends; and there is happiness of a deeper, more spiritual sort. The highest happiness is the wisdom that brings liberation from the realms of birth and death. This happiness is pure, selfless, unshakeable. Persons who practice with the motivation to seek bodhi, the highest and most perfect enlightenment, will first wish to free beings from their mundane physical and psychological afflictions. Then, if causes and conditions are mature, they will help them to realize the more profound happiness that derives from the dharma. For this reason, compassion automatically encompasses loving-kindness and joy, and ultimately grounds itself in the perfect equanimity that is the highest happiness.

We may distinguish five aspects to meditation upon compassion. First is the contemplation of sentient beings. There are three ways in which we relate to other sentient beings. First are those who we deem beneficial to us; second are those who we deem harmful to us (such as our enemies); and third are those who mean nothing to us. The latter group is by far the largest in number. The common mentality is to help and be considerate of people who are good to us and to avoid or wish bad things upon those whom we do not like. As far as the third group is concerned, most of the time we treat them as if they did not even exist. These attitudes are incorrect and do not represent the true attitude of compassion.

The second aspect of meditation upon compassion is to be aware of one's own feelings as well as the motives that underlie one's interaction with others. Basically, we can distinguish two sorts of emotional attitudes: one is to react with dislike to the sentient being and the interaction or relationship, and the other is to react favorably toward the sentient being and the relationship. There should be a third category: the attitude of neutrality, or no reaction, that we feel when we encounter beings for whom we have no real concern. However, as this feeling does not really generate any involvement, we will not concern ourselves with it.

If we look carefully into these subjective attitudes, we will find that they are deeply tied to our sense of physical and mental self. If something is pleasant or beneficial to our bodies and minds (physically, emotionally), then we will take pleasure in it and indulge in it. If something is unpleasant, physically or mentally threatening, then we will loathe and avoid it. It is because of attachment to our bodies and minds that we have such reactions. One should realize that one's mind is really nothing but a sequence of ever-changing thoughts. There is no enduring "mind" (or personality). Similarly, the body is composed of material elements and is itself not fixed or unchanging. Our minds and bodies, as we see them, are false perceptions. There is no need to be attached to them; nor is there any real reason to react so readily to benefit and harm, like and dislike.

The third aspect of meditation on compassion consists of investigating the phenomenon of interaction itself. From where does this interaction arise? What really takes place when we interact with beings? Actually, when people praise or rebuke us, it is nothing more than the sound of their voices coming into our ears. If people gesture, smile, prostrate to us, and so forth, it is only light coming into our eyes. Similarly, if we are beaten or kicked, it is no more than matter encountering matter. Fundamentally, such experiences consist of no more than the elements of the body—or the senses—coming in contact with the external environment. The subsequent perceptions that we form from our bodies and minds and those beings and things external to us are simply illusions, false conjurings. We should strive to see through these feelings of like and dislike and their attendant responses. If we can accomplish this, then we will no longer automatically categorize beings according to subjective likes and dislikes, and we will begin to treat them with true equality.

This attitude itself, however, should not be mistakenly equated with compassion. In fact, if our contemplation were to stop here, it would be very difficult to generate true compassion, for we would constantly be reducing things to characterless interactions of matter. How can we feel compassion when everything is regarded as false and illusion? This brings us to the fourth aspect of our meditation upon compassion. At this stage, we again take up contemplation of sentient beings that are external to us, but this time we do so without immediately projecting our own subjective likes and dislikes onto them. With this clear and detached vision, we then investigate the conditions of these sentient beings. In so doing, we strive to appreciate their sufferings and understand how their actions are the product of ignorance, delusion, and pain. Why do people become hateful, malicious, envious, jealous, arrogant, or violent? Why do they have the emotions and moods that they do? Why is it that they are so out of control? It is because they are ignorant of themselves and are driven by extremely strong selfishness and attachment. We should understand and sympathize with this condition. In a sense, such people are like children. When children meet strangers, sometimes they will be rude, but adults usually will not become angry because they realize that the children do not know any better. When the Buddha experienced rebuke or mistreatment, he did not become angry. Instead he felt compassion, for he realized that these people were not really in true control of themselves. If we can develop this sense of compassion and empathy within ourselves, then we will not react so blindly toward others, but will appreciate their underlying misery and work positively with them to help alleviate the distress that is the true cause of their problems and, hopefully, guide them toward real happiness.

This sense of compassion can be carried to yet deeper levels. For example, it is not only for social or emotional reasons that beings suffer and cause suffering to others. Ordinary sentient beings are dependent and limited, both physically and mentally. Therefore we suffer. Many people know that they should not think or do certain things, but they cannot restrain themselves and do them anyway. They cannot control their minds or bodies. Although our bodies and minds may be false—a combination of elements or a conjured illusion—we are not free of them or sovereign over them. It is as if we had two selves that give rise to an ongoing internal conflict of conscience and will. When the better side fails, people are driven to do harmful things.

To take it a step further, we must also realize that this body and mind to which we are so deeply bound must inevitably perish. This indeed is frightful and pitiable. How is it really any different from being born one morning and dying that evening? Our lives are very short, and over their entire course we are pressed by all sorts of afflictions and problems. This is a matter worthy of deepest compassion.

In the fifth and final part of the meditation on compassion, we strive to universally extend this sense of deep compassion described above to all categories of sentient beings—those we like, those we dislike, and those to whom we feel neutral—throughout all realms and all periods of time (past, present, and future). We call to mind the fact of our interrelationship and interdependence with all beings, contemplate deeply the causes of their pain and loss, foster love and the intense desire to give them what they need, and, finally, celebrate in our minds their fullest spiritual happiness. Working in this way, a sense of compassion can be engendered that is truly limitless. When this feeling is coupled with a pure and powerfully concentrated mind, it can, in turn, lead to samādhi.

MEDITATION ON CAUSE AND CONDITION

Those familiar with Buddhist teachings will likely have heard of the cardinal Buddhist idea that phenomena exist solely on the basis of relational causes and conditions (S. *hetu-pratyaya*; C. *yinyuan*). Meditation on cause and condition is a contemplation of precisely this relational and dependent character of existence. Sometimes, when people hear about this concept of "cause and condition," the word "cause" is misunderstood. Actually, the word "cause" should only be applied in a provisional sense. It is a mistake to think that there is single, one-on-one correspondence between an immutable cause and its immediate effect. For example, it is absolutely wrong, as far as a Buddhist is concerned, to think that existence is an "effect" that can only have been brought about by some absolute "cause" that lies anterior to it. The principle of cause and condition teaches just the opposite: there is no such thing as a "cause" or "effect" in this sense, for such a cause is really itself nothing more than a nexus of relational conditions. Moreover, even though it is the condition rather than the cause that is correctly held responsible for the production of phenomena, there really is no such thing as "condition" either. The point of this contemplation of cause and condition is to train the practitioner to see existence in terms of relational conditions.

There are some differences between this meditation on cause and condition and the contemplations described earlier. The methods of counting the breath and contemplation of impurity start from the perspective of the narrow sense of self. They exhort the practitioner to quiet the mind through concentration on a single object. The meditator may develop the experience of samādhi or the expanded sense of self, but concentration on the objects (breath, impurity, and so forth) used in these meditations may not necessarily be able to lead beyond this experience. The method of compassionate contemplation is even more conducive to the experience of expanded, or great, sense of self, or the feeling that all beings are not separate from oneself. The same applies for mindfulness of the Buddha.

Unlike these previous methods, contemplation of cause and condition—and, to some extent, the contemplation of categories, which we will take up next—deal more directly with the false views and afflictions that are at the core of cyclic birth and death. In this regard, they would appear to have more of a contemplative (S. *vipaśyanā*; C. *guan*), or wisdom, component than a samādhi component. However, this does not mean that meditation on cause and condition is a more profound or desirable practice. As with all of these techniques, contemplation of cause and condition is not to be used indiscriminately, but is targeted for a particular type of individual in a particular emotional condition. Should this practice be given to the wrong person, undesirable reactions might occur, such as feelings of purposelessness, depression, or the notion that one can neglect one's responsibilities.

Meditation on cause and condition is divided into four parts: (1) contemplation of existence and nonexistence; (2) contemplation of the three states of time; (3) contemplation of space; (4) contemplation of motion.

Contemplation of Existence and Nonexistence

The purpose of this contemplation is to understand that there is no such thing as existence as we commonly conceive it. This is achieved by analyzing and refuting notions of existence according to two standpoints: the ordinary standpoint and the more sophisticated philosophical and religious standpoint.

Most people give little conscious thought to the question of existence, yet certain assumptions about existence pervade every moment of their lives. We generally believe that we as individuals have enduring identities, and that the values that determine our relationship with the objects around us are immutable. We simply act and react according to these conceptions, and rarely question their validity. For instance, we assume that our spouses, homes, jobs, clothes, money, personalities, and so forth are as real and meaningful as we take them to be. We and society-at-large share and reinforce these attitudes. Yet these attitudes are really self-conceived and do not have any reality apart from that which we give to them. This is why Buddhists traditionally liken our ideas about existence to a dream. While awake, we know that our dreams do not exist in reality; but as soon as we go to sleep, we unhesitatingly participate in them as reality. Similarly, the things that we recognize throughout our lives to be real are actually no more real than dreams.

Our assumptions about existence, moreover, center upon the sense of self; if the self or the experiencer is not all that we take it to be, then external objects and the values that we place on them—the experienced—have little meaning. So the convictions that we hold about the self are the foundation of our attitudes toward external objects as well. It follows that if we can see through our notions of self, we will consequently see through our attitudes about existence as a whole.

This, however, is easier said than done. Few people take the trouble to inquire into their own existence, because the sense of ego is so profoundly ingrained that such inquiry seems foolish; and of the few people who do intuit that their self may be illusory, fewer still feel any urgency to pursue this further. Most people continue firmly in their ways, looking upon any effort to question existence as an aberration.

Actually, the ordinary standpoint can be refuted easily. By definition, we know that things that are inherently unstable and undergo change cannot be said to have enduring existence. Relating this definition to the self, we can say that the self is false because it consists of nothing more than a continuous series of changing thoughts and impressions. Since external objects depend for their existence on the self (e.g., this flow of thoughts), we conclude that external objects also do not exist. From this perspective, preoccupation with self and external objects seems quite senseless.

While it is relatively easy for most people to see that existence is false from the ordinary standpoint, it is generally difficult to admit the falsity of existence from the philosophical or religious perspective. We turn now to this perspective. Philosophers have postulated that there is such a thing as genuine existence, which they may define as eternal and unchanging, and which they call reality, fundamental substance, God, or Buddha. Mystics and religious leaders, as a result of their meditative experiences, have also affirmed their belief in genuine existence. If they cling to this belief in an ultimate existence, philosophers and mystics will at best be able to attain the great sense of self. They will never be able to go beyond self.

Philosophers reach their conclusion about reality through a reasoning process. Thus the philosophical argument and the resulting understanding of reality are all conceptions. Similarly, we have said that the mystic's belief in genuine existence comes from a meditative experience; but in such an experience, the mind is still active, even if only subtly, and the experience is dependent upon this mentation. Genuine existence for both the philosopher and the mystic, then, is inseparable from mental processes. Now, we know from previous discussion that all mental activity is the product of causes and conditions and, as such, is insubstantial. If thoughts are insubstantial, then the notion of genuine existence itself is unfounded.

Contemplation of the Three States of Time

The purpose of this contemplation is to refute existence by showing that time does not exist. We first explore the relationship between time and existence; we then refute time, and, by implication, we refute existence.

The existence of everything is predicated on an enduring presence through time. Independent of time, existence has no meaning. Yet, our notions of time—past, present, and future—are not what we take them to be. Because it is gone, the past does not exist anymore. The future has not yet arrived, so it cannot yet exist. If neither past nor future exists, we have no means to define the present. The present can have nowhere to originate and nowhere to go; thus it cannot exist.

Let us illustrate this with an analogy, wherein time is represented by a thread. A point in the middle of the thread can be taken as the present moment. The portion of the thread to the left of this point is the past, and the portion to the right is the future. If we cut the thread in two at the point representing the present, then where is the present? Since none of the three states of time can be established, time itself is refuted. It follows that existence is also refuted, since it is dependent on time.

This idea, incidentally, has an interesting implication for practice. Once, one of my disciples asked me what she should do, since she could not seem to progress fast enough. I told her that since time is unlimited, she need not worry. But saying that time is unlimited is really the same as saying that it does not exist, for time is characterized by restriction. If time does not exist, then we can be relaxed about it. We have all the time in the world.

Contemplation of Space

Spatial dimension is defined by the relationship between points or objects. For example, we say there is space inside a room only if the room is enclosed by walls; without the walls, there is no room and, hence, no concept of space inside it. We can say that outer space exists only if there are planets and stars; without them, there are no reference points to define the surrounding space. Thus, spatial dimension can exist only if it is defined by a stationary or moving point. The point provides the index by which we can define space. But, one can also carry this a step further to say that space, and hence additional points of reference, are necessary to define points and objects themselves. Thus, by examining the conditional dependence of dimension and reference point, we can demonstrate the emptiness of all objects.

Contemplation of Motion

The purpose of the fourth meditation is to show that the subject of movement cannot be established. The sense of self arises because of movement in the continuum of time and space. If it can be shown that movement cannot be established, we can conclude that the self—the subject of movement—cannot exist.

The meditation is divided into two parts: (1) the examination of thoughts coming from the past to the present; and (2) the examination of thoughts departing from the present and going into the future. We divide the first part into three stages: (a) what has already arrived; (b) what has not yet arrived; and (c) what is just arriving or about to arrive. "Coming" is defined as movement of the self from the past into the present. Let us examine each of these stages.

If the self has already come from the past to the present, it is like a train that has already passed by. So the self no longer exists. If the self has not yet come, then it does not yet exist. From where can a self originate if in both the past and the future it does not exist? Can there be such a condition as "about to arrive"? As it cannot come from or go to anywhere, the self in the present cannot exist. Since it does not exist in any of the three stages, the self coming from the past to the present cannot exist.

We now turn our investigation to the self departing from the present and going into the future. If the self coming from the past to the present cannot be established, one might suspect that at least the self going from the present into the future would exist. But again our investigation proves this supposition false. As before, the investigation is divided into three stages: (a) already gone; (b) not yet gone; and (c) about to go or just going. "Going," here, is defined as the movement of the self from the present into the future.

If we think of the self or the subject as having "already gone," it is like the train that has passed by. Since it has already passed away, it no longer exists. As before, if the self has not yet gone from the present to future, then it cannot yet exist. Likewise, the condition of "about to go" cannot exist, if the other two conditions are inadmissible. Thus, we must conclude that there cannot exist a self going from the present into the future. In sum, there is no self at all which is the subject of movement.

MEDITATION ON CATEGORIES, OR CONSTITUENT ELEMENTS

The Chinese term *jie*, which we render as "category," is a translation of the Indian Sanskrit word *dhātu*. *Dhātu* itself has many meanings in Buddhist writings, some of which include "sensory field", "sphere," "classification group," "category," "kind," "species," "constituent element," and so on. In this context, it carries the combined sense of classificatory category and constituent element. Meditation on categories (C. *jieguan*) uses a set of six elemental fields of classification as a basis for analysis of body, mind, and the environment. These six categories are divided into basic groups according to whether they are concerned with consciousness or materiality. Those categories, or fields, concerned with materiality can be spoken of as being both internal and external—materiality in terms of the physical body as well as the environment.

The six categories themselves break down as follows. Under the rubric of mind or consciousness, there is (1) consciousness itself. Under the rubric of material form, there is (2) earth; (3) water; (4) fire; (5) wind; and (6) space. The purpose of this contemplation is to demonstrate that our conventional notions about both environment and self are illusory. This is accomplished through analyzing the experiential field of our psycho-physical existence in terms of the six basic constituent categories or elements described above. At first glance, one may think that this is more of an academic exercise than a spiritual one. When combined with extended meditative concentration, however, contemplation of the six categories has a tangible effect on the way in which we perceive ourselves and the world.

Our sense of self and our perception of the environment are inseparably tied to one another. We can speak of self as the physical body or psychological personality; and we can speak of self in more expansive terms as the vast kingdom of self that we ceaselessly strive to build in the world around us. The domain of self extends through our senses to the external environment: everything we see, hear, and touch, as far as one can perceive or even imagine. By dissecting this field of internal and external experience according to the six categories, we can reexamine and transform some of the naive views that are habitually associated with both our narrow and extended world of self. With this change, attachment to the substantiality of self as a whole is diminished. As attachment to self and naiveté about existence diminish, a deep spiritual maturity will emerge. It is this sort of systemic change in awareness, rather than an increase in analytical knowledge, that contemplation of the six categories is intended to achieve.

Meditation on the six categories can take four perspectives: (1) contemplation of the six categories in their uniqueness; (2) contemplation of the six categories in terms of common features; (3) contemplation of pairs of opposites; (4) contemplation of duration of the six categories through time.

These four perspectives analyze various aspects of our involvement with existence in sequential fashion. The first contemplation simply classifies objects in terms of the six categories. The second investigates our basic views about existence—that it is pure, permanent, pleasurable, and endowed with identity—in terms of the insights of the first contemplation. The third contemplation analyzes the implications of action based upon these views. The fourth discusses continuation of action through time.

Contemplation of the Six Categories in Terms of Their Unique Characteristics

The purpose of this aspect of the contemplation is to come to recognize both body and environment in terms of the six basic categories, or constituent elements.

First consider the internal body as being composed entirely of nothing more than the six elements. Muscles, bones, teeth, hair, nails, and all other things having the character of solid material belong to the category of earth. Blood, fluids, secretions, urine, mucus, and all else in liquid form belong to the category of water. Warmth, energy, and vitality of the body belong to the category of fire. Movement of the vital airs, or humors, within the body—breathing, circulation, and so forth—corresponds to wind. This category is called wind, rather than air, because the emphasis is on movement. Air tends to indicate stasis, while wind suggests motion. Furthermore, wind need not be thought of only in the gross physical sense. It may also indicate subtle movement of the *qi*, or "vital energy," within the body. This movement and nourishing function of the *qi*, for example, becomes noticeable as gross obstructions within the body are gradually removed through meditation. Space, the fifth category, is present everywhere within the body—in the mouth, bones, vessels, cells, lungs, and all other cavities and orifices. In essence, the body as a whole, or any portion of it, can be broken down into nothing more than these six categories.

In similar fashion, features of the external environment are also classified in terms of the six categories. For example, such abstract and emotionally charged things as money, cars, girlfriend, or boyfriend are understood to be nothing more than earth, and so forth. By grasping after them and worrying over them, what have you really gained? The sixth category of consciousness is a special category, for it pervades all moments of awareness, regardless of whether we speak of internal or external. Nothing that we experience ever stands outside consciousness; awareness of the body and the self in the narrow sense is consciousness of body and self, just as discrimination, cognition, and grasping of any external object is inherently a function of consciousness. Thus, in a sense, phenomena are themselves grasped, conceived, and experienced only on the basis of consciousness, and have no independent existence outside this context.

Contemplation of the Six Categories in Terms of Common Characteristics

The function of this second contemplation is to understand objects associated with the six categories as, in turn, characterized by four basic qualities: (1) impurity; (2) painfulness; (3) impermanence; and (4) emptiness, or no-self. We call this "contemplation in terms of common characteristics" because all four qualities apply equally to each of these six categories.

Once again, the contemplation proceeds through both the internal and external spheres. Even though we habitually view our bodies and the world around us as attractive and pure, one may contemplate the various organs or components of the body and the objects of the senses as impure and repulsive. Awareness of our bodies and interaction with the environment inevitably involve the vested interest of promoting what is pleasurable and avoiding what is painful. Because of this incessant striving, even pleasure is painful. Thus, by reflecting deeply on our involvement with the fields of the six categories, we become aware of the universality of suffering. Going a step further, we also realize that none of the objects of these six categories endure. They are uniformly impermanent. Finally, looking deeply into the momentary arising and perishing of the six categories, we grasp the fact that none of these items has any enduring self-existence. They are empty and devoid of self. At this point, deep-seated mental anguish will virtually disappear, although physical disabilities and discomforts may remain.

Contemplation of Opposites

Contemplation on the six categories in terms of opposites focuses on activity (karma) as it arises in response to different fields and views of existence. To start, it is important to understand that one's actions will produce either good or bad retribution, depending on the sort of action it is as well as the mental attitude and views toward existence that motivate it. The purpose is to expose and eliminate "dark" karma and its evil retributions, and perform only "white," or good, karma.

As deed and its response are so deeply tied to motive, good karma and karmic reciprocity can be assured only if one realizes the impermanence of the physical body, environment, and consciousness. By recognizing their impermanence, one is freed from selfish attachment and desire, for one knows intimately through unshakeable experience that the phenomena of consciousness and materiality arise only as the transitory conjunction of the six categories, and will remain as such only as long as causes and conditions allow. Using this contemplation to counter evil motives and impulses, self-indulgence is replaced by compassion, and selfish commitment by higher values. While causes and conditions permit, one wholeheartedly dedicates oneself to fulfilling one's spiritual responsibilities. In so doing, one creates white karma and, eventually, achieves liberation.

Contemplation of the Six Categories Through Time

The six categories form, in one instant, a temporary aggregate which we call body and consciousness which, by the next instant, has disappeared and given way to a new aggregate. Thus, although the six categories continue through time, they are never constant. Moreover, since everything consists entirely of the six aggregates, there is nothing that remains constant. We conclude, then, that there can be no self that persists unchanging. There is really no birth, no death, no self, and no existence: everything is just the aggregation of the six categories, and this aggregation is itself false. In this fashion one begins to become tangibly aware of the selflessness of all things.

5

Developing Insight or Wisdom:
The Four Stations of Mindfulness

In the Buddhist sūtras and treatises, the various methods for "stopping," or stilling, the mind are presented as preparatory techniques which are intended to remove gross emotional obscurations, and to help beginning practitioners concentrate their scattered minds and develop samādhi power. As methods of meditation, they are not really designed to foster liberative insight (prajñā) and enlightenment per se, although it is possible that individuals with unusually keen karmic roots may awaken quickly on the basis of these practices.

In the traditional graduated approach to spiritual discipline outlined in the Indian Buddhist and Chinese scholastic systems, the Five Methods for Stilling the Mind are meant to be followed or accompanied by the Four Stations of Mindfulness (S. smṛtyupasthāna; C. nianchu), a set of techniques that are designed specifically to generate liberating insight into no-self/no-mind and emptiness. One could also say, conversely, that the insight technique of the Four Stations of Mindfulness cannot effectively fulfill its function of reaching and uprooting false views without the mental purity and power of samādhi practice.

Why is samādhi power a necessary prerequisite for effective use of the Four Stations of Mindfulness? With the experience of samādhi, the mind is freed of the gross distractions and emotional coverings that normally afflict it, making one's mental awareness quite sharp and clear. This clarity is in itself a kind of wisdom or power of insight—different from our ordinary perception by its purity and its ability to dig deeply and directly into the texture of experience. It is what we call "insight born of meditation" (guan hui), or "mundane wisdom possessed of outflows" (S. sāsrava-jñāna). Such insight is described as "possessed of outflows" because it is still imperfect, and is not yet equivalent to the genuine wisdom that comes with deep realization of no-self. It is called "insight born from meditation" for two reasons: first, because it derives its power of clarity and precision from samādhi; and second, because this kind of mental clarity and precision born of deep concentration is necessary in order to investigate the nature of mind and existence to any real depth. The "mindful observation" *(nian)* that is applied to the Four Stations is none other than this *guan hui*, or pure and deep insight refined by samādhi.

The objects of the Four Stations of Mindfulness are subtle. If one were to try to meditate on them with the usual scattered and opaque mind, they would likely have no impact at all, except to make one even more tired and scattered. Even if one has developed the mental concentration and clarity of samādhi, should one stop practicing and take up the four mindfulnesses only after a long hiatus, one's efforts will also be fruitless. The Four Stations of Mindfulness must be used while the power of samādhi is fresh and strong, and practice must be continuous until results are realized. Otherwise, the clarity and precision of meditative insight will ebb away and one will have to begin all over again.

This idea of using techniques for developing meditative discernment in conjunction with techniques for concentration and samādhi harkens back to the two "wings" or "wheels" of meditative calming (S. *śamatha;* C. *zhi*) and meditative contemplation (S. *vipaśyanā;* C. *guan*) that we discussed earlier. The various methods for stopping, or stilling, the mind are primarily techniques of meditative calming, although several of them can be used to generate meditative insight, or wisdom. The Four Stations of Mindfulness are primarily techniques of meditative discernment and contemplation, although sustained mindfulness of the body can, likewise, produce meditative calm, especially when coupled with the breath.

According to this classic Buddhist concept of *śamatha* and *vipaśyanā,* meditative calm and clarity must be present for discernment to penetrate deeply. Only when meditative discernment penetrates deeply can the root afflictions and illusions of the mind truly be exposed and uprooted. Thus, calming is often likened to a sealed and windless room, whereas contemplation is likened to the flame of a lamp that burns steadily and brightly when the air is still; calming is the soap that loosens dirt, contemplation is the water that washes it away; calming is the hand that holds the clump of grass firm, contemplation is the sickle that cuts it loose; calming excavates the roots of the tree of saṃsāra, contemplation exposes and pulls them up.

Without the mental power and clarity induced by samādhi, discernment and contemplation will be superficial. Any insight that they generate will be shallow and fleeting. You will always remain a word-chasing philosopher, and never will your insights have the power to cause an earthshaking revolution of your entire being. Then again, pursuing meditative calm and samādhi without contemplation and wisdom will result in a kind of brutish obsession with quietude and physical bliss. This can become a kind of addiction that will forever keep you from liberation, for meditative concentration and mundane samādhi can never produce enlightenment. You will always remain at the level of unified mind and the expanded sense of self, unless you have the good fortune to meet a great Chan master, or deliberately take up Buddhist methods for the discernment of emptiness and no-self, such as the Four Stations of Mindfulness.

After receiving ordination, the Chinese Chan master Xuyun (1840–1959) lived in a cave practicing austerities and reciting the Buddha's name, as a result of which he experienced wonderful joy and mental clarity. But it was only six years later, when he happened to meet an accomplished teacher of the Tiantai school, that he realized his error and began the proper study of Chan gong'an.[1] Thus, it is important that one be familiar with the basic principles of "meditative calming and contemplation," or "samādhi and wisdom," that govern the use of such Buddhist practices as the Five Methods for Stilling the Mind, the Four Stations of Mindfulness, and Chan methods of gong'an and silent illumination (mozhao).

THE FOUR STATIONS OF MINDFULNESS
AS A METHOD OF MEDITATION

2. The Four Stations of Mindfulness (S. smṛtyupasthāna; C. nianchu) entails contemplation of four basic objects: (1) the gross physical body; (2) sensation; (3) the mind; and (4) dharmas, or elemental units of psycho-physical experience that constitute experience of body, sensation, and mind. These four are called "stations" (S. upasthāna; C. chu) of "mindfulness" (S. smṛti; C. nian) because the student mindfully observes or contemplates each of these four spheres in sequence, progressing from shallow to deep, from gross to subtle.

The Four Stations of Mindfulness are intended to counteract and uproot four basic "misconceptions," or inverted views about existence: (1) the notion that existence is pure when it is really impure; (2) the idea that existence is pleasurable when it is actually painful; (3) the idea that existence is eternally abiding and constant when actually it is impermanent; and (4) the notion that we and all living things are endowed with a constantly abiding self, when there is really no self. These four are referred to as "inverted" views because they are the very antithesis of the actual nature of existence—that is, that existence, as we know it, is painful, impermanent, and empty, or devoid, of self.

As the most deeply rooted and insidious of all of our misconceptions about existence, the four inverted views deeply determine the way we experience ourselves and the world around us. Indeed, they are themselves the very essence of the ignorance and affliction that generates and perpetuates the cycle of birth and death. For example, our general sense that existence is pure is closely related to the conviction that our own bodies are pure and attractive. Our belief that existence is pleasurable is tied to our naive conviction that sensations we feel are really pleasurable. Our sense that existence is permanent is connected with the sense that our minds and personalities are enduring and unchanging. And, our conviction that we (and existence) are endowed with independent selfhood is based on our own firm sense of ego; namely, that there is a constant and solid "self" or "person" that experiences, makes decisions, and acts in the world. All of these views are, in some measure, tied to ego or self, for they all entail a kind of self-referential organizing of the world around our own persons. One could say that they are the building blocks of our sense of personal existence, or embodiment.

Meditation on the Four Stations of Mindfulness is designed to expose and counteract the four basic misconceptions of existence, thereby provoking a revolutionary reexperiencing of body, mind, and world. The tendency, on an everyday basis, to identify the physical body as the self is something with which most people will be familiar. But our sense of self is by no means limited to the physical body alone. It is also connected with the flow of sensations—that is, the painful and pleasurable feelings that we experience as our bodies and minds interact with the environment. In fact, when we look closely at the experience of our physical embodiment, we find that it is made up entirely of sensations of this sort. It is these sensations that constitute our sensation of physical being.

Progressing to another level, the thought or sense of self goes deeper than the body, since we often perceive and treat our bodies as we would an object in the environment: we say, "my arm hurts," or "my hair looks good." We might think of these things as connected with our selves, but ultimately we will feel that there is a deeper or truer self inside of us. This is what we mean when we conventionally use the word "soul" or "true self."

In the experience of samādhi, our usual sense of physical limitation and embodiment completely disappears. We may feel that our being dissolves, expands outward, and merges with all things. We may feel that we form one essence with the universe, and that this essence is pure existence, God, or ultimate reality. Many religions and philosophies draw their inspiration from this kind of experience. Actually, as Buddhists see it, it is just another kind of "embodiment," albeit a subtler one than that with which we are commonly familiar. It is the embodiment experienced at the level of the great or expanded sense of self, in which the gross sensations of bodily pleasure and pain have been replaced by a subtle sensation of all-pervading bliss and energy. Self is still there and affliction is still there, just in a different form. By using such methods as the Four Stations of Mindfulness, we can actually expose and uproot the naive views that inform these experiences of self and existence, thereby bringing about a true revolution in our being. This comes with the realization of what we variously call "no-self," "no-mind," or emptiness. The Four Stations of Mindfulness are one among a number of Hīnayāna and Mahāyāna techniques of meditative discernment designed expressly to accomplish this end.

Mindfulness of the Body

As presented in the Four Stations of Mindfulness, contemplation of the body bears a superficial resemblance to the meditation on impurity included among the preliminary methods for stilling the mind, since both practices foster the insight that the body is impure. However, there are fundamental differences between the two, and they should not be regarded as identical. As a preliminary method for stilling the mind, the contemplation of impurity is designed specifically to counteract lust and attachment to the body. The practice also entails concentrated mental rehearsal or visualization of the progressive decay of a corpse, culminating in the fixed image of lustrous white bones. In this respect, the object of the meditation is mentally constructed, thematic, and fixed in content. The orchestrated phases of the visualization are designed to counteract attachment to the body and, simultaneously, to provide a stable object on which to establish mental one-pointedness, or samādhi.

While mindfulness of the body may induce insights and experiences of meditative absorption similar to those of the meditation on impurity, the object or field of meditation and the method of meditatively engaging that object are quite different from the meditation on impurity. The object, or "station" (S. upasthāna), of contemplation is the body and its actions, just as they appear. They are not to be intentionally envisioned as pure or impure, pleasurable or painful, sacred or profane, existent or empty, but simply observed as they are experienced from one moment to the next. The method of contemplation, similarly, does not entail seizing upon or seeking to establish a specific sign, image, or insight, but direct and simple observance of the data of bodily experience. Rather than presume what it means to have a body, the aim here is to look directly and afresh at the experience of embodiment—to gain a deep and thorough familiarity of the body by looking closely at its presence in our lives. This silent observance of bodily activity and sensation will quite naturally lead to an understanding of the impure and constraining nature of the body, without the need to establish any foregoing dogmatic assertion as such. In effect, the body itself acts as one's teacher through simple observation and experience.

Ultimately, the practice of mindful observance of the body builds upon the foundation of samādhi, but really aims at generating wisdom that is devoid of outflows—that is, the liberating insight into the Buddhist Four Noble Truths and the reality of no-self. Mindfulness purified and deepened by samādhi reveals that the body is the source of numerous afflictions and attachments. Every person is deeply imbued with the sense of body as the domain of selfhood. From moment to moment, we encounter and organize the world around the perception of our bodies, instinctively obsessed with the protection of the body and the fulfillment of its material appetites. Meanwhile, we are wholly unaware that the karma and the psycho-physical thought-constructs that we engender on the basis of the body keep us bound to the cycle of birth and death.

On one level, we could conclude that the body is impure simply because it is disgusting in the gross physical sense: it oozes all sorts of filth and requires constant effort—both mental and physical—to make it acceptable, even to ourselves. But the idea of the body's impurity actually goes much deeper than this, extending to numerous bodily based habits that are repulsive and distressful: vanity, sexual aggression, sensual obsession, violence, and so forth. This is an ugliness of a much subtler sort. Because our naive identification with the body is responsible for such a large array of negative qualities, to a certain extent it is the root of saṃsāra itself.

Mindfulness of Sensation

If one were to look more closely at the "body"—that is to say, if one were to examine the experience of embodiment itself—one would find that it is comprised chiefly of sensation, which is itself mental in character. Our obsession with the body as the "self," as well as the related conviction that the body and existence as a whole are pure, is closely connected with sensations produced in conjunction with the body. Buddhist treatises typically distinguish these into three basic sorts: sensations of (1) pleasure; (2) painfulness; and (3) sensations that are neutral in character. According to the classic Buddhist schemes of the five aggregates, or *skandhas*, and the Twelvefold Chain of Causation (S. *pratītyasamutpāda*), when a sensory faculty contacts an object (or form), sensations of painfulness, pleasure, or neutrality arise as one of the first elements in the act of cogitation. Whatever we experience, we immediately assess it and react to it according to whether the sensation is pleasant, unpleasant, or neutral—before we even begin to define and act upon the object through the subsidiary processes of associative perception (S. *saṃjñā*) and volition (S. *saṃskāra*). In effect, we have wired into us a powerfully defensive posture toward the world. The first response that flickers through our minds is the question of whether an object gratifies or pleases us, threatens or disconcerts us. At the most primal level of consciousness, perception itself is fraught through and through with obsession, gratification, and fear. We "notice" and cogitate over objects precisely because they impinge upon our world as potential threats or enhancements to our power, attracting us or repelling us accordingly. Objects to which we are habituated and which pose no immediate interest go "unnoticed" as neutral sensations.

Thus, built into the very sensory vehicles through which we "embody" ourselves and the world is a mechanism of self-interest that compartmentalizes all experience into a geography of self/other, pleasure/pain, and threat/enhancement. We habitually seek the pleasant and try to ignore, avoid, or alleviate the unpleasant. Pleasant sensation becomes our overriding obsession. There is great pleasure in eating to appease great hunger, drinking to satisfy thirst, to feel the breeze in hot weather, to bathe when feeling dirty, to appease lust through touch and embrace. People who treasure these pleasures fill their lives with their image, doing their utmost to preserve them and to avoid the opposite sensations of pain and loss. To this end, the dominating quest for pleasure entails a repression of the perception and memory of pain. In our effort to enhance and stabilize the pleasurable, we seek every possible way to diminish awareness of those things that disturb us.

Things that disturb us, of course, break through our protective wall of pleasure all the time, bringing directly the experience of pain. Our effort to forestall these unpleasant intrusions may be reasonably successful; but this attentiveness entails a kind of habitual paranoia and relentless expenditure of energy that is constrictive, exhausting, and painful in and of itself. Worst of all, in conditioning ourselves to seek certain distinctive forms of pleasure, we sow the seeds of our own failure, for the fact of impermanence itself mandates that pleasure in all its forms is unstable and bound to fade. Sensory pleasure, as defined over and against sensory pain and loss, is both limited and transitory, carrying within itself the seeds of suffering. Much like the drug to the addict, pleasure as we know it merely sets us up for the pain that comes with its fading. The more habituated we become to its effects, the worse is our pain. Furthermore, since the mental habits cultivated in this life will continue to condition experiences in the next life, the effects of this prison-like dichotomy are potentially unlimited.

If one were vividly to call to mind the sensations of unpleasantness which we tend to repress, or to ponder just how fleeting and relentlessly addictive worldly pleasure can be, one would feel very differently about the body and its sensations. Some people say that the Buddha was mistaken or overly negative in his statements about universal suffering. Even he himself stated that his teaching of *duḥkha* went against the grain of worldly convention. But unpleasantness and pain are an undeniable part of our experience, and the effort to dismiss consideration of them as "pessimistic" is itself to take an unrealistic view of who and what we are. Worst of all, most people avoid this issue not out of any real philosophical reflection, but merely as part of the habitual strategy to banish all pain and unpleasantness.

To be wise, happy, and fulfilled, ultimately we must confront and come to terms with our condition, not avoid it. Through bold-faced mindfulness, we must open ourselves to the full range of human sensations, allowing ourselves to view deeply the processes by which pleasure and painfulness arise and are selectively mediated. Through this sort of observation, one will come to an intimate understanding of how they mutually condition one another, and how, together, they are capable of generating a relentless cycle of sensory obsession that brings about the worst kind of suffering. In the final analysis, mindfulness of sensation will directly generate awareness that the cycle of pleasurable, painful, and neutral sensation is itself painful. True peace and happiness can come only from looking deeply into its processes and gaining release from its grip.

Mindfulness of Mind

In the foregoing discussions of body and sensation, we have traced the experience of embodiment—or "body as self"—to increasingly subtle levels, beginning first with the conventional awareness of the gross body as self, then proceeding to look at the body as a locus of psycho-physical sensations. With the latter perspective, body is demythologized and revealed to be primarily a mental construct. In this third station of mindfulness of mind, sensory experience as a whole is further reframed within the collective stream of psycho-physical sensations, perceptions, or cognitions, and volitional responses within what we subjectively identify as "mind." Thus the construct of "mind," or "mind as self," becomes the field of focus.

Much as we do with our bodies, we as human beings invest a great deal of faith in the naive notion that the "mind" is a substantial and enduring entity. People may agree that the body or the environment changes over time, but often they will be convinced that their personal character *qua* mental self does not. They may think that they remain, at root, essentially the same throughout their lives—that the mental and emotional traits that identify them as a discrete personality inhere in them as an unchanging substance. In China, there is a common saying used to profess undying love: "The sea may dry up, the rocks may crumble, but my love will last forever." But can such a feeling really last forever unchanged? Is it really as absolute as we wishfully profess it to be? Are we really so consistent? What is the mind really like?

If we examine this thing we call "mind," or "character," closely, we discover an extraordinarily tumultuous stream of thoughts, impressions, feelings, and urges that is constantly changing in response to external perceptions and other internal thoughts. On a day-to-day basis, we operate with the conventional assumption that we assess and manipulate the world around us from a base of absolute subjective integrity: "I" perceive "the world," actively "think" such and such a "thought," and deliberately resolve to take such and such an "action." All the while we imagine that this process is part and parcel of a distinct and enduring self, predictable, and fully under our conscious control. Patterns of regularized perception and response are taken as indicative of the absoluteness of self-identity, while deviations are dismissed as adventitious or deliberate changes of strategy. Thus, we affirm and embody ourselves as discrete, real "minds," much in the same way we do our physical "bodies."

If we investigate or observe this "mind" closely, we find that it is anything but substantial and unitary. The flow of thoughts has a life of its own, "thinking" and swaying us more than we "think" it! Indeed, it is teeming with conflicted feelings and urges, a battleground on which the trenches of self-identity and self-interest are themselves continually being redrawn. Ultimately, there is no unchanging "mind" or "character" that exists outside this fluctuating mental continuum and continual process of self-reification. When you open yourself up to the question of just "who" one really "is" and take a hard look at the "mind," you will inevitably find it to be inchoate and transitory. As with the body, mindfulness of mind forces a powerful restructuring of our mental posture by exposing and experientially compelling us to let go of our naive conviction that mind is changeless.

Mindfulness of Constituent Mental Factors, or Dharmas

Having exposed the arbitrariness of the conventional domains of "body" and "mind," all boundaries between the two and between such subsidiary dichotomies as inner and outer, self and environment, mental and material, are dissolved, revealing in their stead a continually fluctuating continuum or field of psycho-physical sensations, perceptions, volitions, and so forth. Noting certain consistencies in this play of mentation, the Buddha and subsequent meditators delineated these constituent factors of psycho-physical experience into the heuristic categories known as "dharmas." Thus, for example, in addition to our familiar categories of "body" and "mind," our mental and physical experience can be analyzed in terms of the twelve accesses (S. *āyatana*) of sense faculty and sensory object, or the eighteen fields or factors (S. *dhātu*) consisting of the six sense faculties, six sensory objects, and six sense consciousnesses. The most celebrated set of dharmic categories used for analyzing the mind is perhaps the five aggregates, or *skandhas*, of form, sensation, perception, volitional response, and consciousness, discussion of which can be found in most any introductory book on Buddhism.

The fourth station of mindfulness of dharmas entails taking a microscopic look at the continuum of psycho-physical experience from which concepts of self, mind, and body are produced, using its constituent dharmas as the frame of reference. Thus, a given moment of sensory experience might be viewed in terms of consciousness of a particular sense arising from the sense faculty coming into contact with its object. Or taking a forward-moving, cause-and-effect approach rather than a lateral perspective, mentation can be observed in terms of the five skandhas: form coming into contact with sense faculty produces sensation, which is further elaborated by perception, which engenders volitional responses, all of which transpires as consciousness.

The thrust of this practice is to get at the most subtle and afflictive construct of all—the false notion of "selfhood" (S. *ātman*) that undergirds and conditions all saṃsāric experience. If we see that the flow of dharmas—the relationship among body, sensation, mind, factors of form, perception, volition, and the like—keep changing at every moment, then where is the self? Who or what, ultimately, is this "I" that perceives and organizes experience? Is it a bona fide part of perceptive experience? Is it integral to it? Does it stand prior to it? Is it absolute and apart from it? What does looking deeply into this problem suggest that we do about ourselves and our world?

The common, erroneous idea is to believe that the body and the mind are one's own: "*My* body is having these bodily sensations" or "*My* mind is thinking these thoughts." Fundamental to both is the subjective reference point of "I," or the "self." One might thereby be inclined to identify the self with the "body," with the "mind," with individual thoughts, or some hypothetically transcendent "soul." But if one were to truly focus in on and observe the process of psychophysical experience itself—that is to say, the momentary arising and perishing of thought in the mind—one would see that it is but the momentary product of complex causes and conditions. The "I" or "self" is no more than a thought, a mental construct that arises in conjunction with other mental constructs. Ultimately, it cannot be found to stand apart from them or be reduced to any one constituent factor. No enduring or identifiable self can be found in any of these dharmas, or "elemental factors of experience." "Self," or the "I," is found to be a conditioned, baseless, and hence empty construct. This realization is tantamount to the Hīnayāna insight into the emptiness or nonexistence of self in terms of the person (S. *pudgala-nairātmya*).

Upon even closer inspection, the same may be said for all the constituent factors of experience themselves: dharmas arise, operate, and perish in mutual coordination with one another, with none being permanent, absolute, or existing in a priori isolation. Thus the same emptiness and baselessness that applies for self extends to dharmas as well. In the conventional world of saṃsāra, we experience dharmic objects as spatial reifications by falsely projecting the existence of absolute entities into the network of causes and conditions from a dimensional perspective. We experience dharmas as temporal reifications—as enduring entities—by misconstruance of conjunction and dissipation of cause and condition from a temporal perspective. However, in both cases, when examined closely, these dharmas are themselves nothing but junctures of other conditioning factors. They are "empty," subject to change, and devoid of any identifiable self. This is tantamount to the Mahāyāna insight into the emptiness of the selfhood of dharmas (S. *dharma-nairātmya*). As the great Madhyamaka master, Nāgārjuna, states in the opening lines of his *Mūlamadhyamaka-kārikā*, "No dharma whatsoever can be found to originate either on its own, from dependence on another, from both, or from neither."[2]

So far we have discussed the Four Stations of Mindfulness individually, link-

ing them in sequential fashion to the insights of impurity, painfulness, impermanence, and no-self, or emptiness. For a beginner, this might prove the most
effective approach for developing insight. However, as one's practice develops,
any or all of the four insights of impurity, painfulness, impermanence, and no-
self may be contemplated on the basis of each of the four stations. Thus the
stations and their respective insights become mutually interfused.

THE STATIONS OF MINDFULNESS IN RELATION TO THE FOUR NOBLE TRUTHS AND THE DIFFERENT LEVELS OF EMPTINESS

Ultimately, the function of the Four Stations of Mindfulness is to bring realization of the Four Noble Truths, insight into no-self, and liberation from the
cycle of birth and death. At the most advanced stages of practice, contemplation of the Four Noble Truths itself becomes integrated with the Four Stations
of Mindfulness, such that at each station of body, sensation, and so forth, the
Four Truths are plumbed in full, and vice versa. When this occurs, insight into
no-self is said to reach its fullest development, bringing with it the four fruits
of Hīnayāna sainthood—the stage of streamwinner (first substantial taste of
nirvāṇa), once-returner, non-returner, and fully liberated arhat.

But in the same way that they function to bring about the highest goals of
the Hīnayāna path, the Four Stations of Mindfulness—in particular, the fourth
station of mindfulness of dharmas—may also be further adapted to foster the
deeper realizations of emptiness expounded in the Mahāyāna. In this sense, they
become a technique shared by all Buddhist paths and doctrinal systemizations.
They are a common door to the emptiness of no-self, emptiness as the ultimate
reality or suchness of all things (dharmas), and emptiness in its highest and most
inexpressible sense.

Love, kindness, and compassion are the very foundation of Mahāyāna Buddhism and its bodhisattva path. From a general perspective, these virtues are
deeply cherished by other religious traditions as well. However, in the Buddhist
tradition, genuine love and compassion are seen to arise only with proper insight
into the nature of existence—that is to say, its nature as "conditioned origination" (S. pratītyasamutpāda) and "lack of self-existence" (S. niḥsvabhāva). We can
understand this idea from two perspectives.

First, from the perspective of interdependence, we can see that no phenomenon in the world—whether material or mental—exists independently of other
phenomena. All beings and things are intimately connected with one another.
All of the activities and processes that are engaged in by seemingly discrete entities are actually connected to, and affected by, the activities and processes of
other entities—all in an extremely intricate and infinite network. Separation
from this vast system of connections would make existence itself impossible.

On an everyday human scale, we can see the truth of interdependence in the simple fact that no person can live entirely apart from society or from other people. We are born into this world and nurtured in our early years by others—either by our natural parents or adoptive parents. Throughout our lives, we depend on the assistance of others for everything we have, from the basic necessities of life, such as food, clothing, and shelter, to the various forms of knowledge and skill that we acquire in order to make our way through life. Even language and the ability to communicate come from others. We are quite fortunate if we live in a relatively stable society and economy; and if one day we should lose the kind of social stability and protections that we enjoy today, we would begin to understand how precious, but precarious, peace and safety can be.

On a broader scale, countless other aspects of existence, both sentient and insentient, have either direct or indirect influences on our well-being. When we become aware of the connection between human beings and all other forms of life and material existence, how can we not have inclusive sympathy and concern for all beings? It is from this understanding, and from these related feelings of sympathy and concern, that we generate a sense of responsibility for other beings and our environment. We desire to help them and to nurture their harmony and happiness in any way that we can. From the perspective of the Buddhist belief in innumerable past and future rebirths, we can surmise that we must have, at one time or another, lived in close connection to each and every sentient being. They have been our mothers, our fathers, our sisters, and our brothers. All sentient beings have at some time served as the cause of our happiness, and with this in mind, we can only feel a deep sense of gratitude to them. We may also, at one time, have caused all sentient beings grief and sorrow, and for this we can only feel deep remorse. This kind of sensitivity to our connection with others engenders a quality of genuine caring and love that goes beyond the individual's affection for his or her immediate family, race, class, or nation. This sort of love and compassion, extended to all beings everywhere, springs from the knowledge—the living insight—that we are truly all one family. This is the foundation of Buddhist compassion.

From a second perspective, the interdependence of all things also allows us to speak of their "sameness." When we localize or "narrow" our focus on specific configurations within this vast nexus of sentient and insentient interrelations, we conceive the existence of discretely bounded "entities" or "selves." However, since all such entities or selves are, in fact, contingent on each other and the environment at large, not one of them can be said to exist autonomously and permanently in and of itself. It "lacks discrete self-existence" (S. *niḥsvabhāva*). This is the nature of "emptiness" (*śūnyatā*)—it is identical with and inseparable from the fact of conditionality itself. As we penetrate the depths of this conditionality through the cultivation of genuine Mahāyāna compassion and insight, we can come to understand personally and directly that all phenomena are empty of inherent self-nature. This "emptiness" and "interrelatedness" in turn reveals their likeness, their profound similarity. From understanding the interdependence of all things, we thereby go a step further to realize the non-dual, equal nature of existence. This realization is the dawning of true wisdom.

This is the profound nature of the world that we live in; and of course, it is also the profound reality of our own individual lives as we live them from moment to moment. We are all connected to each other and to all things, both animate and inanimate. With this sort of outlook, gained from actual insight into the nature of our existence, one will feel an immediate connection with the world. One will discover that boundless compassion is functionally inseparable from the insight or wisdom of emptiness itself. To live our lives with the true freedom and fulfillment of "no-self" is not to depart from this world, but to live a life of open immediacy and compassion *within* its vast, interpenetrating totality. When wisdom is boundless and able to encompass all modes of being, both particular and universal as well as the empty and the provisionally, or, locally existent; when compassion and skill-in-means are boundless and able to encompass all modes of being and environment as a single body—then one is a perfectly enlightened Buddha.

In the Mahāyāna tradition, all sentient beings (and even the leaves and grass!) are identical in nature to Buddhas. All sentient beings have the potential to realize full enlightenment and to manifest Buddhahood, because all sentient beings are Buddhahood. Persons traveling the path to Buddhahood must cultivate the great wisdom and compassion that sees all beings as one body with themselves. This is not just wishful thinking or philosophical speculation, but a sincere motivation that inspires our actions and compels us to live humanely in the world. Most of all, it is a living experience that grows out of our practice and comes with the gradual transformation of our very bodies and minds. Nor does it come from something external—it is not just infused into us from outside. It comes from our own personal insight into the ground of our own existence, here and now. This transformative insight (prajñā) serves as the ethical impulse of the enlightened being—it is both the motivation and the source of inner strength of the bodhisattva.

III
The Direct
and Sudden Approach
of Chan

6

Chan and the Sudden Path to Enlightenment

SUDDEN AND GRADUAL APPROACHES TO ENLIGHTENMENT

In our introductory chapter on Chan and emptiness, we introduced a distinction between the "sudden," or "instantaneous," approach to enlightenment and the "gradual," or "graduated," approach. We noted that the Chan tradition identifies itself with the sudden path, while at the same time preserving basic principles of spiritual discipline and development characteristic of the more traditional, graduated path. Having touched upon the rudiments of the graduated practice in our discussion of the three disciplines of moral purity, meditative concentration, and meditative contemplation, or insight, we will now turn to the concept and practice of Chan.

The distinction between sudden and gradual representations of the Buddhist path may be considered from several perspectives: a temporal perspective, a spatial perspective, and a thematic or dialectical perspective. From the standpoint of temporal process, sudden refers to what is completed instantaneously, all at once. Gradual implies a time gradient or a step-by-step ascent over time. From a spatial or dimensional perspective, one could say that in the sudden approach there is no motion from "here" to "there;" no shift in position or movement from one realm to another takes place, whether it be from saṃsāra to nirvana, delusion to enlightenment, or so on. In fact, the metaphor of spatial delimitation collapses altogether with the sudden perspective, for "here" is "there," and "there" is "here." The gradual approach, on the other hand, not only sets up spatial distinctions, but represents progress toward enlightenment as a dialectical displacement from one perspective or realm to another—for example, from existence to emptiness, from emptiness back to existence, to both, to neither.

Finally, there is the thematic or dialectical perspective. In a sense, this is not so distinct from the perspectives of time and space, insofar as temporal and spatial designations are here represented as mental constructs. The gradual approach entails a sequence of distinct thematic positions that build on one another or displace one another in dialectical fashion, until the final true vision of highest enlightenment, or emptiness, is revealed.

For example, the *Heart Sūtra* says that "form is identical with emptiness, emptiness identical with form; form is no different from emptiness, emptiness no different from form." To realize this perfect identity—this perfect wisdom or vision of a Buddha—one might begin with the biased view that matter, or form, is real, self-existent. This is our conventionally accepted view of the world. Buddhism, however, teaches that this existence is painful, false, and ultimately empty. Through contemplation of form, one might uproot these illusions and come to realize that form is empty of inherent self-existence, that it is dependently originated like everything else. In so doing, perhaps one goes to the other extreme, clinging to emptiness or effacement of form as ultimate reality. However, Mahāyāna Buddhism teaches that this is a biased and incomplete realization. It is then necessary to correct the attachment to emptiness, to refute emptiness and demonstrate that it itself is not other than form. Form participates fully, as it is, in emptiness. Thus, by stages one gradually and sequentially arrives at the perfect unalloyed Middle View that represents the dynamic vision of true bodhisattva and Buddha.

In the case of the sudden approach, the full and unalloyed vision of perfect enlightenment is presented all-at-once and is apprehended all-at-once, without resort to dialectical shift or temporal development. No conveyance from one mode to another takes place; no process of thematic manipulation or shift of conceptual perspectives is necessary—just an immediate expansion of horizons. Form is already emptiness, emptiness already form. Samsāra is already nirvāṇa, nirvāṇa already saṃsāra. All one need do is let go of such reified polarities and allow them to take their natural place in the totality of cause and condition. In fact, even these polarities are themselves inadequate to express this unalloyed totality of the Middle Way.

According to classical Indian and Chinese formulations of the Mahāyāna path, the bodhisattva's progress to the perfect enlightenment of Buddhahood requires some three incalculable aeons to complete. Over the course of this path, the bodhisattva first arouses the compassionate resolve to strive for perfect enlightenment (S. *bodhicitta*); sets out blindly to practice the six bodhisattva perfections and to realize the liberating insight (prajñā) of emptiness; strives to integrate the two perspectives of ultimate reality and conventional reality, or nirvāṇa and saṃsāra; eventually realizes the stage of non-relapsing and the perfect vision of the Middle Way; and finally arrives at Buddhahood itself. In its most fully developed form in China, this path requires that one pass through some fifty-two different stages of spiritual development, each one marked by the cultivation of particular insights and merits.

While this is the more standard view of the Mahāyāna path vouchsafed in the sūtras, there are also Mahāyāna scriptures which suggest that Buddhahood can be accessed either speedily or instantaneously, without reliance on expedients or a graduated sequence of stages. The *Nirvana Sūtra*, for example, preaches that the dynamic wisdom of Buddhahood is innate. All beings are intrinsically endowed with this Buddha-nature or predisposition to Buddhahood. This very mind is itself Buddha, but beings are not aware of this fact simply because its luminosity is concealed by the adventitious dust of illusion and defilement.[1] Should one hear the teaching of Buddha-nature and resolve to reclaim one's originally enlightened nature, one may, of course, take the approach of countering and unraveling delusion piece by piece until Buddha-nature is gradually revealed. But, since enlightenment is already replete, in theory one might just as well identify with the innate Buddha-nature and manifest the enlightened mind all at once.

In theory, whether the practice is construed as gradual or instantaneous, mediate or immediate, depends on how one construes the nature of the unenlightened condition and ultimate reality. But in practice, it depends more on the karmic roots or capacity of the individual practitioner. If one possesses keen karmic roots and one's mind is already quite pure due to extensive practice in past lives, then in one's present life one may be properly disposed to grasp and make effective use of the sudden teaching. But if one has a dull capacity and one is burdened by complex passions, then progress will be slow, even with a sudden method of practice. As a rule, the more dull the capacity and complex the person, the more complex and involved the practice will be; the more keen and simple the person, the more simple and direct the practice. Someone with exceedingly keen capacity, who is also spiritually ripe, may achieve deep enlightenment at the turn of a word. Such was the case for the sixth patriarch, Huineng, who, at a young age, experienced deep enlightenment upon overhearing a quotation from the *Diamond Sūtra*.

What is more, when it comes to path and practice, we must also ask ourselves what precisely we mean by the term "enlightenment." There are many possible ways to define enlightenment, and different schematizations of the Mahāyāna path may represent it or chart it differently. In some cases, substantial progress of any kind—even moral transformation—can be called enlightenment. Then again, enlightenment may be defined as nothing short of full Buddhahood or non-relapsing (S. *avaivartya*) bodhisattvahood. If one tastes a drop of water from a stream or ocean, one may thereby come to know the taste and feel of water; but it does not compare with diving in a river, drinking up the entire ocean, or becoming the ocean itself.

Even in the case of a sudden or immediate path to Buddhahood, there may be—in fact, there must be—distinctions in level of experience and progress. But how this relationship between gradualness and suddenness devolves depends on how one conceptualizes the path, the practitioner, and the goal to be achieved.

To illustrate this process, let us return to an analogy that was introduced earlier and explore it more fully. Suppose one is trapped in a deep well, with planks over the opening, and dirt piled deeply over the planks. Inside it is pitch dark. One day, the wind blows dirt away from one of the seams, and a beam of light comes into the well, only to be covered up again by the wind. For that moment, illumination has occurred: light has appeared in the darkness, and one now knows the difference between the dark and the light. Let us say that after a moment one manages to scrape away more dirt, so that more light comes in with ever-increasing steadiness, until one finally tears away the planks themselves, so that the whole well is flooded with the light of the sun. Then let us say that one leaps out of the well, to walk freely about the surroundings; or that one ultimately flies up into the sky and becomes one with the sun itself.

There is a vast difference in intensity and degree between the original flicker of light in the well and becoming the sun itself; but qualitatively speaking, the light itself has not changed—it is still one and the same entity. Looking at things from the point of view of the light, one could say that one has known the light the instant the first beam floods the well; but practice and progress are still necessary for the light to reach its fullest extent of power. The same may be said of Buddhahood or the wisdom of perfect enlightenment. The first glimmer of the dharma is, indeed, the stuff of Buddha Mind. But one is not a Buddha in full function. If one were, instead, to focus on the removal of the planks and dirt rather than the quality of illumination, one could even speak of progress being particulate and concrete.

Practically speaking, there is room for many different shades of emphasis and perspective within this rubric of sudden and gradual approaches to enlightenment. Huineng summarized matters this way:

> In Dharma itself there is no sudden or gradual, but among people, some are keen and others dull. The deluded recommend the gradual method, the enlightened practice the sudden teaching. To understand the original mind of yourself is to see into your own original nature. Once enlightened, there is from the outset no distinction between these two methods; those who are not enlightened will for long kalpas be caught in the cycle of transmigration.[2]

The basic concept of sudden and gradual approaches to enlightenment has existed in Buddhist tradition from its inception; however, it was not until Buddhism took root in China that more formal systemizations of this concept developed. In fact, efforts to draw up comprehensive classifications of the Buddhist teachings according to the sudden/gradual rubric is one of the great hallmarks of East Asian Buddhism, for we find it in virtually every major Buddhist school in East Asia, whether it be Huayan, Tiantai, Sanlun, or Chan. Nevertheless, of all these formulations, the tradition that has come to identify itself most avidly with the sudden approach to enlightenment is the Chan school.

"CHAN/ZEN" AS THE "MEDITATION SCHOOL"

As many people will already know, the Chinese word *chan* (*zen* in Japanese and *son* in Korean) is a transliteration of the Indian Sanskrit word *dhyāna*. *Dhyāna*, one will recall from earlier chapters, is traditionally associated with the deep meditative concentrations that are cultivated through the calming (*śamatha*) aspect of meditative practice. Most often, it refers to the states of ecstatic absorption that arise as a fruit of this practice (e.g., the four levels of dhyāna concentration); but its meaning can also extend to the techniques themselves. In either case, dhyāna is understood chiefly to be a mundane phenomenon, for as a state of one-pointed concentration, or unified mind, it still lacks the component of insight into no-self and no-mind that would mark it as supramundane. Thus, especially in the Hīnayāna systems, dhyāna is distinguished as qualitatively different from and inferior to enlightenment itself.

With the Mahāyāna sūtras, the meaning of dhyāna changes somewhat. Raised to the level of one of the six bodhisattva perfections, it comes to encompass both mundane and supramundane, unenlightened and enlightened meditative states or samādhis. The Chan/Zen school draws its meaning from this usage, but pushes its implications even further, with the term dhyāna, or *chan*, becoming synonymous with the enlightenment of Buddhahood itself. Thus the "Chan school" bills itself as the tradition of enlightenment par excellence—a meditative tradition whose very essence is rooted in the cultivation and experience of the living Buddha Mind.

Since at least the time of the Song Dynasty (960–1276) in China, Chan Buddhists have expressed their distinctive character as a "sudden and direct" path to enlightenment through the following set of four axioms: (1) Chan does not take stance in or depend on words and texts (*buli wenzi*); (2) Chan is a separate or special transmission outside the formalized scriptural teachings (*jiaowai biechuan*); (3) Chan emphasizes becoming a Buddha through seeing one's original nature (*jianxing chengfo*); and (4) Chan directly points to the nature of the person's mind (*zhizhi renxing*). As a kind of manifesto of the Chan school, these axioms provide an excellent point of departure for understanding the formalities of Chan as both an institutional tradition and individual practice.

The idea of "not depending on words and written texts" is a familiar one in the Buddhist tradition. From the outset, enlightenment was characterized by Buddha Śākyamuni as something that lay beyond the reach of conventional understanding. It was "inapprehensible" and "inexpressible" not only for its sublimeness, but more important because its very realization required nothing short of a total revolution in the cognitive structures through which we ordinarily process existence. Given this basic distinction, the Buddha was equally careful to differentiate between the Dharma, or "Buddhist Teaching/Law," as a received body of verbal instruction, and the Dharma as the living wisdom or enlightenment (born of religious practice) from which that lore arose and to which it ultimately points back. Likened to the "raft by which one reaches the other shore," the "finger that points to the moon," or the "medical prescription that heals disease," the Buddhist sūtras and their doctrinal formulations have always been characterized as a "means" to achieving the "end" of personal awakening and transformation, not to be confused with the end itself.

Perhaps more than any other Buddhist school, Chan pushes this distinction to the limit by raising contemplative practice and personal experience of enlightenment to a level of authority that is supreme over all else, even the received word of the Buddha himself. When Chan Buddhists forswear "dependence on words and written texts," these words and written texts mean verbal formulations of the Dharma based on and disseminated through the Buddhist scriptures. "Not depending on or taking one's stance" in them carries two senses. On the one hand, it demands that the Chan aspirant should not let the pedantic doctrinal study complicate or distract her or him from putting word into practice. He or she should settle for nothing short of the full transformation of enlightenment itself. On the other hand, it also mandates that teachers of Chan should not be bound by the received word, but should go beyond the traditional conventions of written scripture to use whatever means are appropriate for helping to enlighten their disciples. In the end, the ultimate proof of both practice and teaching lies in directly living the wisdom of enlightenment. Anything short of that is unacceptable compromise.

The second of the four axioms, that "Chan is a special or separate transmission outside of the formalized scriptural teachings," extends this same attitude of independence from verbiage and written text into the area of historical tradition. The term *jiao*, which we render here as "scriptural teaching," became closely linked in China to schools such as Huayan and Tiantai, both of which boasted elaborate systems of doctrine and practice rooted in the Buddhist sūtras. By claiming to stand "outside" this sort of scripturally based representation of the dharma, the Chan school professes to constitute itself differently from those traditions that define religious authority on the basis of the Buddha's spoken word and teaching. Where the doctrinal schools (*jiao*) locate authoritative tradition in the transmission of the Buddhist scriptures, the Chan school looks to a "mind-to-mind" transmission of the living vision of enlightenment itself. Known variously as the "transmission of the lamp or flame" or the "transmission of the treasury of the true eye of the Dharma," Chan claims to be heir to a generation-to-generation transmission of the Buddha's enlightened mind that runs parallel to his spoken word-Dharma. But by the same token stands a priori to and "apart from" it.

Construed in historical terms, this tradition takes the form of a continuous lineage of enlightened Indian and Chinese "patriarchs" that extends directly back to the Buddha himself. To wit, just as Buddha Śākyamuni sanctioned the enlightenment of the first patriarch, Mahākāśyapa, Mahākāśyapa and each subsequent patriarch trained and sanctioned his immediate successor. With the twenty-eighth Indian patriarch, Bodhidharma, the Dharma was introduced to China, after which it gradually reticulated, into multiple lines of transmission. The lineage continues today in the form of the "Chan master" *(chanshi)* and the "master-disciple" relationship—the core organizing structure around which Chan devolves as a tradition.

Institutionally speaking, a Chan master is someone who has awakened to the Buddha Mind through Chan training and whose enlightenment has been tested and sanctioned (C. *yinke;* J. *inka*) by an existing Chan master. Using the flame and lamp analogy, one could say that transmission of Chan Dharma requires that three things be simultaneously present: the enlightened insight of a previously sanctioned Chan master, the enlightened insight of the disciple, and the living reality of the Buddhadharma or Buddha Mind in which both are grounded. If any one of these is missing, enlightenment and transmission cannot be considered genuine, at least by Chan standards. By the same token, the formal granting of sanction is especially key to this, since the very basis of Chan practice and the integrity of Chan as an institution hinges on the idea that the historical transmission preserves intact the "Mind Dharma" of Buddha Śākyamuni. It is this certified wisdom that Chan practitioners seek to "ignite" and verify in their own minds; and, as the embodiment of that light, it is to the Chan master that he or she looks for guidance.

The third and fourth axioms concern the character of Chan practice itself. The Chan school holds that all beings are endowed with the Buddha Mind, that the mind of every being is intrinsically enlightened and pure. Better yet, one could say that all beings do not just possess Buddha-nature; they participate in Buddhahood directly. The delusions and sufferings of saṃsāra are not something that are in and of themselves separate from enlightenment, they participate in it as immediately and as fully as ice or wave does water. When we say that one "becomes a Buddha by seeing into one's original nature," we mean that all of the perfections of a Buddha's enlightenment are manifest the instant that one perceives these afflictions as intrinsically one with the Buddha Mind. Thus the entire project of Chan enlightenment is often summed up in the expression *jianxing* (J. *kenshō*), "seeing into the [original] nature." "Direct pointing at the [nature of] the individual's mind" describes the unique way in which the Chan master—as the living embodiment of the Buddha's wisdom—strives to bring the student face to face with the immediacy of Buddha Mind.

Chan History Revisited: Development of Characteristic Chan Institutions, Lore, and Styles of Teaching

Naturally, there are discrepancies between the way the Chan school represents its own history and what the historical record shows, especially as reworked by modern historians. Chan traditionally traces its origins in China to the Indian patriarch Bodhidharma, who is said to have come to the East around the turn of the sixth century. Following the Indian patriarchal succession, Bodhidharma's "Mind Dharma" is held to have been transmitted through a single line of Chinese patriarchs from Huike (487–593) to Sengcan (d. 606?), Sengcan to Daoxin (580–651), and Daoxin to Hongren (601–674). These four figures, together with Bodhidharma, are commonly referred to as the five early patriarchs of China.

The existence of Bodhidharma and Huike is verified in sources external to the Chan school; but scholars have questioned whether their presence had any direct bearing on the distinctive tradition that a century or two later came to refer to itself as the Chan transmission. With the fourth patriarch, Daoxin, we are on more solid historical ground, for he was the first to settle in a single monastery and gather a large community of followers around him. Daoxin's legacy, referred to as the East Mountain School, was extended even more widely by his successor, the fifth patriarch, Hongren.

After Hongren, the picture becomes quite complex, with multiple lines of descent and claims to the Chan patriarchy arising from among his disciples. According to later Chan tradition, the most elemental split devolves around the two figures of Huineng (638–713) and Shenxiu (605–706). During the eighth century, a controversy arose between the followers of Huineng—that is, Heze Shenhui (670–762)—and various followers of Shenxiu as to which of the two figures was the legitimate successor to the fifth patriarch Hongren. Actually, very little is known about the figure of Huineng himself, to the point where some scholars have suggested that his story and teaching (as recorded, for example, in *The Platform Sutra of the Sixth Patriarch*) were fabricated by later Chan followers.[3]

Whatever the case may be, the Huineng faction—which identified itself as the Southern School of Chan—championed a more radical concept of sudden enlightenment and accused the Shenxiu line or so-called Northern School of lapsing into gradualism. For reasons wholly unrelated to this issue, the "northern" school of Chan died out not long thereafter, leaving the "southern" line of Huineng—or claimants thereof—as the dominant line. To make matters more complicated still, the southern line of Shenhui also did not endure past several generations. Instead, the center of growth in the Chan school soon shifted to several new lines in South China claiming descent from Huineng—one centered around Mazu Daoyi (709–788) in Jiangxi province and the other around Shitou Xiqian (700–790) in Hunan. Over the next two centuries, these movements flourished, producing a long list of outstanding masters who have subsequently been enshrined as the fathers of classical Chan culture. Because of their seminal place in Chan history, the period of the late Tang Dynasty when these individuals were active has long been regarded as the Golden Age of Chan.

Most of these great masters and their disciples are represented in Chan literature as having what we call keen karmic roots. That is to say, their spiritual capacity was very high, enabling them to develop quite rapidly and effortlessly without a lot of involved training. They were naturally endowed with deep wisdom. Sensing this, the masters who taught them did not belabor them with the traditional forms of gradual practice, but used simpler and more direct methods that were better suited to their natural genius. When these individuals in turn became masters, they used similar approaches with their disciples. Thus, acting directly from their store of living wisdom and the legacies of their own teachers, new precedents for Buddhist practice began to take shape.

These masters did not emphasize the slow or gradual methods of ascetic discipline and meditation as taught in the Buddhist scriptures or traditionally espoused in Indian Buddhism. Rather, emphasizing the approach of "pointing directly to the nature of the mind," they used incisive words and actions to compel their students to "let go" of deluded thinking and allow the fully functioning Buddha Mind to manifest. In Chan terminology, the expression is *fangxia*, meaning something like "drop it!" or "put it down!" For the right individual in the right circumstances, such instruction was often enough.

As this distinctive Chan approach caught on, the gradualistic practices appeared increasingly flawed. If a master were to have prescribed the sort of traditional methods of meditative calming, contemplation, and dhyāna that we outlined in earlier chapters, he would have been sharply criticized for burdening his disciples with frivolous tasks, if not downright misleading them. The more traditional gradualistic practice came to be perceived as a vehicle for perpetuating illusion and karma, which in turn just furthered saṃsāric bondage. By comparison, the direct method of just letting go was seen to cut right to the heart of the matter, leaving little room for pedantry and spiritual self-indulgence.

There is an interesting story of a disciple of the noted Caodong master, Dongshan Liangjie (807–869), named Yunju Daoying (d. 902). Yunju engaged in practices deliberately geared to producing samādhi. He would go regularly into the deep mountains and remain there practicing for a long time. When he finally returned and saw Dongshan, the latter asked him why he did not at least come back to get provisions. Yunju replied that he suffered no want for food because heavenly beings supplied him with offerings and protected him. Upon hearing this, Dongshan sighed with disappointment and said, "I thought you were a real human being, but it seems that you are not a man at all. If you lead people, where will you lead them to? If you deceive them, how far will you go in deceiving them?"

Yunju replied, "I see your point. What should I do?"

Dongshan answered, "Come back later tonight and I will tell you." So at night, after everyone had retired to bed he went to his master. Dongshan then told Yunju to try the method handed down by the sixth patriarch, Huineng: "Without thinking of what is good, without thinking of bad, right here and now, where are you?"

For three days Yunju simply sat. Thinking neither about virtue nor about evil, and holding on to no method whatsoever; he utterly emptied his mind until there was nothing left. Every day the heavenly beings that regularly brought him food came to look for him, but to no avail. Where had he gone? He was still there, but with all his charismatic religious powers and meritorious accomplishments forgotten, the heavenly beings were never able to detect his whereabouts.[4]

Most people do not possess the kind of keen karmic roots of someone like Yunju. Hence, things are not so simple for them. They must experience a great deal of complication and hardship in their practice before they can become this plain and tasteless. They practice relentlessly day and night, like someone starving who forever searches for the most meager morsel of food, or one who has just lost his or her parents. Generally, the more dull the capacity and more complex the person, the more involved and tangible the methods must be. Something must be grasped hold of in order to discipline and calm the mind. But these early Chan masters offered nothing much to hold on to at all. Many of them espoused no door or approach whatsoever; hence Chan also came to be known as the gateless, or approachless, practice.

The sixth patriarch is said to have told his followers to "be free of discriminating thoughts" (wunian), or, "without thinking of good, without thinking of evil, what is your original face before you were born?"[5] Mazu Daoyi insisted that "the everyday mind is the Dao," that "this very mind itself is Buddha," and "no-gate is the gate." "If you would seek Dharma," he instructed, "just be without seeking."[6] To reinforce his point to his students, Mazu used all sorts of "strange words and iconoclastic behavior," including shouting and beating. Many of his peers adopted similar methods.

None of these pedagogies, however, offered much in the way of explicit technique. In fact, the early masters seemed to do everything they could to subvert any such dependence on technique. One can imagine the difficulties that students must have faced in their practice. Mazu Daoyi is said to have had anywhere from three hundred to five hundred followers in his assembly, most of whom did not understand his teachings or have any inkling of what he was doing. Among them, only a few were competent to receive Dharma transmission. Danxia, the celebrated figure who chopped up a Buddha image in order to build a fire, had many people come to him to study, but he scolded them so severely that most eventually ran away. Chan master Shigong Huizang kept a bow and arrows by his side, and anyone who came into his room would find himself facing a drawn arrow aimed directly between his eyes. Even the mention of Shigong's name would instill fear in people.

Following the collapse of the Tang Dynasty (618–906) and the eventual reunification of China under the Song Dynasty (960–1279), these tales and aphorisms of the Chan masters achieved increasing circulation. Lots of people were attracted to Chan, and in such a flourishing and, even, competitive environment, different lines of Chan vied to establish their distinctiveness and historicity. Before long the features of an organized and identifiable Chan school began to take shape. Records of the sayings (yulu) of important early Chan masters were compiled and published; formal "lamp histories" (denglu) and patriar-

chal genealogies of different lines were composed; ritual forms and daily procedures designed specifically for Chan monasteries were promulgated in the form
of "pure rules" (*qinggui*), and pedagogical styles of different Chan lineages were
codified. Perhaps out of a genuine concern for the stasis and decay that may come
with institutional wealth, perhaps as an accepted rhetoric of internecine compe-
tition, it also became something of an expected convention to glorify the olden
days and belittle the masters and practitioners of the present day. Ultimately, it
is through such combination of factors that the distinctive teachings of the Five
Houses of Chan took shape—that is, the Guiyang, Yunmen, Fayan, Caodong,
and Linji lines of Chan. Each represented a particular lineage of Chan transmission that centered itself around one or two outstanding masters of the past and
sought thereby to champion its distinctiveness as a particular style of teaching.

Of these five houses that arose during the late Tang and early Song, all but
the Linji (J. Rinzai) and Caodong (J. Sōtō) eventually died out. The Chan that
we find in China and Japan from the thirteenth century down to today is essentially that of the Linji and Caodong schools, as systematized in Song Dynasty
China. The Linji line takes its ne from the ninth-century master, Linji Yixuan
(d. 866). Linji was a disciple of Huangbo Xiyun (d. 850), whose line, in turn,
extends back through the masters Baizhang Huaihai (720–814) and Mazu
Daoyi (709–788) to Nanyue Huairang (677–744), a successor to sixth patriarch Huineng. Apart from Linji himself, the Song Dynasty masters Fenyang
Shanzhao (947–1024) and Dahui Zonggao (1089–1163) are the figures considered most responsible for codifying the Linji style of Chan. The Caodong
school is traced to Dongshan Liangjie (807–869) and his disciple, Caoshan
Benji (840–901). Their line of descent extends back through Shitou Xiqian
(700–790) and the enigmatic Qingyuan Xingsi (660–740) to Huineng. Like
Dahui in the Linji line, the Caodong line found its greatest codifier in the Song
Dynasty master, Hongzhi Zhengjue (1091–1157).

The representation of the Chan historical lineage described here is itself an
historical narrative that is drawn from Chan sources and which is foundational
to Chan's view of itself as a tradition. Central to this tradition is the idea of a
direct and personal enlightenment to intrinsic Buddha-nature; but equally essential to the tradition is the restrictive sanctioning of that experience within the
structure of a formal master-disciple relationship. In effect, it is from this relationship that Chan, as both a practice and a religious tradition, devolved.

The Use of Gong'an and Huatou

In the *Recorded Sayings of Linji*—a text alleged to contain the teachings of Linji Yixuan (d. 866), the Chan master from whom the Linji (J. Rinzai) line takes its name—we find several basic stratagems used by Linji and descendants in his lineage for the training of disciples.[1] They include such things as the "four criteria for differentiating students," the "three essentials," the "four relations of guest and host," the "four classifications [of function]," the "four shouts" (C. *he*; J. *katsu*), and "the eight types of beating with the meditation staff or incense board (C. *xiangban*; J. *keisaku*). Since the text of the *Recorded Sayings of Linji* was probably not circulated as a completed work until the tenth century, there is the possibility that these represent glosses of Linji's teaching style developed by later teachers. Nevertheless, they are certainly rooted in his line and, thus, are illustrative of the distinctive style of training that became associated with the Linji school during the period when the five houses of Chan began to take on definitive shape.

Linji's Chan is described in Chan literature as a style that employed a good deal of "shouting and beating." As a whole, the school is renowned for employing a highly pressured approach to Chan practice centered on intense combative encounters between master and disciple. This fierce, almost martial, quality is readily discernible in the person of Linji himself, as commemorated in his *Recorded Sayings*, but similar behavior can be traced back through his immediate predecessors to the iconoclastic school of Mazu Daoyi. For instance, on the three occasions that Linji dared approach his own master, Huangbo, to ask about the Way, Huangbo simply beat him with the meditation stick. Chan lore presents Mazu as a volatile figure who twisted noses, beat, and kicked people regularly. Many people are intimidated and puzzled by this seemingly violent behavior, especially insofar as it claims to be connected with spirituality. But there is a design to it that is quite consistent with the aims of the "sudden path" of Chan. In his discourses, Linji often used aphorisms that echo the theme of non-striving, or "just letting go": "Just be an ordinary person with nothing to do," he tells us. "Be a person of no rank, no consequence." This teaching, in turn, is coupled with another idea—that of "slaying" or "killing" anything that might cause us to set up deluded expectations or become dependent on things outside ourselves. "Followers of the Way, if you want insight into the Dharma as it really is," Linji says, "do not be taken in by the deluded views of others. Whatever you encounter, whether within or without, slay it at once. If you meet the Buddha, slay the Buddha. If you meet a patriarch, slay the patriarch. If you meet an arhat, kill the arhat. If you meet your parents, slay your parents. If you meet your family, kill your family. You will then attain liberation."[2]

Obviously, Linji is not advocating that one should actually kill Buddhas, parents, and teachers; but what is the point of such a seemingly violent attitude? Can this really be considered a method of practice conducive to Buddhist enlightenment and compassion? Indeed it can. Linji's point is that we must "slay" these things as objects of attachment or self-expectation. We must be relentlessly self-reliant *(zixin)* and cut off all conditional thoughts in our minds until there is nothing further to cut off. When all such discriminations—all such naive views that shape the small self and its world—are exhausted, we will truly be "ordinary, with nothing to do." In one of his discourses Linji explains,

A man of old has said, "If you meet a person on the road who has penetrated the Way, above all do not try to seek the Way." Therefore it is said, "When someone tries to practice the Way, one will not succeed, and, furthermore, the ten-thousand evil states will vie in raising their heads. If one can use the sword of wisdom [to cut down all seeking], nothing will remain. Before brightness manifests, the darkness will already be bright. Hence, an ancient [probably Mazu] has said, "the ordinary mind is the Way."[3]

Thus, Linji's twofold approach of "being an ordinary person with nothing to do" and "slaying" all conditional dependence constitutes a single unified method. Even so, this method is not easy to put into practice. Because we as people are so complex, it is extremely difficult to slay our attachments and self-centered thoughts, much less *completely* let go. Most of us don't even have a clue what this means. What is more, when we attempt to translate it into action, our emotional imbalances may give rise to all sorts of misunderstandings and abuses. To forestall these problems, Linji also stressed the necessity of close interaction between master and disciple.

The intense and highly charged confrontations between master and student, and the shouting and beating that often typify these exchanges, are not used out of some perverse love for punishment or pain. The master does not administer them to torture, brainwash, or break the student; nor does the student use them to rebel or work out some hidden resentment against authority. They are simply intended to help those with incorrect focus or insufficient energy to find the proper integrity and determination necessary to practice effectively. The master helps the student tune the mind and spirit, but the student is the one who ultimately brings the training to its conclusion. In a sense, it is like a chick hatching from an egg. While the chick struggles and presses from the inside, the mother hen pecks on the shell from the outside. By doing so at the appropriate time and in the appropriate way, the hen helps the chick hatch that much easier.

In fact, it is this sort of stratagem on the part of the master that is the subject of the scheme of Linji's four classifications [of function]: depending on the condition of the student, the master will sometimes use words and actions that "snatch away the person"; sometimes he will "snatch away the object or environment"; sometimes he will snatch away both at once; and sometimes he will not snatch away either. Linji explains the function of this approach as follows:

> Among all the students from the four quarters who are followers of the Way, none have come before me without depending on something. Here I hit them right from the start. If they come forth using their hands, I hit them on the hands. If they come forth using their mouths, I hit them on the mouth. If they come forth using their eyes, I hit them on the eyes. Not one has yet come before me in solitary freedom. All are clambering after the worthless contrivances of the men of old. As for myself, I haven't a single Dharma to give people. All I can do is to cure illnesses and loosen bonds. You followers of the Way, try coming before me without being dependent on things. I would confer with you.[4]

To this end Linji made great use of intense, provocative methods such as shouting and beating. Often, these confrontations between master and disciple centered on questions or anecdotes drawn from past Chan masters. However, they could just as well be initiated by something a master would say or do on the spur of the moment. In either case, students were provoked into intense concentration and struggle with specific issues which either spontaneously arose in their minds, or which were given to them as questions by their masters.

Some masters used to refrain from answering any queries that the student had about these episodes. Instead, they might beat or verbally abuse the person without any explanation. Should the student then question the master about this violent response, he or she might be met with another blow. At times this kind of treatment could continue until the student ceased questioning and retreated from the "field of battle." Yet, even though one might withdraw from the master's presence, one would certainly remain unsettled. Should the student eventually return to question or, perhaps, respond to the master, he or she might once again be beaten, thereby leaving him or her even more deeply puzzled.

At this juncture one's whole being might be directed toward understanding the reason for this treatment, to the point where one's consternation about the master's actions even supersede the original question. This sort of thing could well go on for years, ultimately leaving the student in utter confusion, with absolutely nothing sure on which to hold. Should one then decide to leave the monastery and try another master, one may find oneself confronted with further beatings and no answers. However, after years of having the rug constantly yanked out from underneath you like this, in the end you may *truly* become an ordinary person with nothing to do. In fact, this was precisely Linji's own experience. After being beaten repeatedly by Huangbo, he left Huangbo's monastery in despair and went to the Chan master Dayu. After listening patiently to his lengthy story of trial and tribulation, Dayu scolded him saying, "Huangbo is such a kind old granny, utterly wearing himself out on your behalf. Now you come here and ask whether you have done something wrong or not!" With these words Linji realized great enlightenment, after which he was able to return to Huangbo and "pull the tiger's whiskers."

THE USE OF *GONG'AN*

Most people familiar with Japanese Zen—especially the Japanese Rinzai school formalized in the eighteenth century by Zen master Hakuin—will have heard of the use of enigmatic Chan anecdotes and sayings, known as *kōan*, as a method of Zen meditation. *Kōan* is the Japanese pronunciation of the Chinese word *gong'an.* The use of *gong'an* and its corollary technique of *huatou* (meaning "the crux of a saying") was initially developed by Chinese Chan masters. Although masters of all Chan persuasions collected and discoursed on *gong'an*, it was those of the Linji line, such as Dahui Zonggao (1089–1163), who gave it its special place, making it the basis of a distinctive style of meditation known as *kanhua* Chan (J. *kanna zen*) or "Chan involving the investigation of a saying." When the Caodong and Linji schools of Chan were introduced to Japan in the thirteenth century, the use of *gong'an* came with them. Over the centuries that followed, Japanese Zen masters developed their own unique methods for applying *gong'an* to Zen training, culminating in the system of Hakuin prevalent in Japanese Rinzai monasteries today.

The term *gong'an* (or *kōan*), which we often render as "public case," is basically the same term used in ancient times for a legal case or precedent. In the judicial sphere, *gong'an* were records of significant legal events, which detailed both the circumstances of the offense or suit and the deliberations of the magistrate who adjudicated it. In Chan, a *gong'an* is a record of a significant episode in the life of a former Chan master or patriarch, an episode that often bears directly upon the training or enlightenment of that master or his disciples. Much as a current magistrate may review famous *gong'an* of the past in order to hone his or her knowledge for guiding precedents, Chan practitioners will use *gong'an* of past masters to test and further their understanding. For most of the Chan patriarchs, at least one *gong'an* has been recorded. Sometimes there are three, four, or even more. Generally these cases involve key moments of interaction between master and disciple or two eminent Chan figures. They may be moments when, upon receiving a particularly powerful stimulus from his teacher, the disciple becomes enlightened. Or they may describe encounters in which Chan brethren test and reveal one another's relative depth of understanding. Then again, they may record instances when such an opportunity for enlightenment and the meeting of minds arise, but it passes without the student being able to make use of it.

In Chan literature there is a famous story relating Bodhidharma's audience with Liang Wu Di, the devout Buddhist emperor of the Liang Dynasty (502–557). Emperor Wu described to Bodhidharma his many projects of charity and support for Buddhism and asked, "What kind of merit have I received from this?"

Bodhidharma replied, "No merit whatsoever."

A little later Emperor Wu asked Bodhidharma, "How would you characterize true merit?"

Bodhidharma said, "Pure wisdom is marvelous and perfect; its essence is intrinsically empty and quiescent. Such merit is not sought by worldly means."

To which Emperor Wu queried, "What is the ultimate meaning of the holy truth [of absolute reality]?"

Bodhidharma replied, "Empty and vast—there is no holiness."

Emperor Wu then said, "Who is this person standing before me?"

Bodhidharma replied, "I do not know."

Emperor Wu did not grasp Bodhidharma's meaning. Knowing that the emperor did not have the capacity to receive the Chan teaching, Bodhidharma departed.[5]

Once a certain senior monk named Ding asked Linji, "What is the cardinal meaning of the Buddhist teaching?" Linji came down from his seat, grabbed hold of Ding, slapped him, and pushed him away roughly. Ding stood there motionless. Another monk standing nearby said, "Elder Ding, why don't you bow to show your respect?" Just as Ding bowed, he suddenly experienced great awakening.[6]

A monk asked Dongshan, "How does one escape hot and cold?"

"Why not go where it is neither hot nor cold?" said the master.

"What sort of place is neither hot nor cold?" asked the monk.

"When it is cold, you freeze to death; when it's hot, you swelter to death."[7]

A student once asked Caoshan, Dongshan's successor, "What does it mean to say that there is ultimate truth in phenomenal things?"

Master Caoshan replied, "The very phenomena are themselves ultimate truth."

"Then how should it be revealed?" the student asked. The master just lifted his tea tray.

These are just several examples of *gong'an* associated with great Chan masters. From the latter half of the Tang Dynasty (618–907), the period that is often looked upon as the Golden Age of Chan, disciples began to compile lineage histories *(denglu)* and records of sayings and actions *(yulu)* of famous Chan masters in their respective lines. Thus, numerous *gong'an* of this sort began to be pulled together and organized around the different houses or lines of Chan. Today, Chan lineage histories like Daoyuan's monumental *Jingde chuandeng lu* ("Record of the Transmission of the Lamp Compiled During the Jingde Era," completed in 1004) and "Recorded Sayings" collections for such influential masters as Linji, Dahui, Yunmen, Dongshan, Caoshan, and others preserve a rich array of *gong'an* from the formative period of Chan.

As time passed, some of these stories became quite well known among Chan practitioners. They were referred to and discussed on a wide scale, and increasingly came to define a common idiom of Chan culture. In the discourses and writings of Song Dynasty masters (such as Dahui Zonggao of the Linji school or Hongzhi Zhengjue of the Caodong line), we find many examples of masters raising *gong'an* and asking their students to respond to them. Indeed, by the time of the Song Dynasty (960–1279), it became quite common for Chan masters to select from Chan records those *gong'an* that they considered most effective or poignant, organizing them into sets of one hundred or more. Often they would go on to add their own verses or prose commentary to the individual cases and circulate them to Chan students, so that their successors or Chan masters of other schools came to use them, at times adding their own comments to the text. In fact, the *Blue Cliff Record* (C. *Biyan lu*; J. *Hekiganroku*), completed by Yuanwu Keqin (1063–1135) and the *Gateless Pass* (C. *Wumen guan*; J. *Mumonkan*) compiled by Wumen Huikai (1183–1260)—the two most popular *gong'an* compendia in China and Japan—took shape and gained their notoriety precisely by this process.

In the past, as today, *gong'an* have proven an effective approach to Chan training. Originally, they were used throughout all branches of Chan, including the Caodong school, which is often mistakenly thought to give its attention solely to the practice of "silent illumination" *(mozhao)* or Dōgen's teaching of "just sitting, nothing more" *(shikantaza)*. In time, however, their use became increasingly identified with the Linji (Rinzai) line.

Using collections of *gong'an* like those described above, a master might bring up a particular case and ask a disciple to respond to it. Perhaps the teacher will reject the student's answer, even throw him out and compel him to consider it further. Then again, the teacher may confront the student with secondary responses to the *gong'an* offered by former masters, or give him another related *gong'an*. When we examine the sayings and discourses of Chinese Chan masters, this use of *gong'an* seems to have been quite fluid, used by masters as they saw fit at given moments. However, it was also not unusual for Chan masters to discourse or have their disciples work sequentially through *gong'an* contained in such collections as the *Blue Cliff Record* and *Gateless Pass*. This especially became the rule in Japanese Rinzai Zen.

This approach to Chan has occasionally been criticized for leading to a sort of empty formalism or spiritual materialism. It may create the misconception that Chan practice is merely a matter of "passing" a pre-set body of *gong'an*, much as one might plod from grade to grade and finally graduate from college. Or else, in studying the example of the patriarchs, one may mistakenly come to think that Chan practice involves nothing more than dramatizing or imitating their speech and behavior: act like a master and you become a master. These are indeed grave problems. In fact, it is said that the Linji master Dahui Zonggao became so incensed at students' misuse of his teacher's text of the *Blue Cliff Record* that he had the text and its printing blocks burned.

Nonetheless, using *gong'an* is by no means inherently bad. *Gong'an* collections were compiled for two reasons: as historical and literary records of the tradition and as a means (or measure) to help people practice. Of the two, the latter was most essential. Masters such as Yuanwu and Wumen produced texts like the *Blue Cliff Record* and *Gateless Pass* because they found them particularly helpful to their students. What we must understand in order to appreciate *gong'an* properly is the true function they are meant to play in Chan training.

Gong'an, as we noted previously, are records of living encounters between masters and disciples, encounters that often mark a crucial turning point in a disciple's practice. Such incidents had immediacy and living significance for the original participants. As a record or tale, however, it is dead words. When a later practitioner takes up the story, the original incident is dead and gone. There is no way one can go back and reclaim or re-experience the original encounter. One does not approach a *gong'an* with the idea of trying to imitate and become the master and disciple in the story. The tale, however, may be used as a tool, an impetus to create a new situation or living "public case" of one's own. In short, one uses past *gong'an* to generate one's own moment. When this happens, it is a living *gong'an*.

In the recorded sayings and biographical records of the Chan school, we find practitioners of many different generations who grappled with Zhaozhou's *gong'an* about dogs having Buddha-nature. They did not go back and try to relive or reclaim the monk's experience in the Zhaozhou *gong'an*. What Zhaozhou and the monk said and did in the past has nothing to do with them now. Upon reading the Zhaozhou *gong'an*, they may feel a kinship with the monk who posed the question, or even with Zhaozhou himself, but their understanding is their own. Their struggle and their enlightenment grew out of their own particular circumstances—fresh and immediate. Thus, although *gong'an* center around episodes of past Chan "tradition," as tools for practice their thrust is the here and now. It is a mistake to think so much about Chan tradition—what Linji calls "the useless contrivances of former masters"—that you forget to "hoe your own garden."

Enlightenment experienced in the course of Chan practice can be deep or shallow. Regardless of the technique used in practice, it will vary according to the individual. This diversity is not only reflected in *gong'an* themselves, but insights generated from *gong'an* practice will vary according to the individual. For the most part, this is a matter of circumstances and spiritual capacity.

As far as *gong'an* themselves are concerned, some are shallow, some are obviously abstruse. Then there are *gong'an* which are quite elusive, where the meaning progressively changes or unfolds in response to the level of experience of the practitioner. In such instances, several different levels of response are possible, such that the *gong'an* is never simply finished or "passed." Sometimes, different sentences in one and the same *gong'an* will involve completely different levels of discourse.

Persons with shallow insight may not be able to fathom what deeper experiences are like, or they may have an inkling but no clear grasp. Fairly straightforward *gong'an* may present no problem for them, but when confronted with really abstruse *gong'an*, they may feel completely baffled. Or, they may think the meaning is obvious when, in fact, they are completely incapable of appreciating its true subtlety.

On the other hand, persons with deep experience will know what has transpired the instant they encounter a *gong'an*. They will discern automatically the different levels of experience and insight reflected in different *gong'an*. Even though these incidents are themselves dead and gone, for these individuals it is as though they are alive. Their own experience brings life to them, and because of this living insight they know what the *gong'an* is all about. It is analogous to the practice of samādhi in traditional Buddhism. If one realizes the deepest levels of samādhi, all lesser states of samādhi and their characteristics will automatically be known, without their actually being cultivated.

Thus, for persons who are deeply experienced, *gong'an* are no longer relevant. For persons with no experience or shallow experience, they can be quite helpful. If they are not already working in a formal system of *gong'an* practice, such persons may read through the *gong'an* records. When they get to a *gong'an* that they become stuck on, the doubt that is generated can provide a powerful catalyst to their practice. Doubt is what *gong'an* practice is all about, in both its systematic and unsystematic forms. It is the doubt that makes the *gong'an* a living and vital issue, and any "answer" to the gong'an that the student might offer must grow directly out of his or her own struggle with Chan practice and this great doubt.

To this end, working with an experienced master is indispensable, for the master can help the student bring the *gong'an* to life and prevent him or her from going astray. When assigning *gong'an* to students, the master may take a variety of approaches. He or she may begin with shallower *gong'an* and move to progressively deeper ones. Or, he or she may first test the student with deeper ones and move to shallower *gong'an* if the student cannot respond. There need not be a fixed approach—at least in Chinese Chan tradition. In some instances, the disciple may get lucky and give what seems to be a correct response. To test it, the master may bring out other *gong'an* of a similar level. Sometimes, he or she will find the student's experience is false. This sort of incident is more likely to occur if a student reads or hears a lot of *gong'an* anecdotes and is a good actor. There are patterns in *gong'an*, as well as certain characteristic types of behavior. By studying and emulating them, one can come up with some fairly reasonable responses. However, while this may fool some people, especially beginners, those who are truly experienced in practice will soon see through the subterfuge.

Of course, this kind of empty show is useless for one's own practice. The facts of one's condition cannot be changed just by changing the appearance or the words. Actually, a student who has made progress with a *gong'an* should feel it, and both student and master will definitely know whether he or she has made a genuine step or not. Thus, it is a waste of time to put on empty shows. For *gong'an* to be helpful, one needs great integrity: any effort to answer it must come directly out of one's practice and heart. Because we are so emotionally complicated and self-deceptive, this can be a very difficult thing to do on one's own. Since experienced teachers can expose fraudulence and abuse of *gong'an* instantly, they are an indispensable boon to *gong'an* practice.

As a technique of practice, concentration on a *gong'an* accompanied by intense confrontations with a master are intended to generate extreme pressures in order to uncover and completely utilize a person's hidden mental power. It is much the same as physical power. Most people know that they have hidden physical power that is available to them, of which they normally use but a fraction. Under pressure, the situation can change. For example, under ordinary circumstances a person cannot jump far or move very fast. But with a tiger in pursuit or a child in danger, the same person may move a lot farther and faster than he or she ever thought possible. Things like this have happened to almost all of us. You may not know where the strength comes from, but in a life-or-death situation you find the strength to do what must be done. In many respects, the use of *gong'an* or *huatou* and regular interviews with a master is a method designed to put a student in a desperate mental situation—a life-or-death situation—thereby forcing the student to utilize hidden resources in order to save himself or herself. Of course, the issue here is not simply a matter of jumping far and running fast. It is finding a solution to the problem of birth and death.

Chan masters of the past have charted stages of spiritual progress in a variety of ways. Some speak of passing three main barriers, others four. *Gong'an* have been classified accordingly. But these are actually crude, even tentative, classifications. Generally, practitioners over the course of their lives will go through tens, even hundreds, of instances in which doubt and crisis generate pressure and, finally, spiritual breakthrough. Some may come through formal contemplation of *gong'an*, others from issues arising spontaneously in everyday practice. In the final analysis, it is the reality of progress that is most important, not the form and literature of the *gong'an*. *Gong'an* practice should express a spirit of fundamental unity between the individual and Dharma.

What is meant by Dharma? Dharma is the enlightenment experienced by Śākyamuni Buddha under the bodhi tree, and the enlightenment that has subsequently been experienced by generations of Chan patriarchs down to today. On the surface, the content of gong'an may seem absurd, irrational. Yet, it truly corresponds to Dharma and issues forth from Dharma, for the patriarch's mind was one with Dharma. In the practice of Chan, one's own mind must be in harmony with Dharma in order for one to generate its power or energy. This is why it is so essential to work with a living master. The master can correct one's mistaken attitudes and help bring one's mind quickly into harmony with Dharma, so that one can generate its power. When Dharma, master, and student are in harmony—when they are a single unity—enlightenment and transmission of dharma take place.

THE USE OF HUATOU

Huatou is in many respects closely related to *gong'an*. The term *huatou* itself literally means "head, or crux, of the saying." Generally, this has been interpreted as pointing to the most crucial phrase or question in a *gong'an*. Thus, working on a *huatou* entails singling out the most essential element or issue in a given *gong'an* and concentrating on this point, repeating it over and over, while disregarding the rest of the narrative. For example, one of the most famous *huatou* comes from the *gong'an* in which Zhaozhou is asked whether dogs have Buddha-nature. In response to this question, Zhaozhou replies, *"Wu!"* which means, "No!" The *huatou* simply consists of asking, "What is *wu?*"

Huatou invariably are concise questions like this. Although they are frequently taken from *gong'an*, sometimes they are not. Questions such as "Who am I?"; "What was I like before I was born?"; "Who is it that is practicing?"; "All things are reducible to the one, but what is the one reducible to?"; or even, "Which came first, the chicken or the egg?" are all *huatou*. If one is a Pure Land practitioner and has been intoning the Buddha Amitābha's name *(namo Amituo fo)* in the hopes of being reborn in the Western Land of Highest Bliss, one might ask, "Who is it that is reciting the Buddha's name?" In that circumstance it becomes a Chan *huatou*.

Compared to the rather lengthy and diffuse *gong'an* stories, *huatou* are poignantly concise. Thus they are powerful tools for summoning up great energy and quickly bringing one's focus to bear on the key issues of practice. As techniques of Chan practice, the function of both *gong'an* and *huatou* is to generate what we call "great doubt" *(da yiqing)*. This doubt represents an inner uneasiness or anxiety—a feeling that there is something missing or unclear in our lives that we must discover. It is a deep tension caused by the feeling that there is something essential that we need to know—that we *must* know—but that we don't know. This doubt should not be confused with the sort of non-committal waffling that we commonly encounter in our lives. The doubt generated by investigating a *huatou* is not simple agnosticism or skepticism. Nor is it the sort of temporary confusion over moral position or personal identity that we often encounter in everyday life. No simple distraction, explanation, or shift in reasoning can appease it. "Great doubt" is a state of all-consuming questioning that, at its deepest, is irresistible and relentless, admitting no solution other than one that totally gets to the bottom of the matter. Ultimately, the issue to be solved is the "great matter of birth and death."

Of course, there are different degrees of doubt. In a small doubt you may get a glimmer or taste of the immense issues at stake in great doubt, but this condition will quickly pass. Intermediate degrees of doubt will last longer, but the energy and depth necessary for it to grow will not be present. In time, it too will dissipate. In the case of major doubt, however, the doubt mass will continue to expand, consuming everything until there is nothing left but total doubt. At this point it is impossible to stop the doubt. When this occurs, a great explosion will follow. This explosion is enlightenment. Thus, in *gong'an* and *huatou* practice, doubt and enlightenment are intimately related, so that we often say, "Small doubt, shallow enlightenment; great doubt, deep enlightenment; no doubt, no enlightenment."

Because they provide such a specific and intense point of focus, *huatou* can be effective even for one who has never practiced before. *Gong'an* are generally quite diffuse. Often, they involve a complex series of events, making it is easy for the mind to become distracted or caught up in peripheral features. If it is lengthy, reviewing the *gong'an* itself can be a burdensome task. To speculate rationally on its features or meaning will be missing the main issue entirely. For these reasons, it is exceedingly difficult to derive any real benefit from *gong'an* without a significant foundation in Chan practice. Should one try to penetrate a *gong'an* without such a foundation, one really won't know where to begin. In Japan, *gong'an* are often not used until one has experienced an initial breakthrough or a "glimpse into one's true nature" (C. *jianxing,* J. kenshō). That breakthrough is first achieved through a sharply focused *huatou.* After the initial breakthrough, *gong'an* are used to further deepen and illumine the practitioner's mind. This is what we mean by a significant foundation in practice.

Furthermore, the historical context and imagery found in *gong'an* are from the Tang or Song Periods of China. Hence, they appear quite alien to us today. For Chinese or Japanese, or for Chan practitioners who have heard many of these *gong'an* or who are conversant in this culture, the language of the *gong'an* may be meaningful. But for people who do not share this background, using *gong'an* may give rise to all sorts of spurious activities. In such cases, investigating *gong'an* becomes more a study in ancient culture than a grappling with the issue of birth and death. For example, some *gong'an* contain very bizarre and erratic behavior, and students may think that imitating and indulging in this kind of activity is Chan. For this reason I do not normally use *gong'an* with my American students. Or if I do, I will often just use the situation at hand to create a stimulating opportunity—a living *gong'an*—with which to spur the student on.

The Practice of Huatou

In the old days, no conscious preparation was ever given for the practice of *huatou*. Great doubt and its workings were not openly discussed, nor was any definite procedure for using *huatou* taught. The master would just give the student a *huatou* or spark a question in the practitioner's mind and strive to keep him or her working on it. Concentration on one question or *huatou* might last for ten, twenty, even thirty years. Chan master Chushan Shaoqi once said, "Pay no heed to whether it is for a long period of time or a short period of time, a hundred days or a thousand days, under formal monastic restraints or not under formal monastic restraints. From the time you first take up the *huatou*, be utterly decisive and do not let your determination falter, even if after a lifetime of practice you still should fail to get enlightened."[9] Chan master Taixu instructed, "If you have never experienced enlightenment, sit in cold stillness and investigate [the saying], 'What was my original face before I was born?' for ten, twenty, or thirty years!"[10]

This kind of patience and long-term commitment to Chan practice was very much the norm in pre-modern China. Once there was a Chan monk who, upon leaving home, took up residence with a certain Chan master hoping to learn about Chan, but the master just put him to work at menial tasks without giving him any method of practice at all. For a long, long time this monk waited for some instruction, until finally he could restrain himself no longer. He summoned up his nerve, approached the master, and asked for instruction in practice, claiming that he would have to go elsewhere unless he got what he wanted. The master responded, "Who is the person who needs instruction? Find me this person and I will give him instruction!" This question itself was a *huatou*, and the monk—prompted by his years of growing doubt and anxiety—became utterly absorbed in this *huatou*, until he "found the person," so to speak.

In a situation such as this, doubt might be a long time coming, if it comes at all; but when it does appear, it will likely be very visceral and very deep. Under such circumstances, the experience of great doubt and the explosion of awakening need happen only once. If the person's practice is thorough and "well cooked," no further awakening is needed.

Times are different today, however. In this modern world, life is not so simple and routine. People are more preoccupied, stressed, and hurried. Few are willing and able to devote the time and patience necessary to simmer themselves thoroughly on such a low heat. It is the age of the microwave. Thus, despite the old Chan spirit of reticence and innocence, the technique of *huatou* practice has been increasingly spelled out. The purpose in doing this is to make the benefits of Chan practice more accessible to people—to give them a taste of Chan more quickly, so that they may develop the aspiration and commitment necessary for extended practice.

As I indicated previously, the aim of *huatou* practice is to generate a profound and intensely concentrated sense of doubt. When there is great and all-consuming doubt, there is great awakening; small doubt, small awakening; no doubt, no awakening. In rare instances, there are persons who seem to be born with this doubt. The Ming Period Buddhist master, Hanshan Deqing (1546–1623), for example, writes in his autobiography that when he was 3 years old he witnessed the death of his uncle. Seeing his uncle's corpse with no sign of life puzzled him quite deeply. Some time later an aunt gave birth to a child. When he asked his mother where the baby came from, she retorted, "Where do you think you came from?" Hanshan insists that this question remained with him until the age of 27, when he finally resolved it.[11]

Most people, however, do not feel this sort of doubt to any notable degree. Or, if they do, most will take great effort to insulate themselves from it and make it quickly disappear. The purpose of the *huatou* is to actually generate or aggravate doubt of this sort, causing one to concentrate on it and nourish it until it becomes great doubt. Some people think that the wording of the *huatou* itself is the key factor—that effective progress depends on finding the right formula. They may want to change *huatou* time and time again, looking for just the right magical combination of words. To be sure, a master will want to give a student a *huatou* that he or she can relate to, a *huatou* with which the student can identify his or her deeper spiritual yearnings; but ultimately the power of the *huatou* comes from the person, not the *huatou* itself.

No *huatou*, regardless of how lofty or religiously poignant it is, will move people who find things to be satisfactory and who have only a lukewarm interest in the deeper questions of life. These people simply do not care what they were before they were born and what they will be after death. They will likely get nothing from *huatou* practice, no matter how hard they might appear to labor over it. On the other hand, those with keen karmic roots, like Hanshan Deqing, could turn almost anything into an effective *huatou*. Even the most innocuous events in everyday life can provoke profound spiritual doubt and the need to know.

For the majority of people using *huatou*, the essential issue is how to use it to generate and maintain doubt when one feels no real doubt to begin with—how to make the *huatou* a "living" issue. If one is investigating the *huatou*, "What was my nature before I was born?", one should be obsessed with the need to find one's true nature prior to all the conditioned and learned traits that one has acquired since birth. But when such serious and decisive doubt is lacking, even the most intense questioning will likely be concerned more with *how* to experience great doubt than the actual *experience* of great doubt per se. One will then be a step removed from real doubt, and concentration on the *huatou* will become artificial and sporadic. Left to flounder like this, years can go by without any real progress. How, then, does one develop genuine doubt by using a *huatou?*

The dynamics of *huatou* practice are in many ways closely tied to the principles of meditative development that we outlined in Chapter Two ("Meditation and the Principles for Training Body and Mind"). First, one moves from scattered mind and an artificial type of questioning to a simple and unified mind, where concentration and questioning become intensely real and one-pointed. With intense and one-pointed questioning, all doubts and questions are subsumed into a single profound and all-consuming doubt. When this doubt reaches a crescendo, becoming vast and self-sustaining, the explosion of enlightenment finally occurs. Simply put, Buddhist meditation aspires to take the practitioner from the condition of scattered mind to simplified mind; simplified mind to unified, or one-pointed, mind and thought; unified mind to no-mind, or no-thought. *Huatou* practice develops in a similar fashion. But the object of concentration is the questioning and doubt itself rather than the usual objects used for meditative calming and contemplation.

It is extremely difficult and rare to experience great doubt in the beginning of one's practice. Even small doubt is hard to generate. Although we hear of Chan practitioners in whom great doubt arose right at the start of their practice, as a rule most people will begin with no doubt. It may take considerable practice before genuine spiritual yearning appears and the question posed in the *huatou* comes to life.

Concentration on a *huatou* before the experience of doubt is similar in procedure and function to the use of classical Buddhist methods for calming and taming the mind (i.e., the Five Methods for Stilling the Mind). Practitioners strive to ward off wandering thoughts and drowsiness, and keep their attention fixed single-mindedly on the object of concentration—the *huatou*. By repeating the *huatou* over and over, the mind is kept alert and clear. If concentration becomes weak or the mind feels dull and drowsy, one should ask the *huatou* vigorously, summoning power from the anger and frustration sparked by these obstacles. At the same time, it is important not to allow oneself to become overly excited or impassioned, as these feelings may also become an impediment.

Most of all, one must not anticipate great doubt or enlightenment, nor preoccupy oneself with artificial efforts to evoke them. Although anger and fierceness are better than laziness, the key thing is to keep one's mind wholly focused on the *huatou*, not to fight impassioned battles with wandering thoughts. When wandering thoughts are discovered, they should be promptly dismissed; attention should be returned immediately to the *huatou*. In time, such diversions will become fewer and fewer, and concentration on the *huatou* will become like a steady stream, infusing and uniting one's whole being. This is the proper condition for generating great doubt.

Often, people ask whether it necessary to use words to ask the *huatou*. Words seem to lend themselves to speculation or mechanical repetition, both of which would seem to hinder the sort of concentrated doubt that *huatou* aspire to evoke. Actually, the use of language is absolutely necessary. Without words to formulate the question, one will just sit wide-eyed, staring into muddled blankness, without the slightest chance of producing doubt.

Chan master Xuyun interprets the expression *huatou* to mean the "source of all words." *Hua* means "words or speech." *Tou* means "head or source." Thus, *huatou* practice actually entails a search for the source of all words and meaning—the original reality or true nature of mind that is there before all words and discriminations arise.[12]

One might argue that, since the essence of *huatou* practice is to get beyond words, one should dispense with active questioning or forget all linguistic discriminations. But in this search for the "source of words," one must begin with the specific *huatou* question and follow it to its end. One must begin with the concrete. Without something concrete to grasp, without anything to hold on to, the mind has nothing around which to collect itself, and there will be no basis for real doubt to take shape. So that we may securely take hold of the *huatou* and, from it, generate great doubt, it is most necessary that the *huatou* be composed of words.

One must always remember that *huatou* is a method of practice, not an end in itself. Using *huatou* may be likened to unraveling a long, tangled ball of yarn, which is concealed in a basket. You do not know how long the cord is, but you want to straighten it out and find out exactly what is there. So you begin with one end that is in your hand and gradually work your way to the other end. The yarn is elastic and will snap back into the basket if you should let go of it. Thus, you must continue to pull without letting up. And if you do stop for a moment, you must never completely let go. Without allowing yourself to become discouraged, you steadily pull out one length after another, pulling and pulling as though the yarn were endless. Then one day you suddenly reach the end, and—whoops!—there is nothing more to pull!

This may seem foolish—posing a problem for ourselves that ultimately proves pointless and just disappears, like a dog chasing its own tail. There is nothing at the beginning when you take up the "tangle of yarn" and make yourself ask the *huatou*. And there is nothing at the end when you finish and the *huatou* is gone. But working through the yarn was not foolish. A very significant transformation takes place in the interim, a transformation to which the method of the *huatou* is vital, even though it is not the result. Before one takes up a *hua-*

tou, the mind is confused and barren of all wisdom. Through the process of *hua-tou* practice, confusion disappears and wisdom manifests.

Just as with any method of meditative concentration, when thoughts begin to settle and body and mind become unified, one begins to feel unusual energy and power. In the case of the *huatou*, this will be accompanied by a deeper and more intense longing for an answer to the *huatou*, as though one were glimpsing the real urgency and significance of the question for the first time. This kind of concentration may last for varying stretches of time, but will eventually be broken by pain in the legs, exhaustion, the ending of the meditation period, the arrival of mealtime, and so forth. When the practitioner returns to meditating effectively on the method, it will come back again. This is the small doubt.

Thus, the *huatou* is a question that one asks oneself as a means of practice. In the beginning, there is no doubt. Small doubt is sufficient to prod one to keep asking the question. If the mind remains continuously on the question, new power is generated and one can reach an intermediate stage of doubt, in which doubt becomes progressively deeper and more sustained. One may experience this to some degree in ordinary daily practice at home, but it is only when one practices intensely for an extended period of time—as in a Chan meditation retreat—that one can generate the power and momentum necessary to experience great doubt. When great doubt comes, the power is immense. One is no longer aware of one's body, the world, or anything in the entire universe. Only the doubt is left.

At this point, one could say that the practitioner is in the condition of unified, or one-pointed, mind. In effect, the all-consuming doubt concentrates body and mind into one thought, leading one into samādhi. But the questioning and doubt, by its very nature, makes it impossible to settle deeply into a quiescent state of samādhi. Instead, the concentrated power of doubt leads headlong into the explosion of wisdom. Hence, while the *huatou* method avails itself of the traditional logic of *śamatha*, or meditative calm and concentration, in its long-term aim it is quite different from such classical Buddhist *śamatha* methods as the Five Practices for Stilling the Mind.

There is an old analogy in Chan that compares the process of attaining enlightenment to passing a camel through the eye of a needle. It is also said that, to pass into the world of Chan, one must be utterly naked, without a thread of silk on one's body. In effect, this means that, in order to realize Chan, one's mind must be utterly naked, without a single thought, attachment, or reservation. It may not hold on to or retain anything, even its own form. This complete nakedness of mind and soul is comparable to the state of the practitioner who is on the brink of explosion. Doubt consumes and strips this person of everything, even himself. In fact, great doubt is often characterized as the "great mass or ball of doubt" (*da yituan*) or "single mass of doubt." When consumed by great doubt, it seems as though one is surrounded entirely by doubt, cut off from every living

thing in the world. One cannot ignore it or get rid of it, swallow it or spit it out.
Nor can one resolve it. When the bell rings at the end of the meditation period,
one would not hear it. If it were mealtime, one might go to eat, but be oblivi-
ous of the food. Even in bed, one would be absorbed only in the doubt. This
may continue uninterruptedly from day to night, as though one was some type
of mindless automaton. After a few days, however, a great explosion will surely
occur.

How quickly and easily a practitioner produces great doubt depends on the
person's karmic capacity. Great doubt and the explosion of awakening may come
spontaneously to people with keen karmic capacity. Such persons may foster
great doubt and enlightenment even without the guidance of a master. Persons
of mediocre karmic roots, who try to practice on their own may, in time, produce great doubt, but without the guidance of an experienced teacher, they will
most likely fall into demonic states of mind. In the case of persons with dull
karmic roots, even small doubt is extremely difficult to generate.

Since it does provide an effective means for concentrating the mind, *huatou*
can, at least in theory, be used by virtually anyone. But given the difficulty it takes
to generate power from the *huatou* when one's mind is scattered and untamed, I
usually do not assign *huatou* right away. Initially, I prescribe other, more traditional, Buddhist methods of meditation—such as concentration on the breath
(S. *ānāpāna-smṛti*)—to help my students calm and focus their minds. After they
have generated some power of concentration with these methods, I give them
huatou. If they are unable to use the *huatou* effectively, I will have them return to
the previous method of concentration.

In the course of a weeklong Chan retreat, the ordinary student may not be
able to summon enough power and momentum to ignite a truly major explosion of wisdom. However, it is possible for a Chan master to produce a minor
explosion from a small doubt, even though it is weak and intermittent. While
such an experience is in no way equivalent to seeing fully into one's true nature,
a minor explosion like this can be of great benefit to the practitioner, especially
in this day and age, when most people don't have the time, circumstances, or
motivation to devote themselves to steady Chan practice. Although it is incomplete, such a minor experience will shake one up so that one feels mentally and
spiritually reborn. The world will seem quite different from the way one previously experienced it, and, as a result, one's faith and zeal for the practice will
deepen.

Gentle and Forceful Approaches to Huatou Practice

Generally speaking, we can distinguish two approaches to the use of *huatou* as a
long-term form of practice. One is what we call the "gentle" approach, the other,
the "forceful," or "intensive," approach.

The gentle approach is appropriate for practitioners whose minds are coarse and untamed. By steadily repeating the *huatou* to themselves with a soft tone of voice and gentle attitude, their dispositions will become calm and their minds concentrated and supple. In this instance, the *huatou* functions more like repeated recitation of a mantra or the Buddha's name, where one strives to settle one's mind one-pointedly on the syllables or words. It is analogous to tying your mind to a heavy rock and throwing it into a deep pool. By gently and persistently returning one's attention to the *huatou*, the mind settles down into deepening clarity and calm.

The forceful approach is just the opposite. Here practitioners throw themselves into the question with all their might. Because it summons up such intense energy, the forceful approach to *huatou* practice may prove harmful for persons who are unstable or given to excessive swings of emotion. They may drive themselves into such a frenzy that they are ready to kill, or they become so enraged that they bang their heads, beat their chests, throw punches and kick over tables, all the while shouting, "Who am I?" This sort of extreme is wrong and should be avoided. *Huatou*, in the hands of the wrong person, can play dangerously into certain emotional problems, and drive the person in the opposite direction that he or she needs to go, even to insanity. Thus, the forceful method should be taught selectively and, above all, used under strictly controlled conditions. It is an approach that is appropriate only for persons whose minds are already stable and calm, either because of natural endowment or previous meditative practice.

For the majority of people—especially beginners—the gentle method is more suitable, at least initially. However, since the gentle method cannot generate very great power, it will never measure up to the forceful approach, no matter the amount of time and effort put into its practice. To be sure, it is possible to experience a taste of enlightenment through practice of the gentle method, but, in the long run, the power and depth of such an experience will prove to be limited when compared to that derived from the forceful practice. In the normal course of events or when things go smoothly, it may be difficult to tell that the power derived from gentle practice is actually small. But if an incident occurs that truly puts one's mettle to the test, one will know very quickly just how insufficient the power of one's practice really is. When circumstances arise that call for firm moral commitment and action—especially situations involving life and death, fame and fortune, or sexual relations—one may not possess the will power to do what is right, even though the right course of action is clear in one's mind. The reason for this lack of self-control is lack of power from practice.

As such, the serenity and ease that comes with the gentle approach can prove misleading, especially when the practitioner lives in a stable environment where all needs are supplied and the daily routine calls for little external responsibilities or interaction. Things will go very smoothly, too smoothly. One may get up at the same time every day and practice in the morning, until, "Oh! It's about time for lunch now!" Then one punctually stops to eat. After lunch one takes a little break, then practices again until it is time to do the laundry, eat supper, or tend to some other routine chore. In the evening one may study a bit, or practice some more. Then one goes to bed.

Some may continue to practice like this day after day for eight or ten years, and people will think that they are great and seasoned practitioners. At least they will appear dignified and stable, never anxious to get anywhere or do anything. But the reason they appear so stable is because they have no responsibilities for anything or anyone. Throughout the day they just sit around, not participating in any real work or becoming involved in any conflict or crisis that is taxing. Such practitioners appear to have no vexations, but it is not because their minds are truly free: easy circumstances just make it appear this way. People like this can go on for years, deceiving themselves and others into thinking that they are practicing and making progress.

I once met such a monk. He said to me, "I experienced great liberation, great freedom while I was practicing in retreat. I did not have any vexations." I asked him whether he had to worry about food and clothing while he was practicing. No, because others provided for his needs so that he could practice without concern. I asked him if he ever got into quarrels. He replied that there was no one to quarrel with. The fact is, he experienced no vexations because there was nothing in his easy daily doings that could cause him vexation. All his defilements and vexations, however, were still present. They were just asleep. Finally, he told me that since he stopped practicing he had experienced a lot of difficulty. Things were not good at all. I asked him, "If you really attained enlightenment then, why are you not liberated now?"

He answered, "The environment is not right. It is best for me to go back to practicing in seclusion." Actually, though, environment was not the real issue at all. It was his mind. In Chan we wish to reach the point where we can enter any environment with full freedom, where the mind does not fluctuate in any environment.

In comparison to insights generated from the gentle approach, the explosion of enlightenment caused by the forceful method produces much more power. After successfully using the forceful method, you will be capable of bearing great responsibilities and burdens. Even if doing what is right calls for exposing yourself to grave danger, you will do so without the slightest hesitation. Whether armed enemies or bombs, you will enter the most perilous of circumstances if, in doing so, you may solve problems or be of use to others. Having transformed your attachment to self into wisdom and deep compassion, it is quite natural and easy for you to take on great tasks. In the Chan tradition, such a man or woman is known as a *dazhangfu*, or "hero of great vitality."

The forceful approach to *huatou* calls for one to enter an extraordinary mental condition—a condition that, because of its intensity, is not very compatible with ordinary life, and so should not be taken up casually. It must be used in carefully controlled circumstances and under the watchful eye of an experienced

master. The optimum setting is a meditation retreat, where activities are routinized to promote meditation and one is well insulated from outside involvement. At the beginning of such a retreat, the master will tell the participants
that, for the duration of the fixed period of seven days, fourteen days, twenty-
one days, ninety days, or whatever, it is necessary to drop all concern for life and
limb. He or she will say, "Forget whether you are healthy or sick. Do not even
be afraid of death. In fact, look upon yourself as one who is dead already, completely alone. Regardless of whether you have prepared for this retreat or not,
from this moment on simply put your whole being into the practice. Walking,
sitting, standing, lying down—at every moment immerse yourself completely in
the *huatou*. If you use the *huatou*, 'Who am I?', ask it over and over again to yourself with such passion and intensity that you *become* the *huatou*. Don't allow even
an instant of thought of anything else." Practitioners who can develop this sort
of strength and zeal will not even give themselves the liberty to fear death. If
they go on to attain enlightenment, they will never again fear death, under any
circumstances.

In the old days, Chan retreats in Mainland China were almost always geared
to this sort of intense form of practice. This sort of high-pressured approach,
however, is appropriate only for people whose minds are stable and calm. For
persons who have not reached the proper condition, this approach is not very
useful. In fact, it may even prove harmful. Thus, participants were carefully
screened beforehand, and only those who were seasoned were allowed to take
part. When Chan master Xuyun gave retreats, so many applicants applied that
only the most determined persons were allowed to participate. If someone mis-
behaved, had trouble adapting, or failed to put forth the utmost effort, he or she
was often expelled on the spot.

These days, things are different, especially in America, where there is no pre-
existing tradition of Buddhist practice. If I gave a retreat with demands as
intense as those of Xuyun's, participants would leave in droves. This would not
be of much benefit to people, so it is necessary to be somewhat more accom-
modating. Generally, the rules and routine of my retreats are still very strict, but
I use the forceful method of *huatou* practice only on an individual basis, never as
a general rule. I will not assign it unless the individual student has first developed a calm and stable mind and is suited to its intensity. Moreover, as a rule I
only use intensive *huatou* practice on retreats, since they are really the only occasion properly suited to it. When the retreat is over and circumstances return to
normal, it is generally best to discontinue this forceful approach until a special
meditation session is convened again.

Along with the proper supportive environment, it is also essential that one
be under the continual guidance of a skilled and attentive master when using the
forceful approach to *huatou*. The master who leads the retreat must be clearly
acquainted with the particular mental and physical situation of each retreatant.
He or she should be familiar with their personalities, know the level of their

practice, and, most important of all, be attentive to the changes taking place in each meditator throughout the course of the retreat. Does everyone know how to use the method effectively? Is everyone actually working hard and entering the proper condition? Although thirty people may be told to practice with the same *huatou*, inevitably, because of differences in character and ability, there will be thirty different methods being practiced. One person may spend all his time reciting the *huatou* to himself like a child singing; another will use it in a fashion similar to the counting of the breath. Someone may hold his breath when reciting the *huatou*. Another might just give herself up to waiting for an answer, saying to herself, "Well, I don't know the answer to the *huatou*, anyway." While she repeats the *huatou*, she remains in a state of blankness. Another kind of participant may be quite confident that he knows the answer to the *huatou*. Every time he asks it, he feels sure he knows the answer. Thus, with each repetition, he thinks that he has attained enlightenment. But then doubt arises. So he asks the *huatou* again, and a new possibility suggests itself. Then, of course, some might just spend their time dozing off or trying to think up rational solutions.

In all these instances, the practitioners are bound to their particular deluded thoughts and habits, and it is necessary for the master to know them intimately so that he or she may guide them to the proper condition. Whether we are speaking of the forceful or gentle approach to *huatou*, it is almost certain that the practice will go astray without an experienced teacher. Rather than the method turning delusion around, delusion will turn the method to its own particular ends. It is just too hard for the inexperienced practitioner to see beyond the force of habit. A lot of years can be wasted in this sort of self-complacency and pride.

8

The Practice of Silent Illumination

THE HISTORICAL ORIGINS OF SILENT ILLUMINATION PRACTICE

We have spoken in an earlier chapter of the codification that the "gateless gate" of Chan underwent as it developed institutionally during the late Tang and early Song Dynasties. In an atmosphere of increasing sectarianism the different lines of Chan sought to formalize their patriarchal heritages and delineate the distinctive features of their particular brand of Chan practice and culture. Much as figures like Dahui Zonggao (1089–1163) placed the use of *gong'an* and *huatou* securely at the heart of Linji teaching, Song Period masters of the Caodong line gradually distilled the method of *mozhao chan*, or "silent illumination Chan," as the central axiom of Caodong practice. This process reached its culmination with Hongzhi Zhengjue (1091–1157), who was a contemporary of Dahui. Approximately a century later, the Japanese monk, Dōgen (1200–1253) received the Caodong Dharma from Tiantong Rujing (1163–1228), a master in the line of Hongzhi's Dharma brother, Zhenxie Qingliao (1089–1151), and transmitted the Caodong teaching to Japan, where it became known as the Sōtō Zen school. In this chapter I discuss the practice of silent illumination, or *mozhao chan*, as espoused in the Caodong school.

Chan practice that emphasizes *gong'an* and *huatou* tends to make use of forceful methods, such as emotional pressure, shouting, beating, and reviling to push the student into a situation where "one reaches the end of the road but still must press forward," or where "there is absolutely nothing that can be said, but one still must speak." By concentrating all of one's being on a *gong'an* or *huatou*, one is brought to the point of great doubt and, finally, to an explosive experience of awakening. The method of practice is intense and its effect is earthshaking and easily identifiable. Having achieved a breakthrough of this sort, the student has a clear idea of just what having "no thought" or "no mind" entails.

The approach of silent illumination is different. It is more passive in character, and focuses on the development of such qualities as total relaxation coupled with open awareness, perfect stillness coupled with luminous clarity. By gently settling the churning mind of deluded thinking, it seeks to allow the perfect quiescence and luminosity of the enlightened mind to naturally emerge. This mind is described as being smooth and clear like a mirror, cool and bright like the radiant moon, deep and still like a pellucid mountain lake. This is not to say that Caodong Chan dispensed with the use of *gong'an*. Quite the contrary, the historical record shows that *gong'an* continued to play an important role in Caodong teaching, as it did in most Chan lineages. However, they appear to have functioned in a manner different from that developed by Dahui and the Linji line. Moreover, as a signature of Caodong-style training, *gong'an* were given second seat to silent illumination.

Just as with the *gong'an* and *huatou* technique, the practice of *mozhao*, or "silent illumination," did not burst on the scene overnight during the Song Period, but took shape as a gradual outgrowth of the effort to identify the essence of the Caodong teaching. Indeed, antecedents to silent illumination can be found not only among the records of founding Caodong masters, but in documents attributed to the Chan patriarchs of the early Tang Period (618-907) as well. This, of course, is not surprising, given the tendency of later Chan masters to seek historical sanction for their teachings in the example of earlier, often legendary, Chan figures. Bodhidharma himself is said to have taught, "If you wish to cast aside the false and return to true, concentrate and settle your mind in wall-gazing. Self and other, the unenlightened and the saintly, are all as one. Abide securely in this and do not stray."[1] The *Xinxin ming* ("Inscription on Having Faith in the Mind") attributed to the third patriarch, Sengcan (d. 606), states: "The two come when there is [a notion of] one[ness], so oneness also must not be adhered to. When a single thought does not arise, the myriad things are without defect." And again, "All wise ones throughout the ten directions penetrate this essential truth; this essential [moment of] truth is neither pressingly short nor lengthy. An instant of thought is ten thousand years."[2]

In the *Platform Sūtra*, sixth patriarch Huineng says,

Men of the world, separate yourself from views; do not activate thoughts. If there were no thinking, then "no-thought" would have no place to exist. "No" is the "no" of what? "Thought" means "thinking" of what? "No" is separation from the dualism that produces the passions. "Thought" means thinking of the original nature of True Reality. If you give rise to thoughts from your true self-nature, then, although you see, hear, perceive, and know, you are not stained by the manifold environments and are always free.[3]

Yongjia Xuanjue (665–713), a disciple of the sixth patriarch, says in his *Zhiguan song (Song of Calming and Contemplation)*, "Having forgotten all involvement, one is silent and still, yet divine wisdom by nature is incisively penetrating. Dark and incognizant, it [still] shines and illumines. While conforming to primal and true emptiness, one [all the while perceives] with precise exactness."

All of these passages from the early Chan patriarchs are examples of teachings that might be seen as precursors to the practice of silent illumination. One could say that the Caodong line itself took shape as a continuing evolution of this tendency. Dongshan Liangjie (807–869), one of the two founding masters from whom the school takes its name, once remarked that one should not think about anything at all when practicing Chan: "One should not go east or go west, but directly to that place where, for ten-thousand miles around, there is not one blade of grass. Then you will get it."[5]

To have even the slightest thought or attachment in mind is equivalent to there being "a blade of grass." Thus, having no grass means to have no discriminating thoughts, and "ten-thousand miles around" refers to a vast expanse, like empty space. When he heard these words of Dongshan, master Shishuang Qingzhu (807–885), a contemporary of Dongshan, commented, "As soon as you go out the door, there is grass everywhere." In other words, as soon as thoughts arise or "the mind steps out the door," everywhere there is difference and discrimination. As soon as mind fixes on or reifies any feature to the exclusion of others, the dynamic and boundless state of no-mind or no-thought is lost.[6]

Dongshan also states in his *Xuanzhong ming* ("Inscription on the Mysterious Middle"), "Although active and functioning, there is no motion. Although quiescent, it is not fixated. The pure breeze blows over the grasses, but the grasses do not sway. The bright moon fills the sky, yet there is no shining."[7] In a similar but more enigmatic statement, he once instructed, "If you wish to understand this matter, you must be like dead wood putting forth blossoms. Then you will be in conformity with it."[8] Chan master Xiangyan Zhixian (d. 898), a contemporary of Dongshan, was once asked about the Way. He replied, "In the dry woods the dragon sings," and, "An eye glimmers in a desiccated skull."

Dead, dry wood has absolutely no activity, no life, but here it puts forth blossoms; the dragon is known for its great vitality as well as its connection with water. Thus, the images of a dragon singing in a dry wood and a living eye in a desiccated skull seem completely anomalous. Shishuang Qingzhu said of these two statements, "There is joy there" and "there is consciousness there." Caoshan Benji (840–901), the successor of Dongshan, later remarked, "The skull has no awareness, but wisdom's eye begins to shine in it. If joy and conscious awareness should be extinguished, all communication and response would cease. Those who deny this do not understand that purity is in the impure."[9] Both examples point to the cardinal importance of the Caodong image of silence with illumination, illumination in silence.

In the teachings of Shishuang Qingzhu (807–888), this concept of stillness and awareness begins to show evidence of developing into an identifiable technique of silent illumination practice. He is said to have urged his students to become like dead ashes or dry wood, incapable of putting forth flame or growth, or to make their minds like the single plume of a waterfall, with its waters pouring down steadily without interruption. Another favorite simile for meditation used by Shishuang Qingzhu was that of a cold incense burner in a silent and long-abandoned temple. Indeed, Shishuang is said to have encouraged his students to sit in meditation for long periods without moving or lying down, as if they were "dead branches" or "blocks of wood." Consequently, in Chan circles his community was commonly called the "dry, or dead, wood group."[10]

Whether Shishuang Qingzhu's teaching was typical of the Caodong line itself is hard to say. As with most Chan figures of the period, very little information is available about actual practice, and even that is problematic given the late date of many of the sources. As a discrete method of practice, mozhao, or "silent illumination," proper, begins to be taught in the Caodong line only after the line is rescued from the brink of extinction and revived by eleventh-century master, Touzi Yiqing (1032–1082). Records of Caodong masters descended from Touzi Yiqing frequently employ the metaphor of silence and illumination, stillness and radiance, to convey the essence of Caodong Chan. With the advent of the famous Song Period master Hongzhi Zhengjue (1091–1157), silent illumination (mozhao) is finally singled out as the distinctive technique of practice of the Caodong line.

In addition to his well-known Lancet of Seated Meditation and Inscription on Silent Illumination, Hongzhi composed numerous verses on the practice of silent illumination.[11] In one celebrated passage he states that "your body should sit silently; your mind should be quiescent and unmoving; and your mouth, so still that moss grows around it and grasses sprout from your tongue. Do this without cease, cleansing the mind until it gains the clarity of an autumn pool and is as bright as the moon shining in the autumn sky."[12]

Using imagery like this, Hongzhi instructs his students to let go and settle quietly into themselves, leaving behind all entangling conditions and supports, until they reach a point of perfect and unrestrained quiescence. At the same time, this does not imply that mind becomes dark or incognizant. Quite the contrary, it is the distortions of deluded and conditioned thinking that are silenced, not mental clarity or awareness. With this silence, the mind's innate wisdom shines unobstructed, perfectly clear and luminous, without a single speck of dust to impede it. "In this [state of] silent sitting," Hongzhi says, "the mind clearly perceives the details of sensory objects; yet, as though transparent, no constructed image is produced."[13]

Everything is right where it originally is—just as it is—in its own native place. As long as one does not become erroneously fixated on stillness, the more the mind settles down, the more bright and penetrating its intrinsic awareness of things will become. When mind is utterly quiescent, without any grasping or abiding whatsoever, its natural awareness is boundless in both scope and depth. Hongzhi likens this to the point of an arrow fitted perfectly into its protective sheath. This calm and bright awareness becomes so perfectly immediate to the environment that all distinction between subjective awareness and object itself dissolves. This luminous emptiness and quiescence is itself the intrinsically enlightened condition of all beings; and its actualization is great liberation. Thus, silent illumination is the fullest and most direct expression of the unmediated realization of Buddha-nature espoused in the Chan school. Here are two selections from Hongzhi's writings that describe the practice of silent illumination:

The field is vacant and wide open. From the very beginning, it has always been there. Purify and reclaim it; strip and scour it clean! Get rid of deluded conditionings and illusory habits, and you will arrive naturally at a place that is clear and pure and perfectly bright. Totally empty, without fashioning any image or likeness; solitary and sublime, depending on nothing—only in this vastness can one illumine intrinsic reality and relinquish external objects. Therefore it is said, "With perfect and all-pervading clarity, there is not a single thing to be perceived." This field is a deep source of pure luminosity, a place where birth and death do not reach, that is able to emit light and function responsively. Permeating through worlds as numerous as motes of dust— transparent-like, without forming semblances—the wondrous activity of seeing and hearing leaps far beyond that of everyday sound and form. Reaching everywhere, its functioning is without trace; its mirroring is without obstruction. Naturally and spontaneously, it issues forth with perfect impartiality, flowing responsively with thought after thought, object after object. An ancient has said, "Having no mind, one attains in oneself the Dao of no-mind. Attaining no-mind in oneself, the Dao also ceases to be." With lucid awareness, one takes up the task of helping other sentient beings, all the while as though still sitting in utter silence. If you want to know this wondrous activity of entering leisurely into the world, you must investigate in this fashion![14]

And again:

The correct way of practice is simply to sit in stillness and silently investigate; deep down a place is reached where, externally, one is no longer swirled about by causes and conditions. The mind being empty and open, it is all-embracing. Its luminosity being wondrous, it is impartial and precise. Internally there are no grasping thoughts; vast and removed, it rests alone in itself without falling into stupor. Vitally potent, it cuts through all dependency and opposition, all the while remaining perfectly self-possessed. This ease-within-itself has nothing to do with mundane feelings—you must rely on nothing whatsoever. Exceedingly sublime, it brims with an intrinsic spiritual presence; from the moment you first obtain it, you will forever be securely at rest, never again to stray after defiled appearances. Perfectly pure, it is luminously bright; being bright, it is also penetrating. As such, it is able to respond smoothly to whatever phenomenon it encounters, so that phenomenon and the next do not mutually impede one another. Floating effortlessly, clouds come forth on the mountain peaks; shining boldly, the moon glimmers in mountain streams.

Everywhere there is radiant light and spiritual transformation—clearly, with their features unobstructed, they respond to one another with perfect precision, as snugly as a lid fits its box or a sheath fits the tip of its arrow. With further instruction and cultivation, this condition will ripen, until its substance becomes stabilized and penetrates everywhere freely. Round off your sharp corners; cease your theoretical prattling [about right and wrong]. Become like a white ox or tamed ferret that responds naturally to any command—then you can be called a tried and true warrior. Hence it is said, "Having the Dao of no-mind one can be like this; having not yet gained no-mind, it is exceedingly difficult."[15]

THE CONCEPT OF SILENT ILLUMINATION AS A PRACTICE

Silent illumination is a simple method—so simple, in fact, that this simplicity becomes its difficulty. Ultimately, it is the method of no-method, in which the practitioner leaves behind all seeking, all attachment, all expectations, and just lives Chan directly. To practice silent illumination, just drop all busywork and discriminating thoughts and be serenely aware, accepting all things fully, just as they are. Do not hanker after anything or dwell on anything. Simply let your naturally aware mind take everything in, just as it is. This is the natural quiescence and luminosity of Chan. When there is discrimination and clinging, such marvelous quiescence and luminosity are impeded. Mind is naturally silent and still and, at the same time, fully aware. No effort is needed to polish it or make it shine for it to be this way. In principle, silent illumination is very simple. But, because we are so complicated, it becomes a difficult method of practice to master. The greatest problems arise from doing too much. Because we tend to do too much—even in meditation—we may require considerable preliminary training and "unlearning" before we are simple enough to use silent illumination effectively.

Hongzhi Zhengjue instructs that the body should sit silently and the mind should be totally open, yet unmoving. Through this practice, the mind naturally cleanses itself until it gains "the clarity of an autumn pool and is as bright as the moon shining in the autumn sky." He further instructs, "In this silent sitting, whatever objects appear, the mind is very clear as to all the details, yet everything is where it originally is, in its own place. The mind stays on one thought for ten-thousand years, yet does not dwell on any form, inside or outside."[16]

In the practice of silent illumination, we say that you should not use your eyes, ears, nose, tongue, body, or mind. If you find your thoughts dwelling intently on objects of seeing, hearing, smelling, tasting, or feeling anything, you should let go. But even this is not enough. You should not use your discursive mind at all. You should let go of all discriminations, all expectations and regrets, likes and dislikes, desires and goals. You should even let go of the thought of "letting go." Do not think of yourself as an ordinary unenlightened being, nor think that you must rid yourself of vexations and strive for Buddhahood. There should be no thought of enlightenment, no thought of Chan, no thought of gain whatsoever. There should not even be any thought of trying to practice "not-thinking." The "silence" in silent illumination is not one of active silencing or suppressing, but simply letting go and allowing things to take their rest, to be as they are. We simply lay down our mental worries and involvements and remain at peace, free of thoughts, with nothing to do. At first this will be difficult, but as one enters the practice more deeply, this stillness becomes a profound stillness, in which all discrimination ceases and there is no distinction between stillness and marvelous activity. One who experiences profound stillness feels as though wild grass has sprouted from one's eyes, as though boulders have blocked one's ears, as though moss has grown on one's tongue. All complicated human busywork having long since disappeared, wild nature has taken over.

This simile is not meant to suggest that the senses no longer function: that the eyes do not look, that the tongue is motionless, and that the ears shut out all sound. If this were the case, the silence in one's practice of silent illumination would not be profound silence, for the mind would still be conjuring up an image of stillness and effortfully avoiding activity. This is not the complete physical and mental quiescence indicated by the simile. In profound silence and simplicity—with absolutely nothing to do—one is not incognizant, but keenly and totally present. Without a second thought, all things prevail in you and you in all things.

One may wonder how a meditator experiencing this profound stillness would be different from an inanimate object, such as a block of wood. It seems that there would be no conscious awareness or activity whatsoever. There is, however, a fundamental difference between the profound silence of silent illumination and the silence of incognizance; and it is to make this distinction that we place the word "illumination" (*zhao*) after "silent" (*mo*). In truth, silence is inseparable from illumination, and illumination from silence. They are one and the same thing. Even before all thoughts and mental involvement are laid to rest, awareness is already extremely direct, keen, and penetrating. In other words, bright awareness occurs inseparably with profound stillness.

Why is this? When the mind is settled and still, discriminating thoughts disappear; as discriminating thoughts disappear, so do the experiential limitations of past, present, and future, inner and outer, this and that, self and other. With no index by which to mark its passing, time cannot exist. Similarly, with no discursive boundaries between self and other, this and that, there can be no limits or points of reference to define space, so spatial delimitation does not exist either. The bright awareness of silent illumination is not limited by anything at all, since there is no thought of self nor any clinging to features that would separate mind and the environment. One's mind is like a boundless mirror which, though motionless itself, takes in everything, just as it is. No detail is excluded; nothing is impeded. The mirror and the world it reflects are so perfectly fused as to be inseparable.

Hongzhi Zhengjue likens this state to an autumn pond or autumn sky. With the cool and crisp air of autumn, the waters settle, becoming so still and clear that one can see the fish drifting lazily in their depths; the sky so high and clear that one can see the birds gliding gently high up in the blue. He also compares it to the autumn or moon, which shines so clear and high that everything in the land is illumined by its cool and gentle light.

In certain respects, silent illumination, with its distinction between silence and illumining, stillness and observation, is reminiscent of the classical Buddhist practice of "calming" (S. *samatha;* C. *zhi*) and "contemplation" (S. *vipasyana;* C. *guan*), especially as formulated in the Chinese Tiantai school. Tiantai master Zhiyi (538–597) says in his *Great Calming and Contemplation (Mohe zhiguan),*

> One should place one's faith solely in the conviction that this very mind is itself Dharma-nature. When arising [of thoughts] takes place, it is just Dharma-nature arising. When perishing [of thoughts occurs], it is just Dharma-nature perishing. . . . Returning to the source, reverting to the root, Dharma-nature itself is wholly quiescent. This is known as "calming." When one practices calming in this manner, all prior mentation comes to a halt. In the practice of "contemplation," one contemplates that, originally, the mind of ignorance is identical with Dharma-nature. As such, at its base it is fundamentally empty. The entire range of good and evil [deeds] that proceed from deluded thinking is like empty space. These two practices are utterly non-dual. They are not distinct from one another.[17]

In classical Indian Buddhist systems, *samatha* and *vipasyana* are often treated and developed separately. For example, techniques such as the Five Methods for Stilling the Mind or visualization of colored disks known as *kasinas* may be used initially to develop the deep calm and absorption of dhyāna. Once meditative concentration is established, methods of *vipasyana* or contemplation might be applied, such as the Four Stations of Mindfulness. Through the latter, wisdom or liberative insight (prajñā) is developed. Gradually, after the powers of dhyāna and samādhi deepen and wisdom becomes penetrating, their functions fuse and deep enlightenment occurs. In Mahāyāna this is called the "true samādhi devoid of defiling outflows," or the "most supreme of supramundane samādhis." Such an accomplishment comes only from a deeply profound, complete enlightenment, quite unlike short-lived enlightenment experiences of limited impact. Although the path to this samādhi is long and slow, once attained, it never subsides. Samādhi functions constantly within the person, and through the powers of wisdom and skill born of this samādhi, the individual is able to function as a bodhisattva intent upon delivering other beings.

Although we have been distinguishing the two aspects of silent illumination in order to clarify its practice, it is in fact inaccurate to treat silence and illumination as two separate things. To do so would misrepresent the true practice of silent illumination and the sudden path of Chan. To begin with, silence and illumination are inseparable and must be present simultaneously: in the very act of illumining, one relinquishes grasping after thoughts and sensations, and directly takes things in, thereby bringing the mind to perfect silence. Then again, in the very act of silencing and pacifying thoughts, attachment to specific features and objects is relinquished, and awareness comes to illumine all things universally without impediment. Thus, one is always illumining and silencing simultaneously, in one and the same moment of awareness.

It is a mistake to think that first one must develop inner calm and, only then, apply open awareness. As the mind becomes clearer, it becomes more empty and calm, and as it becomes more empty and calm, it grows clearer. The more one is able to forget artificial efforts to cultivate stillness and illumination, the more silent and illumining the mind becomes. But an equally essential point to remember about silent illumination is that, according to Chan, the mind, by nature, is intrinsically still, void, and luminous. It need not be cultivated at all! To put too much effort into trying to stop thoughts or to brighten the mind is to compound delusion upon delusion. If there is any notion of practicing a "technique" of silent illumination, it is not silent illumination at all, but clinging and forceful discrimination. This is the real message of the Chan teaching of silent illumination: it is a method that is no-method. Silent illumination as the causal practice and silent illumination as the fruit of enlightenment are ultimately indistinguishable.

The concept and practice of silent illumination is expressed quite well by two lines from the *Diamond Sūtra:*

Without dwelling in anything whatsoever,
Allow this mind to arise.

In practicing silent illumination, one refrains from grasping or dwelling on any particular aspect of the body, mind, or environment. Thus, as the sūtra says, one is "without dwelling in anything whatsoever." If one were to emphasize this aspect of the practice alone, one could calm the mind and enter the states of unified mind of the various levels of dhyāna espoused in the Hīnayāna tradition. In these states there is deep silence, but little or no illumination, for the mind is still tied to a particular feature—namely, stillness and formlessness. Its ability to illumine universally or be aware of all things is impeded by attachment to the thought of emptiness. In true silent illumination there is illumination in addition to stillness, precisely because mind does not abide in any thought of stillness or emptiness. The meditator must let go of all notions of seizing and not seizing, letting go and not letting go: this is true "non-dwelling." Non-dwelling does not entail turning away from or shutting out the environment. It means to let go of biased attachment and to freely see right through things and take in the whole, so that one is aware of everything, inside and out, just as it is. For this reason the sūtra says, "One should allow the mind to arise and be active." Huineng offers an explanation of this practice and its relation to Chan in the *Platform Sūtra*:

> The deluded man clings to the characteristics of things, adheres to [the thought of] the Samādhi of Oneness, thinks that straightforward mind is sitting without moving and casting aside delusions without letting things arise in the mind. This he considers to be the Samādhi of Oneness. This kind of practice is the same as insentience and the cause of an obstruction to the Dao. The Dao must be something that circulates freely; why should he impede it? If the mind does not abide in things, the Dao circulates freely; if the mind abides in things, it becomes entangled.[18]

At the beginning stages in the practice of silent illumination, letting go and illumining are thoughts, a conscious and effortful practice that is born from the mind's discriminative faculty. As such, the meditator clings to them and invests them with expectations, just like any deluded thought. But as the practice itself matures, this thought of practice disappears. When we truly become ourselves and the method of no-method really becomes no method, there is true silence and illumination. The mind no longer fluctuates or discriminates, and silent illumination simply becomes silence and illumination. This is Chan.

PREREQUISITES AND CAVEATS FOR PRACTICE OF SILENT ILLUMINATION

To practice silent illumination effectively, several important preconditions must be fulfilled. First, one must have a competent master. Otherwise, it is easy to be waylaid by obstacles. Being such an effortless and formless approach, it is easy for individuals simply to indulge their bad habits, thinking all the while that they are practicing correctly. Actually, to forego deliberate effort and practice the method of no-method is by no means equivalent to just giving in to our usual ways. True practitioners of silent illumination know very clearly that they are practicing no-method, and know precisely what "no-method" involves. Without a teacher, ordinary people are likely to misinterpret this as a license to do what they have always done, simply affirming it as Chan. Few will have a clue as to what silent illumination actually means or entails. For this reason, when one takes up silent illumination it is best to have either prior experience with Chan or an accomplished teacher who can constantly check and guide one's practice.

Second, practitioners of silent illumination should spend an extended period of time in intensive practice, preferably in an isolated or carefully controlled environment. Actually, this is as true for the practice of *gong'an* and *huatou* as it is for that of silent illumination. The reasons for this are not difficult to understand. When Chinese practitioners used silent illumination or *gong'an* and *huatou* in the past, they did not work as we do. Normally, they arranged their affairs so that they could attend to their practice all day long, with minimal occasion for distraction. Moreover, life itself was not as complex and fast-paced as it is in today's world. Despite its alleged conveniences, life in modern society is immensely distracting and stressful. If we content ourselves with meditating for an hour or two a day and then spend the rest of our time chasing frantically after this or that, we will never be able to muster sufficient power to make progress in the practice of Chan. Our efforts at calm and clarity will be too meager to transform the dissipation brought on by the rest of the day's activities. Thus, a complete reorientation of priorities and circumstances, preferably in the form of a period of retreat, is necessary to develop initial power in the practice. This period of isolation need not occur in a lonely place miles from civilization. It may just as well be undertaken in the most densely populated area, so long as the immediate setting is free of disturbance and conducive to a regular routine of meditation.

In theory, persons at any level of training may use the method of silent illumination. Indeed, from the traditional perspective of the Caodong school, everyone, including beginners, should just practice silent illumination. There is simply nothing else to be done. But, since silent illumination is so subtle and elusive, persons whose minds are disturbed and whose powers of concentration are poor have difficulty making much progress with it. If someone comes to me having practiced Chan before, I will still not teach this method if the person's mind is not sufficiently stable and open, regardless of how long he or she may have practiced. On the other hand, if a rote beginner comes along whose mind is, by nature, calm and stable, I may instruct the person in silent illumination practice right from the start. The deciding factor has nothing to do with one's sectarian affiliation or professed seniority as a Chan practitioner, but one's power of concentration, simplicity of mind, and clear understanding of just what the practice entails. Before one can take up the practice of silent illumination, one must have a solid intuitive or experiential sense of what it means to let go of thoughts and be aware of what is at hand.

As a rule of thumb, concrete methods such as the Five Methods for Stilling the Mind are intended for less experienced persons. The keener the person's abilities and practice, the more simple and straightforward the method will be. For persons whose minds are complicated and confused, the method of silent illumination will be too formless to be effective in the face of their overwhelming passions. Initially, it is best for them to use the more deliberate methods of gradual samādhi practice, such as the Five Methods for Stilling the Mind, to provide an explicit basis for calming and concentrating the mind. For a more experienced meditator, however, this sort of routinized meditation might prove more distracting and burdensome than helpful. The important thing is that the practice match the individual's disposition and ability. It has often been said that the expedientless and direct path of Chan is intended for persons with keen karmic roots. Inasmuch as the practice of *gong'an* and silent illumination both require a highly concentrated and unified mind to be effective, the Caodong and Linji approaches are similar.

When people first begin to practice silent illumination, they are likely to be confronted by a torrent of scattered thoughts. As soon as one becomes aware of these thoughts, one should try to cease involvement with them. One should not allow oneself to become caught up in their train and carried away by them. One does this by simply noticing them and immediately letting them pass. Try to be fully attentive to thoughts and sensory experiences from moment to moment. Do not deliberately avoid, banish, or suppress them; rather, give free rein to this awareness, allowing it to flow clearly and without interruption, like a stream that sticks to nothing and freely flows into, around, and through all things without impediment.

At the same time, one should be careful of the pitfall of overexertion in the effort to "illumine" things. To "illumine" *(zhao)* does not really mean to "shine," as the sun or moon might put out rays of light. It means simply to be aware. The mind is naturally luminous, so whatever presents itself to our awareness is immediately visible to us. This prereflective awareness is illumination: just let go and look, and let go and look, and let go and look—penetrating directly, deeply, and unobstructedly into events themselves. In a sense, one could say that letting go is the silent aspect of silent illumination, and the unobstructed extension of awareness through all things is the aspect of illumination. But one must remember that they are a single and simultaneous process, not separate aspects. Above all, "illumination" does not entail allowing the mind to scamper after whatever object it wishes. That is the condition of a distracted mind, not one that is tempered by illumination grounded in silence.

In the Japanese Sōtō Zen school of Dōgen, this method of meditation is called *shikantaza* or, literally, "Just sit, nothing more." In the practice of *shikantaza*, one concerns oneself with sitting, and sitting only. When a distracting thought arises, one says to oneself, "All I am doing is sitting; there is nothing else to do, nothing to accomplish. Just sit." Since that is all the person does, he or she simply sits and lets everything else be, even wandering thoughts. Similarly, when involved in other activities—walking, standing, and so forth—the practitioner just tends completely to the action at hand, with no other thought in mind. Ultimately, this very activity is enlightenment; practice itself is enlightenment. There is no other enlightenment to be sought elsewhere.

Another common mistake with silent illumination is to fall into a condition of blankness or stupor, where the mind does not reflect or register anything. This is a lazy, hazy state of blankness. It is a dull and dissipated state, yet it is different from outright drowsiness or sleep. It is like standing on the seashore on a gray, rainy day, not seeing anything anywhere. While immersed in this condition, people often believe that their minds are really motionless and that they are truly practicing silent illumination. They are mistaken.

In certain respects, this error also comes from trying too hard to suppress thoughts and avoid distinctive sense perception. It represents an emphasis on silence, or the notion of silence, as something prior to or separate from illumination. It errs not from too much exertion, but from interpreting silence and "letting-go" to be a lax and disinterested sort of thoughtlessness. Again, silence in the practice of silent illumination does not mean incognizance. Sensory awareness registers quite clearly and thoughts still flow, but in an unobstructed and subtle form. Rather than avoiding thoughts and the sensory environment, one's awareness should penetrate right into the heart of phenomena. What decreases with stillness is not awareness of the world, but the tumult of clinging thoughts and passions that impede our awareness of it. Although the problem of blankness is not explicitly associated with drowsiness per se, it is easiest to slip into this condition while meditating if one is groggy. Otherwise, it will tend to arise in people whose stamina or concentration is weak. Should it go unchecked, this dull blankness can become a habitual condition of practice, and silent illumination will be nothing more than a lazy and disinterested stupor.

Perhaps one of the most serious difficulties with practicing silent illumination is the question of assessing one's progress. Precisely because it is so difficult to determine whether one's mind is truly motionless and open, meditators will frequently overestimate their attainments. What is more, spiritual progress can develop so gradually that it is difficult to find a clear index for it. Thus, it is easy for a silent illumination practitioner to feel that thoughts have disappeared when really they have not, especially so if he or she has never before experienced no-thought.

For example, suppose a meditator goes into isolation in order to make speedy progress, putting his or her total effort into silent illumination. As practice deepens, mental expansiveness, clarity, and brightness grow until, finally, there seems to be no environmental or bodily limitation whatsoever. The daily routine passes smoothly and without vexation. At this point the meditator may be convinced that practice of silent illumination is quite deep. What is more, since silent illumination is both practice and fruit, he or she may dismiss any thought of further effort and progress as spurious. But, really, this experience may be no more than the expanded sense of self and condition of unified mind experienced in the pre-dhyāna states described in Hīnayāna texts. Indeed, there are many levels of samādhi in the Hīnayāna and heterodox traditions that are more profound than this.

Practitioners must have a means to assess themselves, either through contact with a truly experienced teacher or by some other means. Should such a resource be unavailable, it may help to set aside one's practice temporarily and return to the world to test whether one's mind is really unmoving or not. In this way, one can determine whether one's response to the environment is a function of the deluded mind or of wisdom free of outflows. If, in the ordinary world, one free of vexation when confronted with difficult circumstances, then one has made some progress in Chan. Truly accomplished practitioners of silent illumination are like clouds moving through upthrusting peaks, completely part of but unimpeded by anything they encounter. For such people, there is no mind or world to rely on, yet the two interact mutually and spontaneously. Their enlightenment will ultimately be identical to that achieved through practice of *gong'an* or *huatou*. Why might it be so necessary to completely set aside meditation practice in this way? If relatively advanced practitioners meditate regularly for a few hours daily, they will naturally remain calm and stable throughout the day. When such people engage in everyday activities and mix with others, it will be easy to maintain an open and serene mind. However, real accomplishment in Chan—real freedom from defilements—will maintain itself spontaneously throughout all circumstances, without the need for a specialized environment or deliberate efforts at meditation. If one's practice lacks this self-sustaining power when the regular supports for Chan practice are suspended, then one's goal has not been reached.

THE PRACTICE OF SILENT ILLUMINATION PROPER

Presented in theory, the "methodless method" of silent illumination can seem simple to the point of requiring no disciplined effort whatsoever, or elusive to the point of being impossible to put into actual practice. However, there are concrete steps that can be taken to facilitate its development, and it is these that I will outline now. The approach to silent illumination that I teach my students goes back to Hongzhi Zhengjue, the twelfth-century Chinese Caodong master. Dōgen Kigen, the Zen master who introduced the Caodong (J. Sōtō) tradition to Japan, and who expounded the practice of *shikantaza* ("just sitting, nothing more") mentioned previously, lived two generations after Hongzhi. Although he was influenced by Chinese styles of Caodong practice, his practice of *shikantaza* took a somewhat different direction.

Broadly speaking, silent illumination practice can be organized into three stages of development. Of course, this is a provisional scheme that I use to convey the basic principles of the practice. One should be careful not to take these representations to be clearly marked plateaus that every practitioner must traverse or for which every practitioner must aim. Responses to the practice will vary from individual to individual, and progress itself may involve many subtle gradations of experience. The first of the three stages centers on the practice of "just sitting"—just attentively minding your body, poised in the posture of seated meditation. The second stage entails an expansion of one's field of awareness from the body to the external environment. Distinctions between the body and one's surroundings dissolve, so that one sits with bald awareness of this larger, expanded field in the same way that one previously attended to the seated body. In the third stage, subtle reifications of self and object disappear, and everything is present except you. There are no thoughts of self, no dualistic oppositions between self and external environment, and no discriminating or self-grasping thoughts. Hear something, and it is as though nothing is heard. See something, and it is as though nothing is seen. Yet the mind is perfectly clear and unclouded.

The First Stage of Silent Illumination Practice—Just Sitting

The first stage of "just sitting" is a highly physical technique that puts attention squarely on the meditation posture, nothing more. On the surface, this sounds deceptively elementary. But it is not. There are two different ways to apply this method of "just sitting." The first approach is more relaxed in tenor; the second is energetically charged and tense. As a rule, the tense or vigorous approach is best for persons who are relatively new to meditation and who are in good physical health. In the hands of a beginner, the relaxed approach might easily lead to a drowsy and unconcentrated mind—the kind of "stagnant-water" or "deadwood" sitting that we described above. The relaxed approach is more suited to experienced practitioners, to persons with health problems, or to occasions when a meditator needs to regain energy during intensive sessions of practice. In point of fact, however, the two approaches need not be thought of as being mutually exclusive; for as modalities of one and the same technique of "just sitting," they may be applied alternately within a single retreat or even within a single period of sitting. If you become too frenetic or exhausted, the relaxed approach can be used to collect yourself. If you find yourself drowsy or given to daydreaming, you can use the vigorous method to sharpen your concentration.

Good meditative posture is essential to both approaches—after all, you *are* "just sitting." This means maintaining a proper seated posture and equipoise, with the mind attending baldly to the body, right there on the cushion. How does the mind attend to this? It attends directly to the body and its sensations—to the whole of the body engaged in the act of sitting, nothing more. Of course, your attention may from time to time be drawn to different parts of the body, but your sole concern should be just to sit and to experience yourself as sitting, right in that moment, with total body-mind awareness. Individual sensations will come and go, but they should be experienced as an integral part of this whole. With this body-mind whole as the ground of concentration, such sensations will neither disrupt nor distract you.

The Relaxed Approach to Just Sitting

In both the relaxed and vigorous approaches to just sitting, it is best to use the full-lotus or half-lotus posture. But if these are too physically demanding, a looser posture is fine, as long as it is comfortable and the basic principles of proper meditative posture are fulfilled. The eyes may be open or closed; but the head should never be lowered, otherwise you may fall asleep. The area of the lower abdomen and back should be erect and arched ever-so-slightly forward, just enough to bring your spine into proper alignment and give you a bright and alert posture. Just sit straight, relax into the posture, and be your body.

At the outset of "just sitting," one's sense of bodily presence may not be particularly strong, especially if one is slouched and too relaxed, or is too tense and enervated. Under these circumstances, it will be difficult to get the proper feel for the practice. To forestall this problem, it helps to use the most obvious bodily sensations—the sensations of breathing and bodily weight—as a ground for developing the awareness of "just sitting." Of the two, the breath is the more accessible sensation. As in the method of mindfulness of the breath, the breathing can be used as a means to focus your attention in the body and to let you know that you are sitting. There are, however, significant differences between the two techniques, especially insofar as meditation on the breath strives to fix the mind one-pointedly on the breath, to the exclusion of everything else. In this initial stage of "just sitting," the sensation of breathing is used to develop an awareness of the total body. One's attention should stay with the whole body, not just the breath.

The sensation of bodily weight can also serve as a basis for developing the awareness proper to "just sitting." The secure feeling of your buttocks and pelvis on the cushion, your knees and your feet on the floor, the center of gravity in the lower abdomen, can directly bring this weight to your notice. As with the breath, do not focus your attention exclusively on these points, but use the sensation of stability to develop awareness of the whole of the seated body. Again, the idea here is that coarser sensations should be experienced as integral parts of the totality of body and mind.

The Tense or Vigorous Approach to Just Sitting

The tense approach to "just sitting" involves the same basic field and technique of meditation as the relaxed approach, only it is applied in a more vigorous manner. Again, proper meditative posture is essential: tuck in the chin; keep the spine and upper body vigorously erect, with pelvis, lower back, and lower abdomen lifted and poised lightly forward. The muscles of the body should not be constricted, but one's posture should be powerful, and one's attention intensely alert at all times. Once you have settled into the sitting posture, maintain perfect motionlessness. Beginning with the sensation of breathing or the body's weight, strive to be aware of the whole of the body, just as we described above. Remain absolutely motionless and do not flinch, even though you may feel pain, itching, numbness, or soreness. In fact, physical discomfort can itself serve as a favorable condition for practice. By their very power to harness our attention, sensations of pain in the knees, legs, back, and so forth, can be used to reduce wandering thoughts and bring you right back to the fact of just sitting. This does not mean that you should deliberately fix your attention on the pain, much less strive to suppress it or manipulate it. Just relax and allow the body to have pain, but place this sensation within the larger context of the whole body. This may be difficult to do, but it is the best way to deal with pain. With proper attention, sensations of pain and discomfort can be transmuted into a sense of joyful ease. This comes about by reorienting the way that one experientially processes pain. If you continue to sit in this way, you will realize in time that pain is not permanent; it comes and goes. The pain itself will sharpen your mindfulness; and when the pain disappears, the mind will reach a very calm, concentrated, and clear state that is free of wandering thoughts.

At this point, the sense of the body as a hard physical presence may also disappear, resulting in the experience of what we call "lightness-and-ease." In this condition you will feel an unusual bliss. However, it is important that one avoid becoming fixated on this feeling. You should regard this state with utter detachment, and continue to maintain awareness as before. Some people will mistake this feeling for mundane samādhi—or worse, enlightenment itself. However, this is not yet the unified mind of samādhi, much less an experience if no-mind. It is only a pre-samādhi condition. If you continue to sit without becoming attached to it, you will progress beyond this condition. The sense of physical embodiment will dissolve into a transparent awareness, and you will experience an expansive state of mind in which the external environment itself becomes your "body." With this vanishing of bodily boundaries, you will enter into the second stage of silent illumination practice.

The Second Stage of Silent Illumination Practice

The second stage of silent illumination practice comprises two qualitatively different levels of experience. At the first level, the mind becomes clearer and clearer, ever more unhindered by discriminating thoughts. Sensations of physical limitation and heaviness also fall away, so that the field of body-mind awareness comes to merge seamlessly with the environment at hand. Whatever object you encounter in the external environment will feel as though it is part of your own body, as though there is no division between inside and outside. At this point, one's sphere of awareness will seem greatly expanded. However, it will still be limited by the sense of opacity and discreteness associated with objects in the immediate environment. One should go on to subsume external events within one's awareness, just as one previously subsumed specific physical sensations within the body-mind totalilty of "just sitting." In time your awareness will take in the entire universe; and as the limitations of sensory object and field dissolve, you will enter the second level of the second stage of silent illumination practice.

The distinction between these first and second levels is an important one, for it also marks the difference between a pre-samādhi condition and a bona fide experience of mundane samādhi and unified mind. In the first level, the field of awareness expands naturally from the locus of the physical body to that of the immediate sensory environment. Although one may feel that this expanded awareness remains hindered by external objects, one should cultivate the view that this environment is, in fact, infinitely vast, transparently inclusive, and unimpeded—that the whole world is just you engaged in sitting there. In terms of meditative technique, this is a direct analogue to the first stage of just sitting, in which one strives to maintain awareness of the total body by subsuming localized sensations into this larger bodily field. At the first level of the second stage, the method is basically the same, only the holistic scope of "just sitting" is considerably enlarged. One contextualizes events in the totality of the internal-external environment in the same way that one previously contextualized internal sensations within the whole of the physical body.

The transition to the second level of the second stage is marked by an actual experience of boundless oneness between self and the environment. The limited self expands and merges indistinguishably with the universe. Although events and objects in the inner and outer environments are still fully present, nothing interferes with anything else, since external environment is actually you. Just as the physical body ceases to be a burden in the first stage, in the second stage the external environment ceases to be an impediment. One's awareness penetrates right through objects in the immediate environment, without being impeded by their presence. Time passes quickly, and there is just total openness of mind and the clarity of infinite space. Everything is you.

At this second level of the second stage of "just sitting," various extraordinary experiences may occur. One such state is the experience of infinite light— an indescribable kind of light, in which the light itself is you, and there is a sense of oneness, a sense of infinite space, and utter clarity. A second type of experience is that of infinite sound. This is not the familiar sound of cars, dogs, or particular things in the world. It is a primal, elemental sound that is one with the vastness and seems to come from the origin of the universe itself. A pure sound that is unlike any music that you have ever heard before, it is a rich and perfect harmony that comes from all places at once, without any point of origin or reference. I call these the experiences of infinite light and infinite sound.

A third kind of experience that may arise at this deeper level of oneness is that of emptiness, or voidness. Although this sounds like the emptiness of no-self and self-nature that we identify with enlightenment, it is not the same. This is an experience of a pure vastness of space in which nothing at all seems to exist. It may seem that self and object no longer exist, that this is an experience of no-mind; but actually this "nothingness" is itself still conditioned by a subtle sense of selfhood and object. In point of fact, all three of these experiences are products of the unified state of mind that comes with mundane dhyāna and samādhi. They belong to the level of great or expanded self, not to the supramundane forms of samādhi that come with insight into true emptiness and no-mind. When you experience such states, it is imperative that you not become attached to them, much less mistake them for enlightenment itself. As you emerge from them, say to yourself, "This is not what I am seeking."

The Third Stage—Genuine Realization of Silent Illumination

The third stage of silent illumination practice is exceedingly difficult to describe, since it is the inconceivable enlightenment of no-mind itself. At this stage, there is no distinction between practice and realization, nor is there separation between meditative concentration and enlightened insight. The mind is forever unmoved by causes and conditions and free from the illusory thought of self, yet the mind still perceives and responds fully to the needs of others. In so doing, there is nothing artificial, nothing forced or unnatural in its operations. Its wisdom manifests spontaneously in response to whatever arises.

Yongjia Xuanjue, a disciple of the sixth patriarch Huineng, wrote two lines in a longer poem that are useful for helping us understand this third stage of matured silent illumination practice: "In the midst of using the mind, there is no mind to be used; in not using the mind, there is using of the mind."[19] "No mind to be used" refers to the "silent" aspect of silent illumination. "In not using mind, there is using of mind" refers to the aspect of "illumination." In both lines there is neither subject nor object, attachment nor rejection. In the second stage of silent illumination practice, one experiences a kind of non-opposition between self and environment, but there remains a subtle sense of an absolute, of a oneness. Implicit to this objectification, there is impediment, attachment, and selfhood. At the third stage, true freedom from opposition and impediment appears: there is no subjective self, no objective environment, nor is there any subtle sense of a reified absolute. In this state, all dualistic opposition and constraint truly cease. You can interact with the environment without affliction and self-clinging, no matter what circumstances confront you. All things are fully present, and whatever tasks need to be accomplished, are accomplished. By the same token, there is not a hint of self-attachment in this activity—there is just the free functioning of wisdom.

Hongzhi Zhenjue himself gives another description in one of his poems: "Late, late, the fishes have yet to appear; gone far and distant, the birds are no longer seen."[20] Reflecting on this verse, you will see that there is no observer, no subjective human presence. Fish are mentioned, yet they are not seen. You may surmise that the water is so clear as to be transparent, but actually water does not appear here at all. There is no fish or water! If we relate this verse to the experience of silent illumination, the image of fish and water being simultaneously present and absent is expressive of their being silence and illumination, without their being anything silenced or anything illumined. The same applies for the birds and sky. The birds must have flown far away, deep into the sky. The image of birds and sky are evoked, but neither birds nor sky figure substantively in this verse. No fish, water, birds, or sky, yet everything is clearly described. Nothing is there, but this is not a pessimistic, nihilistic nothingness. There is clarity and vividness. In the state of silent illumination, there is the experience of emptiness and no-self, but there is also clarity and knowing.

In Hongzhi Zhengjue's "Inscription on Silent Illumination," the very first lines read, "Silently and serenely, words are forgotten. Vividly and clearly, things appear of themselves."[21] Here, there is also no subjective presence, no observer. "Silently and serenely" describes the ineffability of the undiscriminating mind, the condition of no-mind in which there is no subject and no object. At the same time, the words, "Vividly and clearly, things appear of themselves," tell us that this undiscriminating mind is not frozen in a deadened silence. There is no subjective thought of selfhood, yet things and knowing are ever-present. Wisdom functions freely, even though there is no one who possesses or directs it. There is no concept of "my wisdom." This is not the clarity experienced by ordinary people, which is contaminated by discriminatory attachment. This is the clarity of things as perceived by prajñā wisdom—as they are, in and of themselves.

This outline of the different stages and experiences of silent illumination may seem quite formulaic. However, it is important to realize that we construct it in order to explain the dynamics of the practice, not to imply that there is a hard and fast rule of progression from one stage to the next. In actual practice the order and delineation of the various stages may not be that clearly defined. Moreover, responses to the practice will vary considerably from one meditator to the next. The important thing is not to hanker after specific experiences, but to understand the principles behind this practice so that you may learn to apply it properly, to the best of your ability.

MISCELLANEOUS QUESTIONS ON THE PRACTICE
OF SILENT ILLUMINATION

Students inevitably have many questions about silent illumination, especially since it seems so different from *gong'an* and *huatou* practice. For clarification, some of the more common queries as well as my answers have been included here.

Question: What is the difference between Mahāyāna and Hīnayāna samādhis, and how might this difference relate to silent illumination?

Answer: The principal difference between the two kinds of samādhi is that time, space, the external environment, and mental activities disappear in the deeper Hīnayāna samādhis, whereas in true Mahāyāna samādhi, all of these—except defiled mental activities—remain. For example, a person experiencing deep Mahāyāna samādhi could converse or discourse lucidly. Because the mind is eternally still, one would respond without any mentation at all. The Hīnayāna meditator, however, would experience mental activity and affliction whenever he or she departed from samādhi. These two types of responses—that with defiled mentation and affliction, and that without—are known as "natural response" and "response characterized by mental discrimination or discursiveness." To distinguish between the two is very difficult.

Although the gradual samādhi methods common to the Hīnayāna and elementary Mahāyāna teachings (this may be said of the meditations of non-Buddhist teachings as well) cannot themselves provide access to Chan or genuine Mahāyāna samādhi, the accomplished meditator using silent illumination can indeed enter deep stages of Hīnayāna samādhi, such as the four formless *samāpatti* of infinite consciousness, infinite space, and so forth. However, the novice or less advanced practitioner of silent illumination will likely not be able to enter the deepest stages of Hīnayāna and Mahāyāna samādhi. This is due to the aspect of illumination in Chan silent illumination practice. If silent illumination comprised only the aspect of silencing the mind, attainment of deep stages of Hīnayāna dhyāna and *samāpatti* would be more readily possible. But since the element of illumination detracts from deep meditative absorption, most practitioners of silent illumination cannot enter these states.

Question: What are the differences in the practice and relative efficacy of silent illumination and *huatou* Chan?

Answer: Both are capable of leading to complete enlightenment, and both are sudden methods insofar as neither deliberately sets up cultivation of samādhi as an expedient for reaching this goal. However, the two approaches are in one respect opposite in character. In *huatou* practice, as we know, the meditator must experience great doubt and the world-shattering explosion in order to reach Chan. This is known as the passage from great death to great birth. In silent illumination practice, however, emphasis is directed to what we call *xiuxi*, or "directly desisting and putting to rest." Great death and great birth are only experienced when one cultivates the feeling of doubt to the point where it results in an all-consuming explosion. This is an energetic, forceful form of practice that draws together and exponentially feeds on all of our doubts and passions. Cultivation of silent illumination is opposite in character, since it does not require doubt, but, rather, profound tranquillity, clarity, and immediate mindfulness. Herein lies the outstanding dissimilarity between the two methods. Indeed, since in silent illumination Chan there is no extraordinary experience to use as an index of progress, it is very difficult to judge its correctness and efficacy. This leaves the practitioner of silent illumination open to various points of error to which one involved in *huatou* practice may not be prone.

Question: The idea of silence seems to imply that mind is absorbed in one point or one thought, thereby ignoring or forgetting the surroundings. On the other hand, illumination sounds just the opposite—as though mind is allowed to diffuse actively through the external environment. How can both be so?

Answer: It is misleading to say that silence, in this instance, means that mind reduces itself to or settles fixedly on one point. Actually, it means that, from moment to moment, nothing is retained in one's mind. The mind does not seize on anything; nor does it discriminate or evolve thoughts about anything. In this respect, it is utterly settled and silent. When speaking of illumination, it is all right to say that mind diffuses universally through the surrounding environment, but this does not mean that it is making distinctions or discursively reflecting on the environment. It diffuses fluidly, but it does not seize or dwell on any features.

Furthermore, we should make a distinction between silent illumination as a technique or model of practice to which one strives to conform, and the actual experience of it as Chan. When you are practicing silent illumination, you are mentally keen and clear, but you also drop all discursive involvement with the surrounding environment. Yet, once the practice of silent illumination really matures, it is quite possible to carry on all aspects of daily life and active involvement in the world without impeding this clarity and calm. In fact, you will still not discriminate. Nonetheless, if I point at an object and ask what it is, you will freely and easily tell me. This is because, when one has perfected silent illumination, wisdom actively functions and responds without ever departing from the quiescence of samādhi. In technical Buddhist terminology, this kind of experience, where samādhi and wisdom are perfectly simultaneous, is known as "supramundane samādhi of the Mahāyāna." It is qualitatively different from the mundane samādhi of one-pointed absorption in a single thought or feature. Better yet, it is just Chan, for the Chan school does not make such distinctions.

Question: Is it better not to mix or switch back and forth between silent illumination and *huatou* practice?

Answer: Because they represent two different attitudes—*huatou* quite intense and active, silent illumination more passive—usually these two methods are not intermingled.

Question: What about using each of the two for long stretches of time, one method for a few years, then the other?

Answer: In the past there was no such example, but lately I have been thinking of trying this.

Question: Why was this never done before, and why are you contemplating doing it now?

Answer: People of the past just stuck to one method. They did not want to run the risk of distracting themselves and their disciples, or losing momentum in their practice by switching techniques prematurely. I am thinking of teaching both because people of the past who used one method tended arbitrarily to discredit the other, without having any firsthand experience of it. I tend to be more open-minded about this and feel that both methods have their strong points. For example, one might begin with *huatou* and take up silent illumination later, after one has acquired a taste of Chan. Actually, during the Tang Dynasty—the formative period of Chan—these approaches may not have been so separate. It was only with the emergence of the specific houses of Chan during the Song Period that they became distinct traditions of practice.

Question: Are there any clear indicators that a disciple would do better with one method than the other?

Answer: Yes, there are. If one can effectively calm the mind and let go of thoughts from the start, one may well begin with silent illumination. But if one's mind does not possess this sort of inherent stability, it would be better to use a *huatou.* Then again, if a beginner takes up a *huatou* and is able to concentrate well, but over time is unable to build up great doubt and so runs out of steam, I may have him or her use silent illumination. Actually, there are no rigid formulas. If there were, it would not be Chan.

Question: Can you tell us something about the use of silent illumination and *huatou* in everyday lay life, as opposed to being on a retreat or in a monastic lifestyle?

Answer: When people used silent illumination in the past, they normally tried to attend to their practice all day long. This was possible because life then was a lot simpler and slower-paced. If you have a full-time job, you can't really use this method, because silent illumination requires one to minimize discursive thinking and simply observe. Thus, at best you can only do it in the morning and evening when you sit at home.

As for *huatou*, again, you can't really apply this method when you are on the job. You can still use it for morning and evening meditations, but you will never generate the intense energy that you would on a retreat. This is an important difference, because with *huatou*, it is very important to put all your energy into your practice. It is a very intense practice. Silent illumination is intense and demanding in a different way. In the practice of silent illumination, you try to completely let go of yourself. It is basically a very "loose" method. Beginners might have to exert a lot of energy and use silent illumination in a "tight" or "tense" way in order to settle their minds. But as they become adept at sitting, it isn't done intensely.

Question: Why do you so often have students use the methods of counting or following the breath as a prelude to using *huatou* and silent illumination?

Answer: Of the Five Methods for Stilling or Stopping the Mind, in ancient times the two techniques of meditation on impurity and meditation on the breathing were used most often. During the day of Śākyamuni Buddha, they were called *amṛta*, or "ambrosia," because they were so effective for concentrating the mind. Basically, I teach counting the breath in order to help students calm the mind. If one's mind is scattered—which is a common problem these days—this method will be very beneficial. After a student has made some progress, I might assign contemplation of loving-kindness and compassion or contemplation of impurity if anger or lust excessively plagues him or her. Desire for sex, food, sleep, comfort, and so forth, are closely tied to the body. Thus, meditation on the impurity and repulsiveness of the body is an effective antidote. But, for the most part, these will be exceptional cases. Actually, it is best to proceed directly on the path of Chan.

9

Prerequisites for Chan Practice

GENERAL PRECONDITIONS FOR THE SUDDEN PATH OF CHAN

The Chinese term for practicing Chan is *canchan*, which means to investigate, engage, or dig into *(can)* the heart or living enlightenment of the Chan/Zen tradition *(chan)*. It is often said in Chan that the door to Chan is "no door," the method of Chan is "no method," and the practice of Chan is "no practice." There is a famous story about master Nanyue Huairang (677–744) and his student, Mazu Daoyi. Upon finding Mazu Daoyi sitting intently in meditation, Nanyue Huairang picked up a piece of tile and began grinding it with a stone just outside Mazu's hut. Mazu, somewhat annoyed, asked, "Why are you doing this?"

Nanyue Huairang replied, "I am polishing the tile to make a mirror out of it."

In ancient times, mirrors were made of bronze and had to be regularly polished so that they would reflect. Mazu said, "That's ridiculous, you can't make a mirror by polishing a piece of tile."

To which Nanyue Huairang retorted sharply, "If you can't make a mirror by polishing a tile, how can you possibly become a Buddha by sitting in meditation?"[1]

On another occasion, Linji Yixuan was sleeping soundly at the rear of the meditation hall, while the head monk sat sternly in meditation at the front of the hall. Master Huangbo came in and lightly tapped Linji's meditation platform with his staff. For a moment Linji opened his eyes, looked up, and then went right back to sleep. Huangbo tapped the platform again and walked off. When he came to the head of the hall and saw the head monk meditating intently, he struck him a blow and said, "What do you think you are doing with all your deluded thoughts? That man back there at the rear of the hall is the one who is really meditating."[2]

Linji himself used to teach that one should make no artificial effort in practice, but "simply be an ordinary person with nothing to do." Mazu Daoyi often
taught that "the ordinary everyday mind is the Way." Dazhu Huihai, a disciple
of Mazu Daoyi, is recorded as having asserted that our mind is the same as Buddha. Therefore, for our mind to seek the Buddha is as unnecessary as the Buddha seeking for the Buddha. Likewise, our mind is identical with the Dharma.
To use our mind to seek the Dharma is like the Dharma seeking the Dharma—
also unnecessary. Buddha, mind, and sentient being are not different. There is
no Buddha outside of the mind, no Dharma outside of the mind, and no sentient beings outside of the mind.

When we read discourses on Chan like these, it seems that the Buddhist tradition of the Three Disciplines—purity in observance of precepts of the vinaya,
cultivation of samādhi, and wisdom through meditation—has been turned on
its head. Does Chan really involve no practice or no discipline of any kind whatsoever? Yes, in certain respects Chan truly requires no learning, no practice, no
effort whatsoever. If it did depend on such things, it would not be Chan. But
we are very active, and addicted to artifice, and have far too many things to do.
We must have discipline to help us put an end to these habits. For this reason
it is not entirely correct to say that Chan involves no practice. There are indeed
principles that must be followed.

Shenhui, a disciple of the sixth patriarch, Huineng, said that the precepts
must be used to discipline one's actions. Likewise, recitation of Buddhist
sūtras—especially the *Diamond Sūtra*—and cultivation of samādhi should be used
to eliminate defilements and calm our restless minds. Only then will the wisdom
of no-thought that is inherent in one's original nature truly manifest.

Virtually all the major Chan masters and their followers observed the traditional Hīnayāna precepts of the renunciant and the Mahāyāna bodhisattva precepts. There have been famous household practitioners of Chan, such as Pang
Yun (Layman Pang) and his family, but even though such persons' experiences
might have been quite deep, most never had much impact as teachers of Chan.
Because they were laymen, their sphere of influence tended to be limited, and
major communities of practitioners did not develop around them.

Also, we have examples of Chan masters who deliberately broke the Buddhist
precepts. However, the most celebrated examples of this sort—such as Nanquan's killing of the cat and Danxia's burning of a statue of the Buddha to keep
warm—are all isolated incidents, not regular occurrences. What is more, when
one examines these events carefully, one finds that the actions of these masters
were primarily didactic—intended to make a point to their students, not to fulfill a personal whim. All in all, there are very few examples of influential Chan
masters who made a regular practice of going against the precepts, and fewer
still who advocated that their students engage in such behavior.

To receive either the precepts of a novice or a full renunciant has always been
a minimum requirement for residence in a saṅgha or practice hall of a Chan

community. Thus, in most Chinese Chan temples, the traditional Buddhist monastic precepts were strictly enforced. As Chan grew in popularity during Tang and Song Period China, eminent teachers such as Baizhang Huaihai developed additional codes for a comprehensive system of discipline and daily procedure better suited to the training of monks in large monastic centers. These rules, known as *qinggui*, or "pure rules," supplemented but did not replace the original renunciatory precepts. In fact, moral restraints, strict community routine, collective worship, seated meditation, and regular discourses by and interviews with the Chan master are all essential features of the program described in the pure rules.

What, then, are we to make of the assertion that "practice is no practice" or the sort of iconoclastic examples that we cited above? These sorts of teachings have real significance only for persons who have been immersed in the institutions of Chan training for a long time, or else persons of very unusual capacity. Indeed, Huairang's grinding of the tile had such a profound impact on Mazu only because Mazu had already dedicated so much time and effort to meditation. To any other person they might prove meaningless, if not downright misleading. For this reason, such stories—no matter how frivolous they may sound—must always be viewed within the solemn context of Chan training. To do otherwise is to seriously misrepresent Chan teaching.

There is a famous story about the Central Asian master, Kumārajīva, one of the greatest translators and scholars of Buddhism that China ever knew. Kumārajīva so impressed the Chinese sovereign that the latter forced him to take several mistresses out of the hope that he would produce an heir. Thus, in order to continue his teaching activities, Kumārajīva was compelled to break the precept of celibacy. His disciples asked him if they might take mistresses as well. In response, he swallowed a bowl of needles and, without showing any sign of injury, emitted them back out through his pores. "If you can do the same," he told his followers, "you may take mistresses too."

Then he went on to illustrate for his students the proper attitude that they should have toward his moral lapse. The beautiful lotus blossom grows from putrid muck, but it is the blossom itself that we prize, not the filth. That is to say, even though one may be forced by circumstance to defile the precepts, it is purity that one should continue to prize. Those who are unable to control themselves should keep the precepts and fix their gaze on positive spiritual qualities. In the case of saints like Kumārajīva, who have realized liberation, the precepts are indeed irrelevant, for their minds are pure and are no longer afflicted by the passions. Needless to say, this does not mean that they will wallow in the muck without restraint. Quite the contrary, purity and liberation are still the supreme goal, but it is purification and liberation of others that is the focus now. Circumstances may warrant going against the precepts, but purity and liberation will still be the main concern. The necessary course of action will be chosen out of clear deliberation and motivated out of compassion rather than personal desire.

The idea that there must be certain preconditions for effective practice of Chan is really no different from the original Buddhist teaching of the three disciplines of moral restraint, samādhi, and wisdom. When the activity, or karma, of body, speech, and mind is pure, the Three Jewels of Buddha, dharma, and saṅgha are fully manifest. The genuine Three Jewels, in essence, are none other than the enlightened Buddha-nature that is already inside you. They are fully manifest only when the three kinds of karma, or deed, are purified. To purify the three activities of body, speech, and mind, one must accord with the precepts and calm and clarify the mind through disciplined cultivation of meditation. Indeed, when the three deeds are pure, you, the Three Jewels, everything, are a single totality. If any one of the three deeds is impure, you will no longer be in touch with the living reality of the Three Jewels. The world will appear defiled, Buddha will have long ago entered nirvāṇa, the dharma will be empty words and paper, and the saṅgha will be nowhere to be seen. Thus, when the basic conditions of the three disciplines have been properly met and one's practice has matured, the real import of the Chan aphorism that "practice is no practice" and the examples of Nanyue Huairang and Linji will come to life.

*The Platform Sūtra of the Sixth Patriarch
and the Meaning of the Three Disciplines*

This curious attitude that Chan is "no practice" yet at the same time entails practice is illustrated quite well in the *Platform Sūtra* of the sixth patriarch, Huineng. While it is questionable whether this scripture reflects the original teachings of Huineng, it has always been regarded highly in the Chan tradition, and its message is significant.

The *Platform Sūtra* falls roughly into four sections, each dealing with a particular aspect of practice:

1. Liberating wisdom, or insight (prajñā)
2. The relationship of samādhi to wisdom
3. The practice of seated meditation (*zuochan*)
4. Repentance of past evils and receipt of the bodhisattva precepts

According to our usual understanding of the Buddhist path, the order of these sections seems reversed. In the gradual scheme of practice, one would begin with repentance of sins and cultivation of the precepts (i.e., moral purity), then proceed to seated meditation. Finally, through dual cultivation of meditative calming (S. *śamatha*; C. *zhi*) and contemplation (S. *vipaśyanā*; C. *guan*), samādhi and wisdom are developed, and one arrives at full illumination. However, the approach to practice espoused by the Chan school dispenses with all conditioned views and expedients, and advocates direct identification with the enlightened nature of mind and the world, just as it is: there is no delusion to remove, no enlightenment to attain.

However, only people of unusually keen capacity can accomplish this right off. It is impossible for those with heavy karmic obstructions to achieve this without preparation and practice. Thus, persons with such obstructions must first engage in repentance, receive the precepts, engage in active cultivation of samādhi and wisdom, and so forth. This sequence of steps is reversed in the *Platform Sūtra* because Chan fundamentally emphasizes "no method." The practitioner must not mistake the preparatory conditions for Chan itself, but take them up only as they are needed. In a sense, the more one becomes involved with such preconditions, the more one risks straying from the real spirit of Chan. For this reason, whenever Huineng discusses such things as practice of precepts, vows, repentance, meditation, and so forth, he takes great care to interpret them from a point of view that is in keeping with the "methodless method" of Chan.

In its treatment of the precepts, for example, the *Platform Sūtra* emphasizes the realm of the mind rather than that of the body. Thus, only when there are no wrong thoughts—no deluded thinking whatsoever—is one truly acting in accordance with the precepts. Clearly, it is easier to abstain from wrong actions than from wrong thought. Actions and words are more easily perceived by others and more easily controlled. It is for this reason that Buddhist practice usually begins with the effort to purify physical actions through moral restraint and repentance, then proceeds to disciplining the mind with meditation. If the mind is already pure, however, actions and speech themselves immediately become pure.

It is rare that the mind is pure when the actions are not. There have been occasions in which evil kings or prostitutes have been exceedingly pure in mind while engaging in opprobrious conduct. In reality, however, these people were none other than bodhisattvas who had incarnated in various guises in order to help other beings. They did not act out of compulsive and self-centered urges, but solely in response to the spiritual needs of others. Such highly developed bodhisattvas are exceptions to the rule. Ordinary persons must keep the precepts. The refuges, repentance, and sitting in meditation are discussed in much the same way in the *Platform Sūtra*. "Taking refuge" means to take refuge in the Three Jewels of the Buddha, Dharma, and saṅgha that are already within you, not in Three Jewels conceived as existing elsewhere. Likewise, repentance is "formless," not a repentance that involves the confession and forswearing of specific evil infractions. It simply means not to be tainted by deluded thoughts and actions by identifying directly with one's enlightened self-nature. To sit in meditation is to perceive one's true nature and externally be free of all impediments.

Practicing Chan in the Modern Day

Over the centuries, Chan has been practiced primarily by nuns and monks— that is to say, persons who have left the household life and formally embraced the precepts of a Buddhist renunciant. Although laypersons have certainly pursued Chan practice, those who did so often followed the monastic precepts.

Within the past century, however, the balance of practitioners has shifted from monastics to laypeople. Moreover, when the Chan tradition moved to the West, the characteristics of the practitioner changed further. Americans often approach Chan with the attitude of a dilettante, practicing only for a few days, months, or years, usually with the idea of just getting some experience or seeing what it is like. The majority do not commit their whole lives to the practice as people used to do. We can thus say that Americans, for the most part, do not practice Chan "professionally." At least in Japan, Chan practice remains a full-time commitment, even though it has moved away from the emphasis on monasticism. Thus, it is unfortunate—but true—that Chan has undergone a steady dilution as it has moved from China to Japan to America. Indeed, in China, the criterion of enlightenment was exceptionally difficult to meet. In present-day Japan it is easier, and for Americans the standard is lower still. This reduction in standards corresponds directly to the deterioration of the rigor and depth of attainment in practice. Although it is disheartening and sorrowful, the lowering of standards may provide consolation to those engaging in temporary practice, especially in a culture to which Chan is itself alien.

Irrespective of this general decline, there are minimum requirements which, in any country or at any time, must be considered foundational to any practice of Chan. The most basic are those regulating the body; that is to say, moral restraints and physical posture. Next in order of significance are those requirements which harmonize and unify body with the breath, and breath with the mind, thereby leading to the one-pointed power of samādhi.

The preconditions pertaining to the body may be further distinguished as follows: (1) conditions to be observed prior to sitting in meditation; (2) conditions to be observed during sitting; and (3) conditions to be observed while engaging in activities other than sitting (e.g., walking, standing, lying down, eating, speaking, and miscellaneous actions).

First, one must have very regular habits of eating. One should not eat too much or allow oneself to become too weak and famished. One should not take too much of any substance that stimulates the body—especially drugs—for this can have a detrimental impact on meditation and health. To practice well, the body must be vigorous and the mind, keen and clear. Thus, it is important to pay careful attention to the kinds and quantities of the things that one eats and drinks, as well as the way in which these things are taken.

Work and rest must also be routine and well regulated. Regular hours are best, and one should refrain from exerting oneself to the point of strain or exhaustion. On the other hand, it is just as damaging to do no work at all. Physical exercise and exertion are necessary for maintaining the health of the body.

Sexual relations between couples are necessary and normal for laypersons, but one should contain these activities. Love between couples should not be grounded merely on the physical relationship, but should be based on mutual vision and consideration. If one has sex too often, it will be extremely difficult to develop deep samādhi.

Talking and socializing should be restrained. One is inevitably distracted by chatting with or listening to others. Most of the time, topics of discussion are not very meaningful, especially if one is given to chitchat. This kind of flightiness and distraction can become a terrible hindrance to samādhi. If the mind rushes out through the ears and mouth whenever people come around or thoughts come into the head, how can one possibly make progress with meditation and gain power from the practice of Chan?

The powerful forces of craving and hatred constantly agitate the mind. Although hatred comes and goes intermittently, greed and craving are with us every minute, whether it be in the form of desire for fame, wealth, sensual experience, love, beauty, and the like. If the mind is overstimulated by an excess of the objects of our desire or distraught over their absence, it cannot become calm and settled. If the mind cannot become calm, it will not become clear, and successful practice of Chan will be impossible. Hence, practitioners must constantly remind themselves to let go of their attachments and desires. By preserving a simple environment and reducing desires, the mind will become steadily more calm, concentrated, and clear. This is quite important.

BUDDHIST PRECEPTS AND THE PATHS
FOR THE RENUNCIANT AND LAYPERSON

There has been a continuing history of lay practitioners in the Chan school. Most great Chan masters have had serious lay disciples, both male and female. Some of these disciples were so accomplished in their practice that their deeds and sayings were recorded, much in the same manner as the sayings of the great monastic Chan masters.

In the Chinese Buddhist canon, there is a biographical compendium dedicated to exemplary lay practitioners entitled *Record of Laypersons who Shared in the Lamp*.[3] The Ven. Fu Dashi is perhaps the earliest and best known among this group, although others, such as the famous Tang Period layman, Pangyun, also gained considerable renown. All of these individuals were famed for dedicating their lives to the practice of Chan. Their practice and their attainments rivaled those of the great Chan masters, even though they were householders. Yet, lay practitioners never started lineages or left disciples as the monastic Chan masters did. While certain lay practitioners drank deeply from the stream of Chan and provided indispensable support for Chan monasteries, historically, monks and nuns have been the ones who perpetuated the Chan teaching.

Of course, this may be due in part to the nature of Chinese society and Buddhist institutions in the premodern period. At the same time, however, householders are burdened with responsibilities and circumstances that naturally detract from effective training of oneself, not to mention guiding disciples in their practice. With ties to the secular world, lay practitioners must maintain occupations and responsibilities. To support themselves, farmers still must work the farm; urban workers must hold jobs; bureaucrats must fulfill their duties to the office. Family, friends, and society at large hold laypeople to certain expectations, while laypeople, in turn, feel strong ties of responsibility toward duties and others. These are the non-negotiable conditions of living the life of a householder.

While remaining in the world and being fully attentive to its obligations, laypeople intent on the practice of Chan must define the goals and priorities of life in a very different manner from that of the ordinary person. Outwardly, serious lay practitioners lead the most normal and worldly of lives, but inwardly their sole concern is the practice of Buddha Dharma. Apart from the usual concerns for family and obligations to society, their personal desires are few and they concern themselves only with the minimum activities necessary to keep life going.

Persons who value career more than practice will doubtlessly take a different stance. Extraneous desires and involvements will overcome all else, and there will never be adequate time for practice. This is a common lament of laypersons everywhere: "Shifu, I just can't find the time to practice. I'm too busy." The problem, however, is not really distracting circumstances. It is simply one of priority and determination. When one truly cares for the practice above all else, one will find the time and energy to pursue it. Practice is not just a part of life, but its very core. Every facet of life is practice for a serious layperson. Such an attitude is absolutely necessary for serious practice, regardless of whether one is a renunciant or a layperson.

In terms of daily practice, lay practitioners should strive to live a life of moral restraint and set up a daily routine, just as a renunciant might do. They should observe the five precepts and try to restrain sexual and sensory passion, so that they may establish a calm, honest, and stable life. Specific times of the day should be set aside for practicing meditation, reading or reciting the sūtras, and venerating the Three Jewels. In monasteries and established centers for teaching Chan, daily services for worship of the Three Jewels are held before the morning and evening meals. Periods of meditation are set aside in the morning (before the morning service) and before going to bed at night. When more time is available—weekends or vacations—it is good to visit Buddhist centers in order to hear the Dharma, consult with teachers, or attend meditation retreats. Our center in the United States and temples in Taiwan hold regular day-long sittings as well as offer ceremonies and Dharma-talks on weekends. Eight times a year we hold intensive weeklong Chan meditation retreats. These are open to both monks and laypersons. It is very helpful to involve oneself regularly in community activities such as these, for it will support one's practice in ways that are very difficult to develop and maintain on one's own. Establishing a relationship with a qualified Chan master is especially essential to developing a genuine practice.

In addition to those periods of time dedicated specifically to Buddhist practice, a serious layperson will still try to carry his or her practice into the job. Once someone asked me if it was possible to recite the Buddha's name or meditate while at work. I said that he certainly could try to do so. However, I also warned him that he would either be reciting the Buddha's name wholeheartedly or working wholeheartedly. It is very difficult to combine both; and, if one does not concentrate on one's work, serious problems may arise. In order to maintain practice while working, it is best to just engage the work at hand with one's full attention—make it one's meditation, so to speak—and not try to substitute something else as a focus for concentration. When the work is done and the time comes for one's usual form of practice, forget your work and do the practice wholeheartedly. In this manner, it is possible to forget the past, forget the future, and develop single-mindedness in the midst of the activity at hand. But still, for most people engaged in lay life, this degree of concentration is very difficult to achieve.

What about the requirements for a Buddhist monk or nun practicing Chan? In order to become a good monk or nun, one must have previously been a good layperson. This provides a necessary foundation. Becoming a renunciant is just a natural extension of it. When Huineng first met the fifth patriarch, he was still a layman. He was even still a layman after he received the dharma-transmission from the fifth patriarch. Why did he later become a monk? Tradition of the day believed that the highest level of practice could only be attained by someone who had permanently renounced the household life as a monk or nun. What is more, as we noted previously, the condition of a lay practitioner is not very conducive to spreading and perpetuating the Buddhist Dharma, especially Chan. The first requirement of the Buddhist renunciant is that he or she be free of all attachments. In Chinese tradition, the word for becoming a Buddhist renunciant literally means to "leave the household." Renunciants themselves are referred to as "those who have left the home" (chujia ren). The home is commonly understood to include family, property, and social position. But there is more to it than that. One who has genuinely left home must be willing to renounce everything—to expect nothing, seek nothing, abide in nothing, even their very bodies and selves. This condition is graphically symbolized by shaving the head, changing the secular name for a religious name, and renouncing all possessions except for a set of robes to cover the body and a begging bowl to receive alms.

Of course, even though they leave the secular household, there are some renunciants who take the monastery as their home, the master as their father, and their companions in dharma as brothers and sisters. In a more subtle sense, there are many renunciants who also take their delusions and bad habits as their home. This is not the correct attitude at all. One must be unattached to any kind of family and monastery, and, ultimately, not dwell in anything at all. When it is embraced with the right attitude, the material and spiritual poverty of someone who has left home will facilitate the renunciation of greed and attachment. Only when there is no greed and attachment can there be significant progress in Chan practice.

The second requirement for the Buddhist monk or nun is to hold strictly to the Buddhist moral and monastic precepts. As these have been described earlier, I will not repeat them here. Finally, renunciants must be willing to give themselves entirely to the practice, never once relaxing their efforts or begrudging life and limb. This is the third and final requirement. It is difficult for laypersons to meet this ideal. Most laypeople practice intensively only when they come to the temple or meditation center. Thus, their practice is, at best, irregular. Even very serious lay practitioners who strive to practice throughout their working day cannot usually put all of their effort at all times into the practice. They have numerous other considerations, such as their livelihood, families, and so forth, which distract them from this end. Because Buddhist monks and nuns have renounced all belongings and all thought of past or future, they are not confronted by these sorts of obstacles. Since they have no attachments of this sort, they are able to keep their minds continually on the practice. For them, there is no need to compartmentalize their lives or their time. For a monk, there is no consideration of setting aside time for the private life or pursuit of personal desires. There is no such thing as "free time" or "vacation" from the "work" of practice. Practice is life; life is practice.

Śākyamuni Buddha used to tell his monastic disciples to touch their bald heads whenever they felt disheartened about the monastic path. In this way, they would be reminded that they were different from laypeople. Chan masters of the past often admonished their disciples by saying, "You should practice as if your parents had just died." Great masters before their enlightenment always felt that life meant nothing outside of their practice. Some would think, "If the practice is not resolved in this life, there is nothing else left for me to do. I might as well be dead. If I sleep, I will never be able to sleep well. If I eat, I will never be able to enjoy my food. If I do not come to full understanding, I will never be able to relax, for, in whatever I do, unresolved questions will always torment my mind. Thus, practice is the only recourse that I have."

Linji Yixuan used to say that there is nothing more painful, nothing more agonizing, than a monk who has set out to practice Chan but does not yet know the peace of enlightenment. Those who can appreciate this attitude will, without question, make strong progress. There are other people, however, who after practicing feel that it would be nice just to relax in a bath or go on a nice vacation. They may possibly benefit from their limited practice, but becoming profoundly enlightened is for them quite difficult, if not impossible.

The Institution of the Chan Retreat

If, in the long term, the renunciatory lifestyle of the Buddhist cleric is the most conducive to effective practice and effective teaching of Chan, the institution of the Chan retreat affords laity and clergy alike an invaluable opportunity to advance their skills. Although the veracity of the claim has been questioned, the

Tang Period master Baizhang Huaihai is said to have created the distinctive Chan institution of the saṅgha hall (*sengtang*), in which aspiring Chan monks collectively ate, slept, and meditated in order to devote themselves single-mindedly to Chan practice. Certainly, during the Song Period, the saṅgha hall was a feature ubiquitous to the large public Chan monasteries, and itinerant monks or nuns could enroll there for three-month sessions—the usual length of the scheduled semesters of training.

Later, this arrangement was modified into that of the Chan hall, or *chantang*, a structure that was dedicated to nothing but intensive round-the-clock seated and walking meditation—again, usually fixed to three-month intervals. The precincts of the Chan hall were carefully guarded from disruptions by outside activities or intrusions of personnel from other sectors of the monastery.[4] Their regimen and decorum was also quite strict, designed in such a way as to institutionalize the optimum conditions for Chan practice. Chan Master Laiguo, an eminent contemporary of master Xuyun, or Empty Cloud, once remarked that the strict procedures of the Chan hall played two important roles in his own practice: one was to provide a foundational routine that enabled himself, as a practitioner, to awaken to the mind and see his true nature; the other, to instill in him the self-discipline and sense of responsibility necessary to be an effective example to others.[5]

In premodern China, there was a fairly rigid separation between monastic saṅgha and the laity, their respective activities and roles being quite different. This meant that there was not a lot of opportunity for laity to take part in the life of intensive meditation that typified the monastery Chan hall. In more recent times the situation changed considerably, mainly due to the popularization of the *chanqi*, or "seven-day Chan retreat," as a medium of combined lay and monastic practice. The institution of the seven-day Chan retreat is often thought of as a Japanese phenomenon, largely because of the current popularity of the *sesshin* in the West; but in China it has a long history that goes at least back to the Ming Dynasty (1368–1644). Although it is unclear just when and under what circumstances laity came to be included in these retreats, today their participation alongside of the clergy is a normal state of affairs. In this respect, the intensive seven-day Chan retreat—the routines of which are largely the same as those traditionally used in the monastery Chan hall—affords laity the opportunity to add a dimension of intensified training to their lives that would, otherwise, be the reserve of the professional monastic.

Why a fixed period of seven days? Buddhist retreats are often measured in units of seven days, with full, half, or dark moon days used to mark the beginning of the cycle. Thus, we hear of retreats in China lasting for fixed periods of one week, three weeks, seven weeks, and so forth. The reason for this lies in the general need to attune the practice and the body to the larger rhythm of the natural environment. But in addition to this consideration, seven days is also the minimum length of time necessary for the practice—intensively applied—to have its desired effect. I generally do not hold retreats shorter than seven days, because they amount to little more than dress rehearsals: a weekend or three-day session is simply insufficient to develop the concentration necessary for the method to work its transformative influence.

Between our monasteries in Taiwan and our center in New York, I lead some eight retreats a year, four in each location. Over the course of these seven-day retreats, participants will take communal meals twice a day, in the early morning and at noon. An informal meal, which is literally called "medicine," is provided in the early evening for those who feel the need to replenish their energy or soothe their empty stomachs. The day begins at 4:00 A.M. with exercises, a short dharma-talk, and a period of seated meditation. This is followed by a morning worship service, the morning meal, a period of community work, and four hours of seated and walking meditation. More recently, I have added ritual prostrations to this cycle. The noon meal, which includes a short offering service, divides the morning from the afternoon sequence. The meal is followed by another period of community work, as well as another four-hour stretch of seated meditation, walking meditation, and prostrations. Then come an evening worship service, the evening meal, and a short period of rest or voluntary meditation. The evening concludes with a formal Dharma-talk, followed by an hour or more of seated meditation. The evening boards (signaling lights out) are sounded at ten o'clock. Except for those individuals who choose to continue their practice in the meditation hall, all others retire to their designated spots to rest. Everyone sleeps on the floor.

Just as with the Buddhist monk or nun, participants are required to leave all worldly concerns and attachments at the door—to forget the past, to not think of the future, and to put every ounce of energy into the practice, as if they were going to die tomorrow. Only belongings essential for daily hygiene are allowed. Bathing is permitted but not encouraged, and the reading of books or the use of radios, tape players, televisions, and other media of entertainment are forbidden. Private interviews are held at least once a day, during which students may consult with me about their practice. Otherwise, talking is prohibited, except as is necessary to fulfill specific duties. The sounding of bells or clapping of boards is used to signal all major procedures. In every way possible, the Chan retreat strives to instill an effective use of the assigned method of practice. To this end, I myself typically sit with the students in the meditation hall so that I may personally direct their efforts.

INTERNAL PREREQUISITES: FOUR MENTAL CONDITIONS ESSENTIAL
FOR PROGRESS IN CHAN

Once the external conditions and routines for Chan practice have been established, there is still the question of how the practice should be pursued. What is the optimal disposition for entering retreat? Should one be anxious or relaxed? Should one feel contrite or optimistic? Should one set one's thoughts on Chan enlightenment or not? And, if so, how? Should one start by being easy on oneself and then intensify one's efforts? Should one maintain the same intensity all the way through the retreat? Like fine-tuning a stringed instrument, there are certain mental and emotional "settings" that are optimal for extended periods of practice. These do not bear so much on correct and incorrect use of a particular method of meditation, such as *huatou* or silent illumination, but on the general tenor with which retreat practice, as a whole, should be pursued. If these conditions are met, it will be possible to realize the highest aims of Chan, regardless of the technique that you are using. Short of this, the path will be uncertain and progress will be difficult.

Although we also speak of these mental conditions as a prerequisite for Chan practice, I must stress that they are not something that can be handed to you by way of simple description. Like riding a bike or balancing on a beam, they are an art that unfolds only with ongoing training. When one begins to practice, if one's goals are sound and one is conscientious, the proper conditions will in time arise naturally out of one's practice. For some, this may happen quickly; for others, more slowly—it depends on the disposition of the individual meditator.

Whatever the case may be, it is essential that one not deliberately anticipate or seek to produce these conditions by artificial effort. That will just add further obstruction to your progress. For this reason, at the beginning of a retreat I will generally not mention these requirements. More often, I will work directly with the retreatants in order to help them discover these optimal conditions for themselves. Only when I see that people are in the proper condition to investigate Chan will I talk about them openly.

This is the way things were done traditionally in Chinese Chan monasteries. Very little instruction of any kind was given. So why talk about these preconditions here? It is fine to be silent when right practice is abundantly evident in the people and institutions around you, but not when those traditions are being lost and misunderstanding is rife. I discuss them here to give you some sense of orientation to the Chan path. Just bear in mind that you may read this description or hear these conditions discussed a thousand times; but until you really know what it feels like to be in the condition of right practice you will still have no idea what I am talking about.

Altogether we specify four conditions that are necessary for effective Chan practice. The first is great faith, or confidence; the second is great vows; the third is angry, or resolute, determination; the fourth is great doubt. In effect, these dispositions arise and build on one another in cumulative fashion. Great faith always arises first, followed by great vows and, then, great determination. When there is fierce resolve, it is then possible to generate great doubt. Moreover, only when there is great faith is it possible to have great doubt. Great faith is faith in the teaching of the Buddhist Dharma—that all beings have Buddha-nature.

Great doubt is the compelling need to experience this teaching directly, in truth. Without great faith one will be incapable of making great vows. Without great vows, how can one practice with one's whole being? And if one cannot do that, great determination cannot possibly arise. Therefore, these four conditions do not come into being in haphazard fashion; they do so in an orderly developmental sequence.

Great Faith

The word "faith" has a particular meaning in Western contexts that differs from the way we use it in reference to Chan. The original Chinese term *xin*, which we render here as "faith," has the general sense of "faith," "trust," "belief," or "confidence." In Chan and other Buddhist contexts, *xin* is often combined with the word *jie* ("to understand," "explain," or "comprehend") to make the compound *xinjie*, meaning a kind of "faith, conviction, or confidence that is generated through explanation and understanding." In this respect, the Chan idea of "faith" should not be confused with the idea of "faith" as an affective submission to or communion with a divine being, especially if such faith is thought to bring about some gift of salvific grace. Rather, it carries the more commonplace sense of conviction or confidence in something. Generally speaking, this kind of confidence must be present in anything we set out to do. Without it we will not see the undertaking through—nothing of significance can be accomplished.

In Chan, faith has three aspects: faith in oneself; faith in the method of practice and teaching transmitted from the Buddha Śākyamuni; and faith in one's teacher, who is the living connection to the Buddha Dharma. The idea of "great faith" raises these three to the level of an absolute confidence, or a conviction that assumes priority over all others.

What is faith in oneself? It is believing that you yourself can practice effectively, believing that persistence will lead to enlightenment. It means that you, just like the Buddha Śākyamuni, can eventually become a Buddha. If you lack this self-confidence, if you think that enlightenment can only happen to others who seem superior to you, your practice will falter.

How does such faith or confidence in oneself arise? One way of generating faith is to acquire a good understanding of Buddhist teachings—the principles of Chan—and develop the conviction that these principles are true. In this way, you can come to accept the possibility that practice will lead to enlightenment, even though you yourself may not feel close to it. For "great faith" to arise, however, it is necessary to go on to engage in practice. As one begins to meditate, the mind becomes increasingly settled and benefits begin to appear. Some of these benefits may seem quite extraordinary—changes in the feel of one's body, mind, personality, or the environment that one would hardly think possible in one's usual condition. As a result, you begin to think, "Yes, I too can practice. I too can become enlightened."

Great faith, as well as the other three conditions, is closely related to the process of going from the "small sense of self" to the "large sense of self" and, finally, to the state of "no-self." Great faith starts with faith in one's ordinary, narrow sense of self. After all, who is it that must have faith? It is "I" who must have faith. One must know this commonplace "I" in a clear and solid manner, and be confident that "I" can practice. This firm grasp of the "small self" is the foundation for the initial power of faith and self-confidence. But that self-confidence deepens progressively with the "great or expanded sense of self" that comes with experience of the meditatively unified mind.

The second aspect of faith is confidence in the teaching or method of practice. Simply put, you should know that Śākyamuni Buddha taught this method. Since he was the Buddha—a great human being and the enlightened founder of our tradition—he would not teach us a false practice. However, this kind of conviction is not easy, even for those born and raised as Buddhists. It also requires the sort of educated understanding that I described earlier: to have confidence you must hear and comprehend the basic goals and rationale of the practice. Though you may not have experienced any proven benefit as of yet, you still must develop faith in the method. One could say that the aim of this book is to help you develop this confidence in Chan by explaining to you its goals and principles of practice.

Of course, at the beginning stages of practice this is particularly difficult, since all one seems to get for one's efforts is pain and exhaustion. After trying a method for a while, some people will feel disappointed at not getting quick results and will want a different or "better" method. Other people are simply avid for techniques. They are very acquisitive, collecting and displaying knowledge of different teachings like jewelry. They may learn a few methods from a master, pick some up from books or friends, experiment with this and fiddle with that. Each new technique seems to go very well, but after a while they get bored, and they wander off in search of a new one.

Actually, in Chan, every method is the best method. There is no method that is inherently good or bad; it is really the disposition of the practitioner that makes the difference. The important thing is to have patience. As long as you put the proper time and effort into it, any of the methods of Chan will yield powerful results. If you don't persist, how do you know if the method is effective or not? If your practice has not matured, how can you know if the method is suitable or not? It is only after you have been practicing for a good while that you should think about changing your method, and even then it should be in consultation with your teacher. If one is patient and attentive, one will begin to get the hang of the method. Benefits will start to show, and one's faith will grow, motivating one to practice with even greater diligence.

The third aspect of faith is confidence in the teacher or master. This faith in the master is extremely important. If one doubts the teacher, wondering whether he or she is truly capable or has ulterior designs of some kind, it will be impossible to practice well and gain genuine results. Under such circumstances, one might as well not even bother to practice with the person. To have faith in the teacher is to have faith in his or her instruction, to have confidence in the effectiveness of his or her guidance. It does not mean that you are required to think of the master as a god, as someone endowed intrinsically with spiritual power. Rather, one should look upon the teacher as someone—not unlike you yourself—who has walked the path. Through "mastery of the training," they have acquired the ability, experience, and motivation to help you with your practice.

It is very difficult to have faith in a teacher right from the start, let alone determine the level of the teacher's "mastery." This is especially so if you are a beginner and, as yet, lack the experience to spy out the signs of a truly disciplined and practiced person. If the master is famous, some people may feel that they should have faith in him or her like everyone else. But the faith of most people can only be partial and conditional. They are willing to give the master a try, but what this master says and does may be quite different from what they expect a master should say and do, so doubts or suspicions will naturally arise. For this reason, I never ask people to have complete faith in me as a teacher at the start. Only after practitioners have experienced some results will they begin to feel that I can help them. At that point they will be willing to follow my instructions.

In undertaking intensive retreats, even if for a mere seven days, it is absolutely necessary to have the guidance of a qualified teacher. We often say that intense practice can incite "demonic" states. These "demons" do not come from without. They come from within us, from our conflicting thoughts, afflictions, and defilements; and if they are not properly identified and handled, they can lead us into worse and worse conditions. Under these circumstances—especially after practice has borne some fruit—there is an even greater need for full confidence in the master. Whatever he or she tells you to do, you should do. If he or she tells you to take a rest, you cannot say, "I am very energetic now. I want to continue." If he or she tells you to practice harder, you cannot say, "I'm feeling lousy now. I want to rest." It is not that masters delight in being dictators. It is just that under these circumstances their experience tells them what is happening, and they are the only ones capable of offering reliable help.

In China, when one entered the meditation hall, one was required to give up one's body to the monastery and one's life to the divine protectors of the Dharma. But, in fact, the master personifies both the monastery and Dharma-protectors. If you disregard the master, it is like a pilot disregarding the directions of the control tower: disaster is bound to occur. The teacher is your compass or control tower. Time and again he or she corrects and adjusts your practice, leading you forward. If you cling to your own personal viewpoint or judgment, you are bound to go astray.

What are the signs of a responsible teacher? Every person is different and responds to the practice in unique ways. Thus, in a retreat of thirty people, thirty people will begin to develop thirty different styles of practice. The teacher must recognize this fact and constantly provide guidance to each person, like a hen hatching her eggs. A good master will tend to spend more time with his or her students, observing them and meeting with them regularly so as to stay apprised of their condition. He or she will sit with them and eat with them frequently, and encourage them not only in the evening Dharma-talks and interviews, but spontaneously as the situation demands, even in the meditation hall. With this continuous attention, the practice of both the individual and the group will be tuned to the right pitch, and each participant should be able to derive power from her or his practice in a very short time.

One of the most important functions of the master is to provide encouragement for students when their vigor and confidence in themselves seem to flag. Sometimes this may require stern words or an angry demeanor; at other times, a soft and consoling disposition. Through such encouragement the master helps students over difficult hurdles.

A second way in which the master assists the practitioner is through concrete advice on the use of the meditation method itself. Even though one may have heard explanations of *huatou* and silent illumination practice a hundred times over, it is still very easy for one to distort the practice by falling into old habits or using an approach of one's own invention. If this sort of thing goes unattended, it can have bad consequences. Thus, the master must constantly observe and inquire about the practitioner's use of the method, answer any questions, and remind him or her of its correct use.

Finally, an experienced teacher provides a confident gauge for measuring the students' progress, giving them an authoritative means to confirm whether what they have experienced is good or bad, genuine or false. In this respect, the master also offers a safe refuge from wrongful paths—those paths that can lead to the various physical and mental problems known as "demonic states" or "Chan illness." Above all, you should realize that faith in the master is faith in the "right path" of the Buddha's Dharma, which the master embodies. You must test and walk that path for yourself, but let the master be your refuge and guide.

Great Vows

The second condition, that of great vows, involves defining and establishing one's commitment to the goals of the practice. The Buddhist Dharma is a path of self-transformation—it identifies and takes us from point "a" to point "b." Without definite goals we have no direction. We can have faith in the practice and put forth all the effort in the world, we may travel fast or slow, but without the proper goal firmly in view, we may go in circles, stray off in different directions, or even go backwards. This is the first major reason for making great vows: to know clearly what it is that you seek, and to set your eyes firmly on it. The second is that great vows help us overcome selfishness. They help us overcome the attachments to the small and afflicted self that will hold us back from positive transformation. In the long run, we make vows not for our own immediate sake, but for the sake of all living beings—for the sake of a much greater and perfect world.

Śākyamuni Buddha became a Buddha because he saw that all life is full of suffering—birth, aging, sickness, and death. He also saw in the animal realms that the weaker animals are preyed upon by the stronger. He realized that all saṃsāra—the cycle of birth and death—is characterized by suffering. To him the question of helping living beings liberate themselves from this suffering was absolutely crucial. It is this conviction that ultimately made him a Buddha. He decided to give up his royal status and dedicate himself to finding a way to solve this universal problem. Therefore, he made a vow to leave home and take up the life of a religious renunciant. After practicing for many years, he attained the supreme enlightenment of Buddhahood. If he were selfishly motivated, after his liberation Śākyamuni Buddha would not have bothered to turn the Wheel of Dharma. But he did remain in the world to teach others the Way, and these teachings have been handed down to us today.

On the surface, the quest for enlightenment seems to be self-centered: "I want enlightenment. I want liberation." But properly understood, enlightenment and liberation have nothing to do with this narrow and selfish "I." Profound altruism and concern for the well-being of the world characterize even the "great or expanded sense of self." Enlightenment goes even beyond that, coming only when one lets go of the self completely and perceives the utter selflessness of no-self, or no-mind. In point of fact, if we are not willing to leave behind the small self, it is impossible to become enlightened. Great vows take one from the narrow self through great self to the door of no-self. It is for this reason that all bodhisattvas aspiring to Buddhahood make great vows when beginning their practice. This is known as "arousing the mind or resolving to seek perfect enlightenment" (S. bodhicitta). Bodhi means the perfect enlightenment of Buddhahood; citta means the mind or resolve that seeks to embody it.

The most common formula for expressing the resolve to seek perfect enlightenment is the four great vows that we recite daily:

1. Sentient beings without limit I vow to deliver
2. Afflictions without end I vow to sever
3. Approaches to Dharma without number I vow to master
4. The unexcelled enlightenment of a Buddha I vow to attain

The first vow is the most important. If you think only of helping others, naturally your own vexations will be lessened. If you have the benefit of others solely in mind, naturally you will strive to learn all approaches to dharma so that you might help them. Finally, if you insist on helping all beings to the point where all afflictions of selfhood vanish, at that time sentient beings will also disappear. Then you will have attained Buddhahood, for there is no affliction, no self, no sentient being to be saved. All Buddhas and bodhisattvas, and anyone who wishes to seriously pursue the Mahāyāna path, make these great vows every day. Of course it may not be possible to accomplish these goals so quickly; but we can derive great energy from them. The power of the vows pulls us forward, because they are always kept in front of us.

Aside from the four great vows, specific vows are also very important. Often, people hesitate to make vows because they are afraid they will break them. This is especially so when impediments to one's practice are at issue. Naturally, one should not make vows lightly; but it is wrong to hesitate to make them at all because one is afraid of breaking them. It is precisely because of our weaknesses and failures that vows need to be made frequently. The emphasis should be on the effort to keep making progress, not just the momentary consequence of accomplishment or failure. Through vows we can summon our powers to confront our specific weaknesses and keep moving forward. Without them we go nowhere.

Often, I admonish my students to make a firm vow to practice to the best of their ability each time they approach their meditation cushion. When sitting well, it may not be so necessary to keep reminding themselves of this vow. But if their energy wanes or turbulent emotions and pain appear, vows become a very effective means for focusing the mind. Many vow not to stir before the sound of the bell; some pledge to sit straight through two, maybe three, periods of meditation without moving or getting up. But then pain in the legs becomes unbearable, the mind can't concentrate, and finally they give in. Does this mean that they should take it easier and never try again? No. One should tell oneself, "This time I failed in my vow, but next time I will make the same vow and do better." So with each sitting, by making such a vow, one's sittings improve and one's faith and energy grow.

Great Fierce or Angry Determination

The third condition of great determination or perseverance is closely connected with great vows, but is a little bit different. Once the vow is established, great determination is manifested in the resolve to persevere (jingjin) in its realization—to practice hard, to go forward single-mindedly and without deterrence. Often we speak of this as a fierce or angry (yongmeng or mengli) determination; but this should not be understood as a kind of hate. Rather, it has to do with will and forward-moving perseverance.

Basically, everybody has great inertia. When we run into difficulties, we become disillusioned and disappointed. When tired, we want to sleep. However, practice is like rowing a boat upstream: if you don't row continuously you will drift backwards. When you cook rice, you cook it steadily until it is ready—in one cooking. If you cook it for a while, turn off the fire, then later turn it back on again, you definitely will not get good rice. It is the same with practice. For the method to work its transformative effect, you must do it consistently, with uninterrupted and single-minded perseverance—not sporadically.

There are people who are able to work so hard that they forget to eat or sleep, and these are not just Chan practitioners. Someone who is passionate about football may play or watch the game with such rapt attention that time will pass in a flash. They will not even notice that they are tired, sore, or hungry. Chan practice should be approached with the same natural intensity and vigor. But most people are likely to slacken and take a break long before they get to the point of forgetting the environment, forgetting food, and forgetting sleep.

There is a kind of Chan practitioner who, on the surface, looks quite dedicated and accomplished. He lives in a center for practice or in a hermitage, so that his lifestyle seems to be centered on the practice. Outwardly he appears very serene and stable, with very few vexations. Actually, though, his practice may be very weak. In the morning he practices for a while and then thinks, "Oh! It is about lunchtime, I may as well stop." After lunch he takes a break to digest, then sets about practicing again. Suddenly he thinks to himself, "Ah! I must do the laundry." Or perhaps someone comes to visit, and he interrupts whatever he is doing in order to entertain his guest. Finally he resumes his practice; but then supper-time comes. This goes on all day until he goes to bed, perhaps with the thought that he has really worked hard today. The next day it starts all over again. This may go on for a long time—eight years, ten years, even longer. Because he lives a cloistered life, more and more people come to think that this person is a well seasoned practitioner. And yet, the whole reason that he appears so free of anxiety is due to the fact that he has no responsibilities at all. All day long he just sits around and has no involvements or conflicts of any kind. By practicing Chan like this fellow, one can go on for a decade and still be exactly where one started. In fact, I have met persons who lived in hermitages or monasteries like this.

There are other practitioners who work very hard for one or two days, putting every ounce of energy into their practice, as though their very lives were at stake. Maybe they have even vowed to reach enlightenment within a certain number of days. But after a short while their excessive intensity leaves them utterly exhausted. They suffer headaches, or they find that their bodies are so sore that they can hardly even sit up. So they think to themselves, "Maybe enlightenment isn't that easy. I had better take a good rest and prepare myself more effectively. After I build up my energy I will return to practice." As a result, they give up the practice and decide to take a rest for a month or two. Maybe they then return to intensive practice; but after a couple of days of torturous overexertion, they break off again, just as before.

The point here is that meditation and retreat mean nothing if there is not proper perseverance. There is a saying in Buddhism that practice should be like a well-tuned harp, neither too intense nor too lax. Both examples are flawed in this respect. Actually, though, this balance is not easy for inexperienced persons to find. For the most part it is very easy, especially for beginners, to make excuses for oneself. However, rarely will exhaustion or discomfort be the real problem. The other extreme is less frequent; but it is still not unusual to find persons who, out of a kind of vanity or self-loathing, place unrealistic demands on themselves. What one needs is a good master who knows the proper pace and intensity of practice and who can help you discover what it means to be "fine-tuned" in one's efforts.

If you are too lackadaisical, too easy on yourself, a good master will spot it and use strong, perhaps even fierce, methods to goad you onward. If you are too intense, to the point where you become exhausted and scattered, he or she may instruct you to lay off a bit in order to refresh yourself, then prick up your energy to the right pitch. With this kind of manipulation and guidance, the master will in time bring the student directly to the proper condition of fierce determination and perseverance. When this condition appears, you will feel it very clearly: pain and tiredness will no longer be a problem, and your practice will develop a strong and self-sustaining power.

Great vows pull us forward while great fierce and angry determination pushes us from behind. But how, in principle, are we to define and generate this angry determination? A lot of people mistakenly think that angry determination is equivalent to developing anger or loathing for oneself and the world. But this is not the case. Such a flawed understanding can only arise if great faith and great vows are not properly formed. Great determination may arise from our sense of failing and our desire to change, to be sure; but how we identify personal failing must be based on how we identify our goal, which in the case of Chan is the quest for the perfect compassion and wisdom of a Buddha.

When confronted with weaknesses in one's practice, one might reflect to one-self as follows: "I haven't done justice to Śākyamuni Buddha. He suffered tremendously to discover and transmit this path to us. Now that I am on this same path, how can I not strive as hard as I can?" Thinking in this way, if one still cannot summon the determination to practice hard enough, one can also physically prostrate oneself in remorse and contrition before the Buddhas.

A second point that one can dwell on is the thought of how rare it is to be born as a human being, capable of hearing the Buddhist teaching. Imagine! Out of all the people in the world, you are one who has learned of the path, heard the dharma, and developed the desire to follow it. You should realize how rare it is to have such good karma, and throw your whole being into the practice so as to make the most of this good fortune.

One can also reflect on how fortunate one is to have a good environment for practice and a qualified person to guide one. If you don't seize the opportunity now, when can you be sure that it will come again? What other time are you waiting for? If you are a layperson, your opportunity for retreat is even more precious, since monks and nuns have their whole lives set aside for practice, while you do not. This is all the more reason to strive hard.

Finally, one can reflect solemnly on the brevity of life itself. You have no idea when you or your loved ones are going to die. Were you or they to die right now without your accomplishing the goals of this practice, it would be unfortunate indeed. Who knows where your karma will lead you in your next life? But if you give the practice all the energy you have, at least you will have done justice by yourself and others, even if you don't become enlightened in the process. Thus, recognizing the brevity of life, you should put your whole being into the practice.

During the daily cycle of the Chan retreat, special time is set aside for collective morning and evening worship services, with a shorter tableside service at the noon meal. During these services, we chant such things as the Three Refuges, the Four Great Vows, the *Heart Sutra*, hymns of offering to the Buddhas and all sentient beings, praises of the virtues and merits of the Buddhas and bodhisattvas, the Ten Vows of Samantabhadra, formal prayers and dedications of merit on behalf of all beings, and so forth. These are punctuated with ritual prostrations, bows, and acts of reverence such as the joining of the palms. Many people wonder what this kind of service is for—why it should be included in a retreat geared toward self-transformation and Chan enlightenment. Actually such services have always been part of the Chan monastery, even for those in the sangha and Chan halls. When approached with the proper attentiveness, these services provide us with precisely the sort of opportunity for self-reflection and contrition that we have described here. They can help settle our minds and focus our sense of faith and vow so that we may generate the fierce determination necessary for effective progress. Great and angry determination is itself nothing less than right earnestness and diligence with respect to the removal of one's obstacles and the realization of one's vow.

Great Doubt

Great doubt is usually a condition that we associate with the investigation of *huatou* or *gong'an*; and since we have already discussed great doubt in relation to this method of practice, there is no need to repeat that information here. Simply put, great doubt is the intense condition that arises with proper use of *gong'an* and *huatou* and naturally culminates in the "world-shattering explosion" of enlightenment. It is the successful application of that particular technique which brings about the transition from the "unified mind" of great self to the "no-mind," or "emptiness," of enlightenment.

However, we also noted that it is not uncommon for great doubt to arise spontaneously out of one's practice, even without deliberate use of a questioning device like the *huatou*. This will often happen automatically when the mind becomes unified and concentrated: the practitioner will naturally begin to develop a strong spiritual interest and drive. Great doubt takes shape as this urgent need to know, this need to resolve a deep anxiety or sense of lack that can only be alleviated by a complete experiential revolution in one's being. In effect, this is a condition of maturing practice that can come just as easily out of the use of silent illumination or any other method. In the case of silent illumination, one can think of it as the intensified absorption into the method that marks the transition from one level of silent illumination practice to the next, especially that which is experienced as one passes from the "unified state" of self and environment to the total "dropping off" of body, mind, and self that occurs with the third and final stage of silent illumination.

Once the conditions of great determination and great doubt arise, exhaustion is no longer a concern for the practitioner. For once seized by the condition of great doubt, the practitioner's endurance will know no bounds. No harm can touch the body of the practitioner no matter how hard he or she works, since he or she is in total harmony and union with the universe, and the power of the universe is naturally available to him or her. But just as with the condition of fierce or angry determination, this condition is something that one must be brought to through the natural course of practice. You cannot instill it in yourself artificially, as though through injection or willful manipulation, and to be overly anxious in this way will cause great obstacles to your practice. Above all, to attempt to generate great determination and great doubt without the guidance of a reliable master will at best be fruitless; at worst, you can do great damage to yourself. On the other hand, a reliable teacher will bring you to that condition naturally and in due course.

10

What It Means to Be a Chan Master

To act like a Chan master or talk about being a Chan master is a very easy thing to do; but to actually become a Chan master is difficult. What is a Chan master? In effect, it is to develop the viewpoint of Chan and to use Chan methods to become master of oneself. The Chan school drew its inspiration or "heart" from India, but developed its characteristic form and institutions in China. One of the first marks of being a Chan master is to be personally versed in both the heart and form of Chan. Properly speaking, though, this constitutes a practitioner of Chan, and not necessarily a Chan master. A Chan master is someone who not only masters himself or herself, but uses Chan methods to serve as master to others. Thus, we ordinarily think of a Chan master as someone who is actually engaged in teaching Chan, or someone with disciples that revere him as a teacher of Chan and have gained some attainment themselves.

This is a rather general statement of what it means to be a Chan master, but to fulfill that role effectively a person must have a number of other basic qualifications, to which we will turn now. These include: (1) acquiring right views; (2) acquiring bona fide realization produced through practice; (3) acquiring formal transmission within an orthodox dharma-lineage; (4) acquiring the influence or power of meritorious causes and conditions; and (5) skill in the use of expedients to accommodate and guide others.

ACQUIRING RIGHT VIEWS

What does it mean for a Chan master to acquire and possess right views? There are three basic aspects to this idea. First, one must have a firm understanding of and belief in the principle of moral cause and effect. This also implies that one will take moral retribution as a guiding principle for one's actions. Second is to have one's outlook on worldly events conform to the teaching of cause and condition, or dependent origination. Third is to take emptiness of self and objects as one's ultimate point of reference.

The first person to introduce Chan to China was the Indian patriarch, Bodhidharma. Chan tradition attributes a short treatise to him known as the *Two Entrances and Four Practices*. The two entrances refer to two basic approaches through which one may enter and realize the heart of Chan—namely, ultimate reality. The first entrance is known as entrance by principle; the second, entrance by practice or action. Entry by principle refers to sudden or immediate enlightenment. One does not need to rely on any explicit method or effort. In fact, to try to negotiate enlightenment through dependence on the medium of discriminating thought and intentional practice is to impede its very manifestation— to go south when one wants to go north. Thus, in the entry by principle one directly lets go of deluded thinking and comes immediately to enlightenment.

Entry by practice or action comprises four practices: (1) correctly responding to enmity; (2) acting in accordance with causes and conditions; (3) having nothing to seek or gain; (4) acting in accordance with the Dharma (i.e., emptiness or *śūnyatā*). These four practices correspond closely to the three criteria for right views outlined above. The first of the four practices describes how to respond to anger that is directed to oneself from other people. Basically, it views anger as something that is more complex than an incidental display of temper, seeing it instead as a mutual problem rooted in past karmic causes and conditions. Thus, when you become the object of anger, you should regard it as possible retribution for evils that you have done to this individual in past lives. Such a position illustrates perfectly the idea of approaching relations in terms of the principle of karmic cause and effect.

The second of the four practices—acting in accordance with causes and conditions—corresponds to the idea of viewing events as dependently originated products of complex rather than singular factors. Whatever situation befalls you—whether success or failure, fortune or misfortune—it inevitably entails a network of influences that are beyond your immediate control. Not only does this include karmic factors from your own past lives, but the coordinate contributions of many other persons around you. Hence, there is no reason to become either proud or elated, or despairing or dejected, over the way events turn out. You can take earning a Ph.D. degree as an example. One may struggle for many years to gain the skills necessary to earn one's profession and degree, but many other people and factors also enable this achievement—parents, teachers, fellow students, and so forth.

Once I knew a person who, after an especially long period of study, finally got his Ph.D. degree. At the celebratory dinner that followed—with his parents, teachers, and friends all there—he was asked to give some words of acknowledgment.

He recounted how, for many years, he worked so hard to overcome obstacles and realize his goal, attributing all his success to his own diligence. By the time he finished, his teacher had walked out and his father, too. They were outside chatting how they had worked so hard to raise him, train him, enable him to make his way. If even a Ph.D. is not simply a personal accomplishment, how much more so becoming a Chan master or a Buddha. If any of us succeed in achieving enlightenment or becoming a Chan master, we must realize that lots of beings have contributed to that process, including our incarnations and efforts over many prior lifetimes. It is not the work of one individual or moment.

The third and fourth of the four practices correspond to the third aspect of acquiring right view, namely, taking emptiness of no-self and formlessness of dharmas as one's point of reference in day-to-day activity. By the word "self" we mean not only self in the abstract or philosophical sense as essential soul or entity, but the phenomenal self who is the supposed referent and arbiter of our thoughts in the course of everyday action. In effect, we are referring to the palpable sense of "I" or "me and mine" around which we structure experiences, events, and sensations in our daily activity. Emptiness, or formlessness, means that no thing—no "self" or "entity"—has absolutely discrete, permanent, or inviolate existence. "Self," for example, cannot be found to exist apart from the perception of an "other."

By feature or form we mean the datum or attribute that one seizes on to demarcate the existence of things. Marklessness means that there is no such absolute or inviolable mark or sign that can be isolated as a discrete and unchanging entity. Everything in this world—all domains of experience of all beings— are interconnected in mutual dependence and also engaged in a constant process of fluctuation, influenced by changing causes and conditions. Thus both self and object are empty of inherent existence or boundary.

The upshot of this teaching of marklessness is that one should not reify or be attached to any event or thing, regardless of whether it is pleasant or unpleasant. Emptiness, in fact, is another way of speaking about marklessness or formlessness. The *Heart Sūtra* says that "form is itself identical with emptiness; and this very emptiness is itself identical with form. Form is not different from emptiness; emptiness not different from form." This passage introduces the concept of emptiness. Emptiness does not mean annihilationism or nothingness, that things are absolutely effaced in a state of nonexistence. It simply tells us that no object is eternally existent or an absolute discrete entity unto itself. Everything is mutually codependent on and conterminal with everything else, through the fact of dependent origination via cause and condition. Hence, individual "entities" are empty of any discrete own-being.

When we consider together the three aspects of right view described above— moral retribution in the form of karmic cause and effect, events as dependent on complex cause and condition, and emptiness as the ultimate ground and goal of practice—one can see how the teaching of cause and condition, or dependent origination, serves as a central thread that unites all three. On the one hand, it is the foundation for effective ethical action and the cardinal Buddhist values of loving-kindness and compassion, for the inseparability of our own being and experience from that of others allows no other posture. On the other hand, the realization of emptiness and liberating wisdom is, in and of itself, the profound realization of the interdependence of cause and condition. Although Bodhidharma's *Two Entrances and Four Practices* and our discussion here treat these three aspects as discrete perspectives or levels of practice, in the eyes of a Buddha they are one and the same function.

EXPERIENCE OF REALIZATION THROUGH CHAN PRACTICE

Acquiring bona fide experience through Chan practice *(xiuzheng)* has two senses to it: one is to be thoroughly trained in the culture of practice *(xiu)*, and the other, to have an authentic experience of enlightenment born of Chan practice *(zheng)*. Both are a kind of experience. If people practice Chan for a long time, but do not attain enlightenment through that practice, can they be considered Chan masters? Actually, they cannot. Having experience in practice, one also must have the experience of its fruition: enlightenment. Only then can one really act as a Chan master.

There are altogether three aspects of religious discipline that are fundamental to effective Chan practice, the contents of which are none other than the traditional Buddhist Three Learnings: moral restraint and purity *(śīla)*; cultivation of meditative concentration (samādhi); and wisdom (prajñā), or right views. The first aspect, moral purity, or restraint, concerns making our everyday life very stable and routine. This is a necessary foundation for effective practice. To achieve it one must have a lifestyle and outlook that is securely grounded in moral principles. The means for developing such a foundation is the Buddhist precepts, or moral restraints.

If teachers' lifestyles and relations with people around them are not stable, their meditation practice will suffer problems, not to mention their ability to teach Chan. When not properly restrained, the power and self-confidence that builds up through practice may lead to all manner of complications. If one is in a position of teaching others—a position of authority—moral inconsistencies may jeopardize the climate of trust and respect so necessary to the master-disciple relationship. In either case, by spontaneously acting on one's urges—especially where others are involved—one will end up destroying other people's practice along with one's own. Anyone familiar with the Chan or Zen scene in the United States will know of many such episodes that have transpired in recent years. Some of these people in the name of Chan enlightenment have been less socially responsible to others than the most average citizen, leading people to wonder what value Chan has for the world—especially if it only seems to foster this kind of childish self-inflation.

At the same time, however, Chan tradition is indeed filled with stories of the iconoclasm of past Chan masters—stories that seem to celebrate the intentional breaking of traditional Buddhist precepts against sexual involvement, drunkenness and meat-eating, theft, verbal and physical violence, and so forth. In the *Platform Sūtra*, the sixth patriarch himself refers to the "formless precepts"—the idea that one's actions should answer first and foremost to the living principle of emptiness and enlightenment, unencumbered by discriminatory thinking and restraint. This is, indeed, an important part of Chan tradition; but there can be problems with this kind of understanding. Upon reading these tales, there are many people who think that being a Chan master is all about being uninhibited when it comes to matters of desire. They think that one should not entertain questions of self-restraint—especially restraint that is socially imposed—but directly indulge whatever urge may arise. This, they surmise, is being true to one's original nature. Thus, original nature is equated with the will of the so-called individual; illusion and suffering, with conventional inhibitions imposed by society.

When I first came to the United States, there was a student of mine who wanted me to take up living with her. She insisted that a lot of Chan masters do this kind of thing in Japan and the United States: "Chan enlightenment must mean that you are free of these kinds of restrictions or hang-ups. If you are unable to do this, then you can't really be a Chan master."

So I said, "Fine, then I guess I'm not enlightened."

More recently there was a wife who came to the Center to see me, and she took an incredibly strong liking to me, so she professed her love to me and tried to embrace and kiss me. I scolded her, telling her I am a monk and can't do this kind of thing. Eventually, she mocked me saying, "You are not a master. You are just a monk. I am the master!"

In the *Transmission of the Lamp* collection, a hard-practicing monk stayed in a hut behind a devout lay practitioner's house. To test his practice, the layperson ordered her beautiful daughter to sit in his lap and embrace him, and then report to her his reaction. Having done as requested, the girl returned to say that the monk sat stone-faced, without the slightest response. The mother then went to the monk and asked him what he thought and felt, to which he replied that the daughter's touch was like a dry log leaning against a cold stone. Hearing this, she beat him with her broom and drove him out of the hut, yelling after him that she had been wasting her time supporting him in his practice.

Although the story can be understood to illustrate the pitfall of becoming too attached to spiritual piety or vanity, does it also mean that I and other monks should, as a rule, embrace and show romantic affection toward other people we may come in contact with? Does it imply that indulging passions without restraint is a norm to be emulated by all? There have been enough scandals in Chan history to suggest that some people have believed this to be the case.

On the one hand, the conscientious monk in the story may have deserved what he received from the woman. Sensing his inner conflict and lack of self-understanding, the wise mother rebuked him. In such a situation, her response was perhaps appropriate. Maybe it even provided a powerful impetus to the monk's Chan practice. On the other hand, the monk was adhering to the guidelines and precepts that he formally took upon becoming a Buddhist monk.

Chan masters are human beings and members of society at large, and as such they still need to follow certain criteria in their lives and actions. My way is the path of a Buddhist monk. If one is not an enlightened Chan master or even a good monk—if one does not have a degree of genuine self-perception—think how destructive such indulgence might be for both oneself and those around you.

The next aspect of practice is cultivation of samādhi, or meditative concentration. Samādhi refers to a certain mental stability, power, and purity that develop with meditation practice. This kind of inner stability and power is necessary to ease the influence of internal and external circumstances and give one a firm mental foundation. Buddhist tradition places great emphasis on samādhi, or meditative concentration, as a basis for enlightenment; and yet, in the *Platform Sūtra* it says that true Chan or "meditation" *(zuochan)* does not involve sitting in meditation. Sitting in meditation cannot ultimately produce enlightenment and make one a Buddha.

Again, the disciple of the sixth patriarch, Nanyue Huairang, demonstrated this point quite effectively to Mazu Daoyi when he likened Mazu's effort to attain Buddhahood through meditation to polishing a brick in order to turn it into a mirror. Sitting in meditation can't produce enlightenment. It cannot deliver enlightenment at will, like some kind of tool or magical spell. But it can make our minds very calm, open, and clear, under which condition it is much easier for enlightening insight to occur. Hence, it is an indispensable part of Chan practice.

Once, a prospective student came to me to inquire about attending a Chan retreat. The first thing I told him was that everyone was required to sit in meditation for some fourteen hours a day. He wondered why such rigorous meditation was necessary. I told him that meditation was the very heart of Chan practice, to which he responded by bringing up the example of the Mazu story from the *Transmission of the Lamp.* When I asked him what his point was, he said, "I have come to get enlightened, not to sit in meditation."

I told him, "In that case you might as well go practice at home. You can just as easily not-sit at home." But the student said he needed a master, so he came here. So I told him, "Unfortunately, I myself have not discovered any kind of method that can enlighten you effortlessly." If I had such a method, I would just teach that and there would be no need for this sort of hard and painful retreat.

It also says in the *Platform Sūtra* that if you are free of false discrimination between good and evil and your mind is truly liberated from deluded thinking, then and only then are you really enlightened. But who is really capable of this? Are you? If so, then perhaps you do not need to sit in meditation or observe precepts. The *Platform Sūtra* has been circulated among Chan practitioners for well over a thousand years now, and many people have read this passage about being free of thoughts of good and evil. But by merely reading it and thinking about it, how many have really been actually freed from delusion in this way? Therefore, practice of Chan still requires firm foundation in self-restraint and meditation; and if anyone will bother to look at the institutional setting in which Chan practice has been pursued over the past millennium and a half the importance of these disciplines to Chan tradition will be obvious.

Now we come to the third point of practice: the experience of awakening, or enlightenment, itself. This involves two aspects: one is wisdom or insight; the other, liberation. What is Chan enlightenment? It is, in fact, liberation. Seeing into one's original nature is not just a quick cerebral grasp of how the world works, even though we use "sight" as the chief metaphor. It entails a complete revolution in one's being—a sense of "liberation" from the grip of craving, hatred, and delusion, and the afflictions that attend them. Thus, in the Mahāyāna sūtras, realization of emptiness itself is referred to as a "gate to liberation" (S. *vimokṣa-mukha*).

If you don't have an enlightenment experience that involves both wisdom, or illumination, and a sense of liberation, then it is not truly Chan enlightenment. Nor is the recipient a Chan master. To be a true Chan master—to teach others correctly and well—one must develop genuine compassion for their delusion and pain. This requires that one have both a thoroughgoing insight into Buddha-nature and the profound sense of liberation that comes with it; without them it is impossible to develop this heartfelt sense of compassion. Should you go on to teach students without it, you can do them a lot of harm.

TRANSMISSION WITHIN AN ORTHODOX DHARMA-LINEAGE

The criterion for being a Chan master is that one must have transmission within a true or correct Dharma-lineage. Again this comprises three basic requirements. First one must have a bona fide master to guide and certify one's progress in Chan practice. Second, one must actually obtain the sanction or "seal" *(yinke)* of this Chan master. "Sanction" here means that the master, on the basis of training and sanction under a prior master, is qualified to recognize one's enlightenment as genuine. This is the idea of the mind-to-mind transmission that is central to Chan. Third is receiving permission of a Chan master to teach as a Chan master. In point of fact, a lot of people may receive certification of enlightenment; but an enlightened practitioner is not one who can necessarily serve as a Chan master; that is, one who teaches Chan to others. So a full-fledged

Chan master must determine whether the duly trained Chan practitioner can really take on the responsibility of being a Chan teacher. Only then can the person become a functioning Chan master. This need for an enlightened teacher poses something of a problem. When I myself was practicing, I often wondered how one could recognize a bona fide Chan master. Without having achieved any enlightenment myself, how could I know? Actually, in such a situation, we really have no means of knowing whether someone is a genuine Chan master. We may scrutinize the person's demeanor and actions to spy out any impressive or special qualities, but these are only matched to our naive notions of what we think a spiritual master ought to be. Since one has no clue what Chan is, one can't really see the Chan master either. This can be a very painful situation, especially if one spends years with someone who fails to bring genuine progress in the practice, or who deliberately misleads students. Regrettably, there have always been people ready to pass themselves off as enlightened Chan masters, so this poses an even greater problem for Chan aspirants. As a student struggling on the path, you are like a blind person unable to see. Without having reached a certain level of training, it is impossible to distinguish who is a good and who is a bad teacher. When the eye of Chan has opened a bit, the situation will change.

There is actually a story about Song Dynasty master Dahui Zonggao. Dahui searched many years for a good teacher. Eventually he met a famous layperson of the time known as Zhang Shangyin, who encouraged him to come meet his own teacher, Yuanwu Koqin. Dahui ended up studying with Yuanwu for many years. After a long period, he finally achieved enlightenment, but only after many years of not really knowing what his teacher was all about. Years later Yuanwu touchingly asked Dahui what his impression of him was when he first came to him. Dahui answered, "You looked like a crude butcher ready to carve up a fat pig." So who do you think the butcher and the fat pig were?

This business of sanction, or *yinke*, by an experienced Chan master is very important. When one has a transformative experience of some sort, it is wrong to declare on one's own that it is Chan enlightenment. This is useless, since you don't have any standard of judgment to begin with. One needs a truly experienced master to check and approve it for you. Just by looking at your demeanor—how you speak, your mannerisms, the way you carry yourself—a skilled teacher can tell whether your experience is genuine or how deep it is. Unfortunately, there have always been bad teachers, too. Even in the Tang Dynasty, Linji (Rinzai) mentions the existence of numerous dime-a-dozen Chan masters who, after a bit of Chan dramatics, are ready to "sanction" anything that comes across their desk. Most experiences of people who think they are enlightened are false, or at best incredibly shallow; and if such a person goes to a master who doesn't have proper sanction and a stable enlightenment himself, it is a big problem, especially if that master casually gives his acknowledgment.

About seven years ago a student came to me who had practiced for many years, his express reason being to get my approval of his enlightenment. When I asked him, "Why are you here?" He said, "You are a Chan master; you already know what I am here for." When I refused to play his game and give my approval, he said, "I came here thinking that you were enlightened; now I see that you are not." He rejected me as a Chan master because I did not approve him as the master! This kind of person is incapable of learning anything from anyone. Ultimately, genuine sanction is not an easy thing to obtain. You can't get it from just anyone. The word *yin* in the term for sanction (*yinke*) means "to seal or stamp." It refers to the seal of office by which an emperor or magistrate might put official approval on some document. In Chan we speak of seals made of pure gold and seals made of bean curd. There are a lot of seals around made of bean curd.

Formal permission to teach comes after receiving sanction of one's enlightenment or understanding. It amounts to being given approval from a genuine teacher to go out and teach others. This also is not a simple matter. In Taiwan today there is a Chan master who claims to be able to enlighten a student in five minutes and to train a Chan master within a week. In the space of a year he sanctioned more than one hundred students. This is quite an accomplishment. Throughout his entire career, Mazu Daoyi, the most prolific Chan master in history, had no more than 120 sanctioned students! There is a teacher in the United States who represented himself as a Chan master and gathered quite a few students, when in fact his master never formally gave him permission to teach. This, however, was not widely known. Should a person who has not received permission to teach go ahead and do so without formal approval to teach? There are circumstances that might allow for this. If the person is practicing hard and continues to do so after his or her master dies, perhaps the time might come when it is appropriate to teach, even though the master is not there to give official approval.

POSSESSING THE INFLUENCE OR POWER
OF MERITORIOUS BLESSINGS

Having received sanction of one's attainments in Chan and approval to teach Chan to others, there are still factors that must be put into place for one to function as a successful teacher. To begin with, one must have the right time, space, and general environment for teaching Chan. If one were living in mainland China during the Cultural Revolution, it would be utterly impossible to teach. One would probably be defrocked and sent to a communal farm deep in the countryside. Even today in China, Buddhist groups are not allowed to sponsor activities outside officially sanctioned monasteries. Hence, generally speaking, one must have a social climate that is conducive to Chan practice.

On a more immediate scale, one must also have a place to teach Chan, specific times set aside for people to come and practice Chan, and the medium for getting out the word and generating interest. Take the example of a weeklong Chan retreat for thirty or forty people. You need a facility that is suited to this kind of activity; you need money for food; and you need the human resources to advertise, plan, and run the retreat. The same criteria apply to establishing permanent centers for teaching Chan.

At our first center in Queens the street noise was incredible, especially during Fourth of July celebrations. At our first session we allowed participants to exercise outside the center grounds. By the fifth day, most people were looking pretty ratty. One neighbor was overheard wondering whether some insane asylum had recently turned its inmates out on the street. For fear of alarming people, we stopped letting students take walks outside the center during retreats. Over the many years that we have been holding retreats at the Chan center in Queens, our neighbors have never given us any trouble, and most have ended up being quite supportive of our presence in the area. But the location, noise, and size of the place have still been constraining. Thus, we recently purchased a large facility in the countryside of upstate New York which we now use for retreats.

A second requirement for the Chan master is the ability to coordinate one's instruction with the level and character of one's audience. There are very few Buddhists in the United States today. Most people do not have a background in Buddhism or any experience with Buddhist practice. Once in New York I was on the street, and a couple of tough-looking kids came up and asked me what I was. I told them that I was a Buddhist monk and asked them if they were interested in studying Buddhism or Chan. What they wanted to know was whether I could teach martial arts. In introductory meditation classes I usually begin by pointing out the physical, mental, and spiritual benefits of meditation practice. Then I ask what people's interests are: how they came to the practice of meditation and why. Ordinarily one gets all kinds of answers, from the desire to improve sleep and ease stress to an urge for deeper spiritual understanding. Not too many people know much about Buddhism, and those that do don't have a very clear understanding. Is there a basis for teaching Chan here? I would say there is, but traditional cultural forms and institutions of Chinese Chan cannot be foisted unilaterally on Americans. One must teach to and accommodate their own interests and problems, allowing Chan practice to directly address and take shape in this climate.

A third requirement over and above audience and place is the need for what we call "external patrons and protectors" (waihu). In traditional Chinese Buddhism, this refers not only to a supporting staff that tends to the daily operation of the monastery, but also supports it financially and materially. A lot of people—including many Americans—think that there is something decadent about these sorts of material concerns. You might come up with a time and a location to teach the dharma, but, frankly speaking, without the necessary material and human resources to make it happen, there will be no teacher, no teaching, no facility, and no audience. When I first came to America, I wanted to teach and hold Chan retreats as soon as possible, but my first students and I did not have our own permanent center or means of support. We did hold retreats, but it was difficult to find a place. Rent was also expensive. If we didn't have a group to support us financially and to assist in the holding of these activities, it would have been impossible to continue. Hence, it is a bit selfish to think that Chan practice involves nothing more than you, your meditation cushion, and your relationship with your teacher. You owe a lot to those people who have given resources and worked tirelessly to provide you with these circumstances. You should be grateful and willing to share the burden in return. For this reason, we refer to the good fortune of having a proper time, place, audience, and resources for practicing Chan as "acquiring the influence or power of meritorious blessings." It is not just a matter of the Chan master's personal determination and effort, but our collective vows, the purity of our practice, and—above all— karmic causes and conditions.

SKILL IN THE USE OF EXPEDIENT MEANS TO ACCOMMODATE THE ABILITIES OF ONE'S AUDIENCE

The last requirement for being a successful Chan master concerns the ability to meet the particular spiritual needs of one's students. Altogether, four subcategories of this requirement can be distinguished. First, the Chan master needs a firm intellectual foundation in Buddhism. Second, he or she needs knowledge of the world, or what one might call practical knowledge. Third, he or she needs powers of keen observation. Fourth, he or she needs the power to intuitively sense and respond appropriately (*ganying*) to the condition of one's students.

Everyone has heard that Chan does not depend on words and texts; it points directly to the nature of the mind. Because of this, many think that a Chan master does not need to read books or actively pursue the study of Buddhist doctrine and history. All he or she has to do is curse, strike, and discombobulate people. Supposedly, that is enough for Chan training. This is the myth and rhetoric of Chan, to be sure; but you need to know that in its advancement of the "wordless teaching," Chan has generally worked within the context of a larger Buddhist culture. Moreover, when one looks closely at the historical record, one finds that the great Chan masters were all extremely well educated in Buddhist sūtras and doctrine along with the lore of their own tradition.

So what is this rejection of words all about? Not depending on words and texts simply means that one does not make the mistake of thinking that words themselves are a repository for truth or enlightenment itself, that truth can be purchased simply by manipulating words. In looking for living enlightenment, one looks for immediate life-context understanding and not secondary description. Hence, one does not rely on the words and texts of someone outside oneself to understand one's original nature. But this does not mean that one does not use language or rely on discriminatory knowledge and books altogether. In fact, that would be impossible. How would you even come to know about Chan—much less set out to practice Chan—if you didn't hear or read about it from others? How, as a teacher, would you instruct students in the development of right views, lifestyle, and practice? Would there be a Chan master or Chan student without a traditional discourse of words and symbols that define them as such? So, really, it would be very difficult for someone who doesn't have knowledge of Buddhist doctrine and Chan lore to be a Chan master.

Then again, if one doesn't have knowledge of world events and everyday affairs, one cannot act in sympathy with people—one cannot understand them or accord with their needs. Once a person asked me for advice on how to control his children and his wife. When I answered, he was surprised to find my ideas useful to his particular situation. He asked me how I, with no wife or children, could give such fitting advice. I replied, "Does a surgeon or doctor need to be ill and operated on to be a good doctor or surgeon?" Simply being open to and engaged with people may be enough. For a Chan master to relate to people well, he or she must take an active interest in and know something about the world, for this is really the ground of our spiritual vexation and progress.

The third factor—the power of observation—means the ability to read the mental and emotional state of one's students. Sometimes one can know students' states of mind from their demeanor or actions, without any need for speech. Knowing the appropriate method to deal with the situation, the master may adjust their states of mind with a gesture or a word. This is much easier in the case of students with whom one has practiced for a time. One gets to know them very well through the daily practice, and there is no need to speak with them directly. When it comes to disciples who have practiced with me in Chan retreats, it is easy for me to direct changes in them under just about any circumstance; but I cannot always do this with people whom I haven't had the time to observe closely and whom I don't know that well. There is nothing mysterious about this. It probably holds true for teachers of any sort. When students have studied with a teacher for a long time, the teacher comes to know their strengths and weaknesses, and it becomes much easier to give them useful advice.

The fourth factor—how to respond expediently to the situation of the student, in keeping with the student's needs of the moment—is, of course, closely related to the previous factor of observation. At issue here is the affective aspect of the Chan master's interactions with the student; namely, how to give kindly encouragement when such encouragement is needed, or to scold and beat when that is most beneficial. Many people imagine that it is routine for Chan masters to beat and scold students; that this is something of a rule in Chan, done for its own sake. Actually, this is more myth than fact. The masters I have known rarely do this sort of thing. It is not only wrong, but also potentially quite harmful to beat someone who shouldn't be beaten. If you are going to do it, it must carry a clear message and have a clear use—it must produce the desired result. Otherwise it is flawed.

In intensive Chan retreats, the setting where one most often finds this kind of close interaction, beating and scolding are used to adjust the tenor of the student's practice, to instill what we call "right mindfulness." The bottom line is the question of how effectively the student is using his or her particular method of practice, whether it be a beginner's struggle with the *huatou* or a more advanced student's use of the "methodless method." As was stated in an earlier chapter, a good analogy is to be found in a hen's hatching of a chick. When a chick hatches, it begins to peck at the egg from the inside. When it is just about ready to emerge, the mother bird might cluck and peck from outside to help it along, but if she were to peck too soon, she would kill the chick. If the student is beat under the proper circumstances, in the end the student will be very grateful.

Looking over these criteria, we can say that it is really easy to become a Chan master; and yet, at the same time, it is also very difficult. Why is it easy? Because Chan does not depend on words and letters, and does not require theoretical knowledge. As soon as you have right views and right methods, it is fine. However, to complete all six of the criteria described above is quite difficult. If one can perfect certain items among the six, it might be sufficient to be a common Chan master; but to be a really effective Chan master—to have a major impact of the kind that ancients such as Mazu Daoyi or Dahui Zonggao had—it would be inadequate.

The Ten Oxherding Pictures

People who have never undergone Buddhist training or have never had a taste of "entering the gate" of Chan often like to speculate about enlightenment. But lacking a clear sense of what the dharma actually entails, they tend to delight in the exotic and cook up all kinds of strange fantasies. There is such a thing as "enlightenment," or "awakening," to be sure. The Chinese word for it is *kaiwu*, which means to "open forth and awaken," or simply "to awaken." This expression has been used in the Chinese Chan tradition for centuries—at least since the Tang Dynasty (618–907). But although it figures centrally in Chan tradition and its literature, enlightenment is not something that can be comprehended—let alone reached—by philosophical speculation or flights of the occult imagination. Should you even be tempted to conjecture or fantasize about it, you will actually be moving farther and farther away from it. You will be heading south when you should be going north!

There is an old saying in Chan: "The instant you open your mouth, you are wrong. The moment your mind flickers, you are off the track." The aim of Chan training, like any form of Buddhism, is to investigate and transform the very ground of one's being. Since this entails the reversal of some of our most deep-seated assumptions about existence, to begin by trying to mold Chan to old habits of egoistic thinking is like "heading south when you want to go north." In order to underscore the incompatability of this discriminating mind with the no-mind of Chan practice, Chan masters down through the ages have made a tradition of "not depending on words and letters" and refusing to speak too openly about enlightenment.

This, of course, is not to say that Chan tradition decried altogether the use of scripture, literature, or systematic effort to organize Chan teachings. In fact, it is a rather interesting touch of irony that the literature of the Chan school is far more voluminous than that of any other Chinese Buddhist school. This literature, however, differs substantially in style and content from that of other traditions: it prefers the conceit of historical interaction between master and disciple—the living idiom of Chan practice and enlightenment—to the systematic expositions of Buddhist doctrine and scripture that typify the more scholastic schools, such as Tiantai and Huayan. For example, among the most representative forms of Chan literature, the "recorded sayings" or *yulu* collections, purport to contain oral discourses, exhortations, and anecdotes associated with specific teachers and their communities. The Chan lineage, or "transmission of the lamp" histories *(chuandeng lu)*, organize selections from this same material into capsule biographies arranged in sequences of historical dharma-transmission; and *gong'an* collections, such as the *Gateless Barrier* and *Blue Cliff Record*, borrow selectively from both. Even so, this rhetorical emphasis on orality and immediacy did not obviate systematization. The literature of the different Chan houses or lineages shows distinct evidence of efforts to identify and organize the salient features of the Chan path. As lineages such as the Caodong and Linji took on greater institutional and ideological definition at the hands of their successors, their systems were formalized to the point of becoming emblematic of their school's distinctiveness as a tradition.

Thus, even though Chan emphasizes wordlessness and immediacy of action, one must realize that there is logic to Chan training, and numerous influential masters of the past have sought to articulate these principles for their students. At times, these formulations of the Chan path suggestively parallel the representations of the Bodhisattva path developed in the Tiantai and Huayan traditions, which only goes to show that they did not develop in isolation from the culture at large. But in contrast to the philosophical language of the scholastic schools, Chan representations preferred the use of more ambiguous forms of imagery and symbol, perhaps in keeping with the idiomatic "encounter-style" relationship of master and disciple. In the Guiyang line of Chan, for example, different levels of training and enlightenment are expressed through the manipulation of different circular configurations. In the Linji line there are the so-called three mysteries, or three essentials; the four shouts; and the four permutations of host and guest. In the Caodong school, there are Dongshan's five ranks, or five positions of lord and vassal, with Caoshan's accompanying five diagrams. Chan masters in these different lineages were expected to be thoroughly familiar with their respective schemes of the path. In fact, early records of the Caodong school even suggest that exposition of the five ranks was itself a formal part of dharma-transmission. Whatever the case may be, the success of these different formulations caused their popularity to extend well beyond the confines of their respective schools, leading to the creation of a richly eclectic culture that was shared among the different Chan lineages. Thus, the imagery of "guest" and "host" that is so central to the Linji school often appears in discourses of masters from the other four houses of Chan. In turn, eminent masters of the Linji line, such as Dahui Zonggao, not infrequently commented on the five ranks of the Caodong school.[1] Today, the Japanese Rinzai (Linji) school includes study of the five ranks as a formal part of its kōan (C. gong'an) training.

Of the various symbolic schemes devised to express the dynamics of the Chan path, that of the oxherder and the ox is perhaps the most popular. The image of "herding the ox" is an old one in Chinese Buddhist lore. The Yijiao ching ("Sūtra of the Bequeathing of the Teaching") likens the Buddhist practitioner to an oxherder who—ever watchful, ever patient—herds his ox with stick in hand, never letting it stray. In Chan tradition he becomes a model for the meditator, who must constantly guard his or her mind to prevent it from straying into defilement.

In one of the most celebrated examples of this ox metaphor, Mazu Daoyi (709–788) is said to have once asked a monk tending the fires in the kitchen, "What are you up to?"

The monk replied, "Tending the ox."

"How does one tend the ox?" Mazu pressed.

The monk answered, "When he strays into the grass, I pull his nose back onto the path."

"You really do know how to tend the ox!" Mazu replied.

Similar instances where Chan practice is likened to "tending an ox" appear among the sayings of other masters of the Tang Period, including Baizhang Huaihai and Guishan Lingyou (771–853). The analogy seems to have been a pertinent one, for by the time the Chan tradition was reaching its full institutional development in the Song Dynasty (960–1276), "tending or herding the ox" had become a well-known metaphor for Chan training.

Precisely when and where people first began to illustrate the stages of Chan practice with graphic representations of harnessing, taming, and riding the ox home is not easy to determine. Historically speaking, two sets of oxherding diagrams, titles, and didactic verses have proved the most enduring—one by the Linji master Kuo'an Shiyuan (twelfth century), the other by a late eleventh- or early twelfth-century master of uncertain provenance known simply as Puming.[2] Although these are the only versions extant today, Chan records of the Song Period indicate that many variations on the oxherding formula were in circulation at the time when Kuo'an and Puming composed their respective schemes. D. T. Suzuki in his Manual of Zen Buddhism counts four distinct versions. The Japanese Zen scholar Yanagida Seizan has found evidence for as many as six. Not only were they produced by persons of different lines—including the likes of Foyin Liaoyuan (1032–1098) and Foguo Weibai (eleventh century) of the Yunmen school, Qingju Haosheng (eleventh century) of the Caodong school, and several other figures from Kuo'an Shiyuan's Yangqi branch of the Linji school—but the number, title, and conceptual organization of the stages varied considerably.

There were versions with as few as five, six, or eight pictures, and versions with as many as twelve. Some depicted the ox itself changing color from black to white, much like the famous diagrams of "taming the elephant" from the Gelugpa school of Tibetan Buddhism. Others kept it entirely black. Some had the ox and oxherder completely vanish, to be replaced by an empty circle signifying the inconceivable substance and function of perfect enlightenment. Others appended additional diagrams depicting the reemergence of phenomena, ostensibly in order to emphasize the enlightened bodhisattva's continued activity in the world.[3]

Of the various sets of pictures and verses that circulated in China during the eleventh and twelfth centuries, all have vanished except for those of Kuo'an Shiyuan and Puming. In China and Korea, Puming's version has received the most widespread attention. By contrast, Kuo'an's set has seen only sporadic publication and comment, as when the Ming Dynasty Buddhist reformer Yunqi Zhuhong (1535–1615) included it as an appendix to his reprinting of Puming's verses and diagrams. In Japan, the situation is the reverse. Kuo'an's diagrams and verses were introduced when Chan (Zen) was transmitted to the Japanese isles during the Southern Song (1127–1279) and Yuan (1279–1367) Periods. There they were published together with Sengcan's *Verses on Faith in Mind (Xinxin ming)*, Yongjia's *Song of Enlightenment (Zhengdao ge)*, and Changlu Zongze's *Treatise on Sitting in Meditation (Zuochan yi)*, and circulated in medieval Rinzai Zen monasteries as one of "four foundational works of the Zen school."

With the recent publication of several English-language translations, Kuo'an's ten oxherding pictures and verses have, in turn, become popular among Western practitioners connected with Japanese Zen.[4] Given the current high level of interest and familiarity that the system enjoys among Westerners, I will confine my comments to the ten oxherding pictures and verses of Kuo'an Shiyuan. In the form we find them today, Kuo'an's original pictures and didactic verses are interspersed with prefatory cases and "harmonizing" verses by various later masters in the Chinese Linji line. The harmonizing verses are attributed to Shigu Xiyi (twelfth century), a grand-disciple of the Linji master, Dahui Zonggao (1089–1163).[5]

THE TEN OXHERDING PICTURES

As the central theme that unites the sequence of oxherding pictures, what does the metaphor of the ox and oxherd mean to the Chan practitioner? Certainly, the quality of attentiveness is an essential virtue for good oxherding. In the Chan context, it is not difficult to understand its applicability: it signifies the extraordinary mindfulness and persistence required to train the mind. Every time the mind wanders from the correct practice or proper attention to the activity at hand, the meditator catches it and patiently pulls it back. Such a person never gets upset. He or she doesn't regret what has passed, doesn't anticipate the future, but, remaining constantly alert to the mind's deviations, catches the wayward mind and gently puts it back on track. In fact, the very awareness that the mind has wandered is itself proper practice, for as soon as it is detected the problem is already corrected. This is watching and reining in the ox. But what is this ox? Who, precisely, is the herder, and what is the significance of their journey homeward?

The oxherder is the practitioner, not in the conventional sense of a total human being or personality, but in the more specific sense of the inner "self," or "I," who is engaged in and motivated to practice. The path is the right direction to go—the course of spiritual growth that leads back to one's original "home" of intrinsic enlightenment, or Buddhahood. As the proper course to follow, it may also be considered part of the method of practice.

These images are fairly easy to comprehend. However, that of the ox is more ambiguous. Generally speaking, one could say that the ox represents the mind and its activities. It is the primary object to which the practitioner directs his or her attention, and that which he or she strives to cultivate or domesticate. But what exactly do we mean by "the mind" here? In Chan, we often speak of the mind as inherently enlightened, and equate "seeing the ox" with a "glimpse into one's original nature." Thus, on the one hand, the ox may be seen as the great white ox of enlightened Buddha-nature. Seeking, discovering, taming, and riding the ox home would then signify the process of awakening to and actualizing one's true nature to the point where it is fully integrated with all aspects of life. On the other hand, the ox is characterized as wild and unruly, and must be forcibly restrained from wandering off into the weeds of desire and deluded thinking. This image seems more suggestive of the mind of vexation than the mind of enlightenment. Full enlightenment is achieved only after the practitioner succeeds in finding the ox, harnessing it, subduing it, and herding it down the road to his true home, where it finally disappears.

Both views are admissible, for, conceptually speaking, the mind of affliction is not separate from the mind of enlightenment. As Huineng says, "Deluded, a Buddha is a sentient being; awakened, a sentient being is a Buddha. . . . If the mind is warped, a Buddha is a sentient being; if the mind is impartial, a sentient being is a Buddha."[6] In fact, affliction and enlightenment define one another— you cannot understand, much less perceive, one without the other. In the third frame of the oxherding pictures, when the practitioner sees the ox, he not only discovers his true nature, but also comes to know what vexation really is. The subsequent process of harnessing, taming, and herding the ox home involves a simultaneous effort to subdue the mind of vexation and further actualize the mind of enlightenment. Moreover, one will notice that, as practice progresses, the ox, the oxherder, and the relationship between the two changes radically.

In Puming's version of the oxherding pictures, the ox is depicted as gradually changing from black to white. Ultimately, in the tenth and final frame, ox and oxherder disappear altogether. In the seventh of Kuo'an Shiyuan's ten diagrams, the ox vanishes, leaving only the practitioner. In the eighth, they both have disappeared. What does this signify? Originally, there is no enlightenment to be attained, no person to seek it. Ox and person do not really exist at all. They are illusory distinctions. In Chan, we say that there is really nothing to do, nothing whatsoever to attain. However, people don't understand this deceptively simple fact, so they feel they must learn what it means to "have nothing to do." This is Chan practice. The ox is the manifest object or concern of the practitioner, whether it is the mind of enlightened insight, the mind of affliction, or both. The oxherder is the inner voice, or sense of self, of the practitioner. Possessed of the resolute urge to seek enlightenment, the oxherder applies the harness and whip of Chan meditation to the ox. The successive transformations that take place in the relationship among ox, oxherder, and the journey home describe the profound evolution in one's understanding of enlightenment, vexation, self, and practice that occurs over the course of spiritual development. Ultimately, the ox is not really an ox, the person not really a person. As the dualistic distinction between the two vanishes, they revert to one. Yet even this perfect unity cannot be spoken of as "one."

Thus, to try to define the ox strictly as the enlightened mind or the mind of vexation can be misleading. One should not lay too much weight on the fact that, in Kuo'an's ten diagrams, the environment and practitioner reemerge after ox and oxherder vanish, whereas, in Puming's, they do not. Both intend to chart the Chan path to its full completion in the marvelous and inconceivable function of full enlightenment, but they convey it differently. Rather than be confused by such differences, it is more important to be aware of just how the relationship between ox and oxherder, self and objective, changes over the course of the ten pictures.

As a final word of caution, one must still be careful not to inflate the importance of such formal representations of the Chan path, for it may create the impression that there are hard and fast definitions of enlightenment and spiritual progress to which everyone's practice will conform. This is simply not the case. People's responses to training will vary according to their individual karmic capacities, as well as manifest causes and conditions. Some may develop very quickly and steadily, others slowly or intermittently. Likewise, the form and circumstances of their enlightenment experiences will vary. Thus, although schemes such as the ten oxherding diagrams and the Caodong five ranks provide valuable sense of the aims and tenor of the Chan path, in no way should they be considered definitive.

The discussion below is an interpretive commentary on the diagrams and verses of Kuo'an Shiyuan, together with their appended prefatory cases and harmonizing verses. Since these materials are readily available in other English works, translation of the original text will not be included here.

1. Looking for the Ox

圖　牛　尋　(一)

In this first picture, the oxherder is depicted in the countryside or wilderness outside of town. He carries a harness and is looking about anxiously, trying to decide which direction to go. He has discovered that he has lost his ox, his most prized possession; and he has set out to find it, but doesn't know where to begin. This illustrates the growing sense that deep in our being there must be a true and unchanging nature, a nature that we have lost and desperately need to reclaim in order to be at peace. Thus, the basic mentality for seeking enlightenment is present. It is strong and real, but undefined. One is anxious and frustrated, not knowing where and how to look, as though lost in a wilderness. Often, persons in this condition will feel more afflicted than they did before they ever began to think about religious practice. Not many people will be willing to seriously face up to this torment, much less put themselves through the hardships required to tread the path to enlightenment. Some may be partially convinced that there is a splendid white ox somewhere and that it is worth taking a half-hearted look. They may start out and then stop, start out and then stop again. Others may be totally convinced and plunge into the search unhesitatingly, as if they had no other recourse. Do you believe in such a search? Do you believe that there is such a true nature? Is it worth seeking? How would you feel if you searched for it until your dying day and never found it? Will the whole effort have been a waste? These are very real questions, the kind of questions that an individual in this condition will ask, and must ask.

2. *Seeing the Tracks*

圖 跡 見 (二)

Here the oxherder has found hoofprints of the ox, but the ox itself is still not to be seen. Some tracks go off to the east, some to the west. Others start and then suddenly stop, or turn, leading the oxherder into all sorts of dead-end byways. Seeing them, the herder becomes ever more confident that the ox is out there, and now he has an inkling of just how he might proceed. However, he is still confused about which direction to take or which trail to follow.

This scene depicts persons who have come into contact with an enlightened teacher or who have read about Chan practice in Buddhist scripture. They have developed a firm belief that Buddha-nature is real and that Śākyamuni Buddha and the Chan patriarchs experienced it and left valuable teachings to point the way. Realizing that those who attained enlightenment in the past were once ordinary persons like themselves, they develop the confidence that they can accomplish this too. Nevertheless, not having any experience themselves, they are not sure how to proceed. What is the best method to search for enlightenment? Precisely how is Chan to be practiced?

For many people, practice at this elementary stage will be erratic. If results don't come soon, they may begin to have doubts and wish to change their methods. Sometimes they will work hard, at other times grow lax and drop their practice. Frequently, they are not at all sure if they are heading in the right direction, or making any progress at all. Sometimes, efforts will be rewarded and practitioners will feel quite confident, "Yes, I definitely can achieve enlightenment this way." Other times, they will feel completely despondent, often far worse than when they started. With persistent effort, however, they will eventually sort out the confusing array of hoofprints and begin to get an idea, through experience, of just what proper practice entails. They will develop some power and skill in their practice, and with the appearance of these positive signs, their confidence in it will become more firm.

3. Glimpsing the Ox

圖 牛 見 (三)

In the third picture, after searching for a long time, the oxherder gets a glimpse of the ox's tail sticking out from behind a tree. He is overjoyed to spot the ox, but he still does not have the beast in his grasp. In fact, he hasn't even clearly seen it face to face.

Getting a glimpse of the ox is equivalent to seeing one's basic nature for the first time. It is like making a long and exhausting journey to a famous mountain and finally spotting it in the far distance. It is close enough to see, but too far yet to climb. Just how high it is and what the actual terrain is like are still not clear. Proceeding onward, from time to time one may lose sight of it in the trees and mist, but at least one has seen the mountain and knows that it is always there. At this point, faith is firmly established.

In the Chan tradition, we speak of "seeing into one's true nature" (C. jian-xing; J. kenshō) as a form of "enlightenment," or "awakening" (C. kaiwu; J. satori). This idea of Chan or Zen "enlightenment" is quite popular in the West these days. However, as simple as it may seem, a great deal of vagueness and confusion surrounds the term. Few people have a clear idea of what they are referring to when they use it, not to mention what it takes to achieve it. Some books give the impression that it is a simple thing to accomplish, or that it is an easy and instant solution to all one's problems. Actually, a lot of harm can come from too much emphasis on this word, especially when differing interpretations are so abundant. One must be aware that its usages are far from uniform and that they cannot necessarily be equated. Within the Buddhist tradition alone, the term has a wide range of meanings, depending on which Buddhist school, doctrinal system, or text one happens to be studying. Some Mahāyāna scriptures speak of sixteen different levels of insight into emptiness (S. *śūnyatā*), or schemes of the Bodhisattva path that involve anywhere from ten, to thirteen, to even fifty-two stages of development. Any one of these stages may be characterized as a kind of enlightenment, or enlightenment may be reserved for one or two stages that are regarded as key watersheds in the bodhisattva's spiritual development. The Hīnayāna, likewise, distinguishes four stages of sainthood, culminating in the condition of arhat, or complete liberation from saṃsāric rebirth. In both Hīnayāna and Mahāyāna, the criteria for distinguishing different levels of spiritual progress are quite complex and closely bound up with their respective doctrinal systems. There are experiences that may be called enlightenment which are equivalent or far superior to seeing into one's true nature. There are experiences that may be called enlightenment which do not involve seeing into one's nature at all. Thus, while one may be able to draw certain rough correspondences between these different systems, for the most part each understanding of the term "enlightenment" is unique to its particular scheme of practice and must be understood within this context.

The meaning of enlightenment also varies widely among different religious traditions. Many instances of enlightenment may be little more than somatic responses to a particular regimen of practice. Ascetic exercises, breath control, and concentrated prayer may induce visions, intense experiences of joy, or the sensation that the body is light and free. Are such things to be considered bona fide enlightenment experiences? They may, indeed, represent positive signs of progress in the practice: the individual's mind is brighter and more open than usual, and, for a while, this person may feel free of the usual vexations and weaknesses of character. Generally, after a few days, hours, even minutes, the situation will change. Greed, hatred, and the usual afflictions will reappear. Even so, such experiences are valuable. At the very least, they may deepen the practitioner's commitment to the spiritual path. But according to Chan (and the Buddhist tradition at large), they are not enlightenment. They are just feelings, often little more than conditional neurological reactions to meditative postures and techniques.

Be that as it may, in certain respects Chan practice is especially prone to this sort of overinflation or misinterpretation of meditative experiences. Given the traditional reticence of the Chan school to provide any formal discussion of enlightenment, when a beginner hears that Chan espouses a sudden path to enlightenment, it is easy to mistake an unusual meditative experience for enlightenment. There are many people who, when they speak of Chan enlightenment, are actually referring to this sort of shallow, emotional response. Traditionally, such mistakes are forestalled by the presence of a Chan master. Indeed, this is why Chan practice has always taken the form of training directly under an experienced master. If people were to seek confirmation for these experiences from a truly capable Chan teacher, the teacher would more than likely scold them for their presumptuousness. Even if these experiences do represent progress of a sort, to acknowledge false enlightenment does more harm to students than good.

What, then, does the Chan tradition mean by the expressions, "seeing into one's true nature" or "enlightenment"? Seeing into one's true nature is to achieve a mind of perfect equanimity. In its being perfectly equal, this mind is also empty. Emptiness does not mean blank extinction. It means that the ordinary narrow mind of selfish attachment has been seen through and, as a consequence, has momentarily opened forth and vanished. The Chinese word for "enlightenment" (*kaiwu*) is a compound containing the two words to "open up" (*kai*) and "awaken" (*wu*). The barrier between self and other dissolves, or "opens up," and one "awakens" to the all-pervading openness and equality of emptiness. Even the idea of enlightenment itself vanishes. Thus, if a person thinks he or she has been enlightened and is elated over the idea, or feels that he or she has made a great personal accomplishment, the chances are he or she has not really seen into his original nature.

However, even when defined in this way, one should not think of "enlightenment," or "seeing into one's nature" as a single monolithic experience that never changes thereafter, or that it is the same for all people. This is not really what "sudden" enlightenment means. Indeed, even though one glimpses one's true nature, generally one will still be partially blind. In Chan, we speak of this stage as "having opened one eye." One might also describe it as the eye opening for a moment and then closing again.

Imagine walking at night. It is raining hard and pitch black. Suddenly, a bolt of lightning flashes across the sky, briefly illumining the terrain around you. Previously, you groped and stumbled your way along in the dark; but now, because of the lightning bolt, you are aware of your immediate surroundings and direction. You can walk with more assurance, but only for a short distance.

Is this experience a big event? Is such a person a sage, a saint? One could say that during the time that the eye is open, which may be no more than a split-second, this person has gained an inkling of what it means to be a completely enlightened sage. But really, he or she is still just a common person and continues to suffer the same vexations as other ordinary people. Of course, there are people who open their eyes completely and never close them again. But this kind of individual is very rare. For the most part, the initial glimpse into one's true nature will not be very deep; nor will it mean the end of further searching and practice. Be that as it may, this experience does mark an important watershed in a person's practice. One could even say that it is really the beginning of genuine Chan practice. Having had a taste of one's true nature, one will never forget its flavor. From this point on the practitioner will have a keen sense of what vexation is and the direction in which true practice lies. In fact, this is precisely the idea that Chan masters have in mind when they equate "seeing into one's true nature" with "entering the door of Chan."

Such questions about the meaning and nature of enlightenment are extremely important, for they address misunderstandings that potentially can have disastrous consequences. For instance, if a person who has had an "enlightenment" experience believes that he or she no longer has any vexations or no longer needs to practice meditation, he or she may doubt that the experience was of any value when vexations return. It is equally possible, after vexations reappear, that such persons may deceive themselves and others by putting on airs of a Chan master, or by claiming that "vexations are themselves enlightenment," or that "there is no enlightenment to attain."

There are a number of ways a genuine Chan master may help students avoid such pitfalls. One such way is to let them know that, although these initial glimpses into one's true nature are good, they are still very shallow. Practitioners at this stage are like newly hatched chicks. They know enough to open their mouths to eat, but have yet to grow a single feather on their bodies. How can they think of flying at this point? If the fledgling tried to leave the nest, it would tumble to its death or become the meal of a larger animal. If its siblings followed its example, the situation would be even worse. People who have shallow enlightenment experiences and then think they are qualified to practice as they wish or tell others what to do endanger both themselves and others. It must be impressed on these persons that one must continue to work hard at one's practice. This discipline of continued practice is the safe nest for practitioners.

Another way to help such individuals is to remind them of the five precepts: not to kill, not to steal, not to engage in sexual misconduct, not to deceive or speak falsehood, and not to indulge in intoxicants. Truly great masters who are deeply enlightened need not pay deliberate attention to the precepts. Because of their highly developed powers of wisdom and samādhi, they will never be apart from the spirit of the precepts, even, if on occasion, they may seem to contravene them. Their entire being is imbued with selfless loving-kindness and compassion. However, for persons who have just had their first glimpse of enlightenment, the precepts are like the nest that keeps the chick safe. It is dangerous for them to leave the precepts prematurely.

To some people this may seem like a double standard. One hears, for example, of Buddhist groups where monks drink alcohol and call it "wisdom soup." Such activity is often justified by the traditional Mahāyāna Buddhist claims that, for the enlightened person, vexations are themselves enlightenment, or that vexation itself may be used by a teacher as an "expedient device" (S. upāya) to break down a student's narrow conceptions of spiritual discipline. It is true that great masters are keen at targeting a student's attachments and devising methods on the spot to help them. Some of you will already know the tale of how master Nanquan once cut a cat in half as a means to teach his disciples. But, if a lesser master tries to imitate great Chan masters in this way, it leads to problems. I consider myself to be a lesser Chan master, so I am not going to do such things. Indeed, when one really thinks about it, only one great master in a thousand years killed a cat; and even then it was a single occasion. He did not kill cats as a rule. Generally speaking, masters and students alike should maintain the precepts, for the precepts safeguard one's own practice and provide the basis for harmony and trust in the spiritual community. Master Xuyun, who was probably the greatest Chan master in recent history, strictly adhered to the precepts.

A third way to avoid error after the initial glimpse into one's nature is to adhere to the outer forms and rituals of Chan practice. Having definite forms of procedure, attire, and behavior helps to create a better environment in which to practice. Of course, I am mainly referring to monks and nuns, but this holds true for lay practitioners as well. By respectfully maintaining proper ceremonial form and demeanor, a Chan student will not stray from the practice. Nor will his or her actions encourage others to do so. Actually, if a person who has never had a deep enlightenment experience continues to practice hard and adheres to the precepts and all the outer forms, to a certain extent he or she is in a position to help other people. I am sorry to say that, in Taiwan, practitioners do not keep up these outer forms. Today it seems that most practitioners are sloppy in their practice.

Most of all, however, it is one's basic attitude toward practice and enlightenment that is important. I always tell students that they should emphasize the process, not the result. The process of practice itself is really the final result. Thus, one should never be attached to experiences, good or bad.

4. Getting Hold of the Ox

圖 牛 得 (四)

Applying the halter, the oxherder harnesses the ox. Now the beast is in his grip. But the ox is unruly. It bucks the halter and constantly tries to wander off to graze in the fields, so the oxherder must apply the whip and keep a firm hold on the reins in order to restrain it.

One can say that at this point the practitioner has met and come to know the ox in all its fullness. Both eyes are open now. Although they will not close again, at times they may get heavy and not see things clearly. Even so, they are always ready to open up again. Persons at this stage will have had a full experience of their original nature. Nevertheless, the subtle predispositions, or defilements (S. *vāsanā*), that foster vexation still remain in their minds, even though their activity is considerably suppressed. When practitioners at this stage encounter conditions that stimulate these predispositions, vexations will arise and they may lapse. Fearing that they could fall back into their previous condition of moral and spiritual darkness, they redouble their efforts. In heart as well as deed, they become true keepers of the precepts.

Where does such a person stand on the Chan path? Is he or she qualified to teach others? One can say that practitioners at this stage have gained control over their vexations and are able to maintain conformity with their true nature. Thoughts of enmity may from time to time appear, but they will never allow themselves to be driven to harm someone as an ordinary person might do. Thoughts of lust may arise, but such thoughts will not carry over into word and deed. The oxherder has the ox in the harness, and, although it might pull mightily against it, he will not be willing to let it go. This in itself is a great accomplishment, for it means that one has the determination and capability to manage practice on one's own. But one is by no means finished. If one knows of a master who is more advanced, one should continue to study with him or her so that one can make rapid progress. However, if there are no other teachers available and people who are not as advanced come to ask you for guidance, you can and should try to help them.

5. Herding the Ox

This fifth picture is the true oxherding picture. The oxherder, with whip in one hand and reins held lightly in the other, either leads the ox gently along the path or walks alongside it. From time to time, the ox still shows a tendency to stop and nibble the grasses along the road, so the herdsman must be alert and not allow himself to become too frivolous or self-satisfied. But the ox readily responds to command, so the oxherder does not have to struggle as fiercely as he did before. In certain respects, the oxherder does not seem to be expending much effort at all. The ox just appears to follow along. Actually, however, attentive practice continues, but it is now even subtler. It has become part of everyday life and is not so manifestly visible.

圖　牛　牧　(五)

The main focus at this stage is the development of one's power of samādhi. After the initial insight into one's true nature, it is necessary to deepen samādhi, for when vexations do arise, the unshakeable power and calm of samādhi enables one to disperse them quickly. Most important of all, it is through deep samādhi that one reaches down and uproots the suppressed seeds or predispositions of vexation. The method of practice at this point is different and more subtle than the usual *gong'an* or *huatou* practice described in previous chapters. *Gong'an* and *huatou* methods make use of a certain amount of samādhi power—they skirt its surface, so to speak. But they are fundamentally different from true samādhi concentration. One can think of *huatou* or *gong'an* practice as a method for gathering up one's vexations or wandering thoughts and squeezing them all into one concentrated spot, one unified question or problem, until there is no place to push them anymore, at which point they explode. We use the sensation of doubt to focus the mind, draw together these vexations, and concentrate them until they explode. The strength of the explosion depends on the force behind it. When blowing up and bursting a balloon, the balloon may burst into many pieces, or it may only develop a small hole and slowly collapse. It depends on many factors, among them how much force one applies. In *gong'an* and *huatou* practice, the goal is to concentrate the mind, and then—ultimately—to blow this concentrated mind to bits, so to speak.

It is analogous to throwing a rock into water. If a person with keen karmic roots and relatively little vexation uses the "doubt" method, it is like throwing a big rock into a little puddle. The water is scattered and all that remains is the rock. That's the aim of the method. However, if the person practicing has many vexations and doesn't really penetrate the method, then the result will be like throwing a pebble into a lake. There will be a splash, but not enough to displace the water and see the bottom of the lake. Focusing on the *huatou* and the doubt sensation involves concentrating the mind on a single object, just like samādhi practice. In fact, if the doubt is all-absorbing, the explosion at the end will momentarily touch or skirt samādhi; but the experience is not the same as samā dhi proper, which entails the deliberate cultivation of a much deeper, unmoving concentration. Thus, *huatou* and *gong'an* are useful for bringing about and deepening the initial Chan glimpse into one's true nature. Moreover, in some cases— for those individuals of particularly keen capacity—the resulting experience may be quite thorough. But at this later stage of "herding the ox," initial insight must be deepened with sustained cultivation of samādhi proper.

6. *Riding the Ox Home*

圖家歸牛騎(六)

While initial experiences of glimpsing one's true nature are equivalent to *seeing* one's intrinsically enlightened Buddha-nature, they are not the same as actually becoming a full Buddha. To reclaim and fully actualize one's original Buddha-nature is to "return home." Seated at ease atop the ox, one is now securely on one's way back home.

In this picture, the oxherder rides lightly perched on the ox's back. The ox still has a halter, but the reins lay loosely at the oxherder's waist, who plays the flute with a self-absorbed and carefree air. He doesn't bother to guide the ox at all, for the ox is completely tame and familiar with the way home. At this point, practice is effortless, like no practice at all. The individual's six sense faculties are purified of the taint of vexation. When such people come into contact with things in the environment, vexations do not arise. They are lucidly aware of the world around them, intimately aware of it; but the world does not generate feelings of greed or anger in them. People at this level will feel close to all that they see, touch, hear. It is as if body, mind, and the whole world are perfectly complete. It is a Buddha-world, where every object speaks and proclaims the Dharma. There are no words to describe this. Nor is it necessary to describe it. It is just so.

Practitioners at this stage know that practice is still necessary, that there is a mind that needs cultivation and goals still to be reached, so they continue to practice. Practice, however, is effortless. There is no need to urge oneself to practice, no need for one to even deliberate about practice. Nothing can come between oneself and the practice of the path, no matter what happens, no matter what one does. When practitioners reach this stage, they are safe. Precepts, samādhi, and wisdom become part of their being. One no longer thinks or says, "I need to practice." Could people at this stage really do something normally considered evil or a flagrant breach of the precepts? The answer is clear. If samādhi and precepts are truly part of their being, vexations will not be able to influence them to break the precepts. Those who deliberately—out of passion—commit destructive and unwholesome acts would simply not be at the level of the person depicted here in the sixth picture.

7. *The Ox Is Forgotten, but the Oxherder Is Still Present*

圖人存牛忘(七)

In the seventh picture, the oxherder and ox have returned home, but we see only the oxherder. The ox is off sleeping, but where we do not know. Although the ox is not to be seen, the situation is quite different from the first picture, in which the ox was missing. Here, the oxherder sits contentedly at home, in full possession of himself and with no worry whatsoever. At this stage, one no longer perceives vexations to tame or enlightenment to cultivate. Truly, one has reached what sixth patriarch Huineng describes, where attachment and aversion no longer afflict the mind. The practitioner stretches out his two legs and lays down to sleep.

At this point vexation is gone, as well as the determined and anxious personality that struggled with vexation and sought to strengthen enlightenment. Although there is no longer any distinction between inner and outer, nor any tendency to grasp either vexation or enlightenment, practitioners still sense a feeling of "self." One could say that the elementary stages of practice are like learning to swim. At first, people struggle against the water and must work hard to stay afloat. But, by the stage of the seventh picture, the water is gone. The swimmers have become one with the water, so harmonized with it that they are no longer aware of it. Is there still swimming then? At this stage, swimming and self-cultivation, as we might normally understand them, cease, but the person is still there.

There is a story about a monk from the Ming Dynasty (1368–1644) who had no temple of his own or any fixed place to stay, so he just wandered around. One day, he came across a monastery fronted with fine statues of the divine guardian kings who protect the Dharma. Thinking, "What a fine place to rest," he lay down and fell asleep at the foot of the statues. He was snoring loudly when a high government official arrived at the monastery. Hearing the snoring and spotting the monk, the official became enraged. "Who is this?" he cried. "What kind of monk shows such laziness and impropriety!"

The monk woke up and hearing this replied, "It is only I, a monk with nothing to do."

The official retorted, "What! A monk with nothing to do! How can you have nothing to do? You have meditation. You can recite sūtras, do prostrations, or offer prayers. How can you dare say a monk has nothing to do?"

The monk replied, "What does that have to do with anything? Why should I do any of that?"

The official's anger turned to bewilderment at these strange words; and, before long, he realized that this was no ordinary monk. He really was a true monk, a monk with nothing to do.

8. Herder and Ox Both Forgotten

In the eighth picture, neither person nor ox is to be seen. There is nothing in the picture but an empty circle. If the ox represents the awareness of one's true nature, and the oxherder the subjective intention of the practitioner who takes it as the object of cultivation, then it stands to reason that both the ox and the oxherder must disappear when one truly identifies with one's original Buddha-nature. When the subjective self really is self-nature, there can be no sense of a

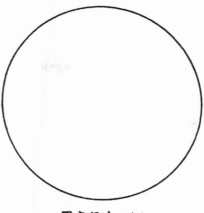

圖忘俱牛人(八)

self-nature to realize or a self that realizes it. As long as there remains a notion of the two becoming one, or as long as there is the concept of a "one" present, it is not really "one." When "one is really "one," there is no sense of "oneness" whatsoever. When self is really the original self-nature, there is no self, no nature. Thus ox and oxherder are actually both unreal. They are a perfect totality, one; and that one is not even one.

Who experiences the original nature or the true self-nature? It can only be experienced when all sense of a distinct self is left behind. If there is still a sense of some original self-nature to be experienced, that is not the true nature. The original enlightened nature exists as an object to those who do not really understand it. For the person who has experienced it, there is really nothing to talk about. One's condition before enlightenment and after enlightenment is different. Before achieving truly deep enlightenment, you only have an image or fleeting memory of what original nature is like. After deep enlightenment, you *are* the original nature. When you reach home and come to complete rest, or you arrive and settle on the distant mountain to which you are journeying, you *become* the home. You *become* the mountain. Is there still a home or mountain to return to? No. At that point, you do not know where home or the mountain is. You do not even think about them.

We talk about and refer to ourselves all the time. Maybe you think that you can grab hold of yourself. Maybe you can grab hold of your nose and say, "This is me, myself." But if it really is you, how could *you* grab hold of something else and say it is you? If it is really you, how could it be objectified as separate from yourself, something other than yourself? So, when we aspire to think or talk about enlightenment and original nature, it must be something other than original nature. It is a reified thought or idea of original nature. When you really are you, and self really is self, there no longer is a self or self-nature. There is no person cultivating and no cultivation that needs to be done. Since there is not even a notion of "oneness," of course there will not be "two." At this point, do you exist or not? Does Chan exist?

There are no words to describe this experience or communicate it to others. In fact, there is no way to even conceive of it. It is utterly different from our normal discriminatory and discursive consciousness. Ordinary consciousness is always conscious of something. There must be a dualistic structure for conscious awareness to take place. It is fruitless to try to grasp the experience of the original nature through words or ordinary mental processes, for it is beyond all concept of big, small, near, far. Since it can only be known after all such relative distinctions are laid to rest, it is damaging to even think of it as absolute. Many people talk about realizing absolute truth or the great unity of all things, but if you experience a feeling of "great unity" or "absolute truth," you are simply at the level of an expanded sense of self, where you experience the world in terms of your own inflated views. This is not the true self-nature that is "no-self," beyond self.

In the seventh picture, there is just the oxherder depicted in repose with nothing to do. Now, in the eighth picture, not only is there nothing to do, there isn't even any person to be in repose. Although the circle in this picture is blank, it would be more appropriate if there were no picture at all. The presence of a circle suggests that there is something still there—a great unity, an absolute. In Chan literature, there are anecdotes in which a disciple asks a question and the master responds by drawing a circle and then erasing it. If you have a circle, then attainment still exists, and that is not true enlightenment.

One would think that this is the end, the highest level attainable in terms of eliminating vexations and achieving wisdom. In some sense this is so, for one has achieved the fundamental wisdom that eradicates the source of all personal vexation. It is the root of Buddhahood. But such wisdom is incomplete. One is yet far from being a Buddha. A Buddha has a deeper wisdom, a powerful function that enables him to respond with great compassion and precision to help undo the vexations of others. Thus, the eighth stage is not the end of the path. The aim of Buddhism is not simply to disappear from life. Should this take place, it is not true Buddhism, nor true enlightenment. It is an unhealthy nihilism that is possibly the product of certain hidden problems.

Some people experience a glimpse of their original nature and then fall prey to very negative attitudes. They become reclusive and shy away from daily life, perhaps even thinking, "The world is useless to me," or, "The sooner I die the better." I have seen quite a few people act this way. Such a mentality is definitely a step off the right path. One woman didn't want to go back to her family or have anything to do with her husband. Another, the chairman of the board of his company, was ready to quit his position and give up everything, including his family. This is wrong. Such people have big problems, problems that did not originate with their glimpse of emptiness, but which existed from before and persist in coloring and twisting their experience. Thus, for certain persons who are mentally or emotionally unstable, an experience of emptiness or glimpse of their true nature can be quite dangerous. It can play into their existing problems in a harmful way. As far as the right path is concerned, it is essential to realize that spiritual development does not end with formless extinction. The *Heart Sūtra* says that "form is emptiness and emptiness is itself form." Actually, the eighth stage leads automatically into the ninth, in which the world of phenomenal distinctions is spontaneously reaffirmed.

9. *Reverting to the Origin and Returning to the Source*

圖源本還返(九)

In the ninth picture, suddenly a spotless world of green hills and blue streams, luxuriant bamboo and dainty plum blossoms, reappears in the circle. It expresses a return to awareness of the manifest world after the deeply interiorized experience of absorption in the oneness of the original nature. When awareness returns, everything is perceived that ordinary persons perceive, but it is not the same as before. This awareness emerges as pure wisdom that illumines everything lucidly and precisely. Whatever it encounters, it sees it for what it is, without the interference of vexation.

There is a famous saying in Chan that in the beginning, before one deeply engages the practice, mountains are mountains and rivers are rivers. Then, at a certain point in training, mountains are no longer mountains, rivers no longer rivers. In the eighth picture, mountains and rivers, person and ox, all vanish. But in the end, mountains are again mountains and rivers are again rivers. The mountains and rivers that are perceived before and after deep enlightenment are the same, but with one important difference. Before enlightenment they are perceived with attachment and discrimination. Now there is no such attachment. At this level all things can be used to help beings on the path to enlightenment.

Yangshan Huiji (807–833), a disciple of master Guishan Lingyu (771–853), once asked the latter, "If everything in the world suddenly appeared before you, what would you do?"

The master replied, "Green is not yellow, long is not short. Each thing abides in its own place. It has nothing to do with me." This is to say, phenomena are perceived, but they are phenomena of other beings, not something that entails any experience of vexation on one's own part. In fact, practitioners at this stage do not think of the world in terms of such dualities as enlightenment and vexation, noumenal principle and phenomenal manifestation. Their sense of self and the external world has changed completely. One will notice that, in the ninth picture, there is no oxherder or practitioner depicted anywhere. Things are just as they are, in and of themselves. The deeply enlightened individual gives them their own existence and assumes his or her own existence, forgetting self entirely and affirming the spontaneous function of the world without feeling compelled by vexation to impose any boundary or confused relationship on them.

However, this is a very subtle point that can be easily misunderstood. Some people may take it wrongly and go to the extreme of assuming that all distinctions and conventions are meaningless and can be dealt with as one chooses. There is no need to be responsible to or for anything. One can take other people's wives or husbands, belongings, and simply do what one wants to do. Actually, this kind of cavalier attitude conceals an insidious and misguided selfishness. To one who is truly practiced, other people's wives and husbands are still other people's wives and husbands. Worldly conventions are still valid and should not be disregarded. At this stage, the practitioner wants what is best for all, wants all things to be just as they are, fully. Because the afflicted self has been transformed, one doesn't have any compunction to treat others in an irregular way.

Of course, there are times when Chan masters do create confusion by saying or doing contradictory things. Usually, this occurs while interacting with students. For example, there is the famous tale of the monk who burned a wooden statue of the Buddha, or the monk who purposely broke his master's leg by rolling a wheelbarrow over it. When hearing these things, people may think they are standard Chan behavior. Actually, their significance is quite different. These are but isolated incidents in Chan history, usually involving a seminal transaction between a master and a student. We do not see disciples, as a rule, behaving like this all the time. A Chan master will act like this in order to certify that the student's condition, at that moment, is not the everyday condition. What is more, such behavior on the part of a student is not characteristic of the ninth stage. It is more typical of the seventh or eighth stage. If I made a habit of going around saying, "Bananas grow underground and ginger grows on trees. Fish fly in the sky and sheep swim under water," people would think that I belonged in a mental institution. The person at the ninth stage honors worldly conventions; he himself has no problem with them whatsoever. One could say that his attitude is quite affirmative: of all the myriad phenomena that surround him, there is nothing that is not perfectly complete, just as it is.

10. Entering the Marketplace with Open Hands

圖手垂鄽入(十)

The tenth and final picture depicts a rotund, smiling, self-contented monk carrying a cloth bag. His hand is outstretched to a destitute old beggar. In an odd way, roles are reversed here. Usually it is the itinerant monk who seeks and receives alms. But, here, the monk is doing the giving. The ordinary person is the beggar, the one who needs and receives. Like Santa Claus, the monk distributes freely from the wealth stored in his bag. This illustrates how the fully liberated practitioner is able spontaneously to generate great compassion and skillful means to meet the needs of living beings. These are natural fruits of progress, not some things calculated or developed for ulterior purposes.

The homeless monk in the tenth picture is a mysterious figure. One does not know who he is or where he comes from. Every place is his home. This illustrates the power of the enlightened bodhisattva to manifest in any form, or take on any personality and walk of life, in order to help living beings. At any time and any place, enlightened ones are prepared to assist others. There is no definite form that they take. They may present themselves as Chan masters, laypersons, or even someone who is despised by others. All of this flows quite naturally from their being. Without artificial calculation, they do what is appropriate to the dispositions and needs of others. Beings who encounter them may develop fixed ideas or images of them, but enlightened bodhisattvas will have no such fixed images of themselves. When an enlightened being takes on a particular incarnation, naturally that form will limit him or her, and there will be only so many people that he or she can help. But they can reappear later, or in another life, in a different form. As far as this enlightened person sees it, however, nothing substantially has changed.

In Taiwan, I know a woman who claimed to have been introduced to the meaning of Buddhism and its practice by her daughter. She was very grateful for this. I asked her how old her daughter was. She said, "Eight years old." I thought, "This must be a very special daughter," so I went to see her. She seemed a very normal little girl. I asked the woman, "Why do you think your daughter 'enlightened' you to Buddhism?"

The woman replied, "Since my daughter was born, various things that have happened to her have steered me toward a deep appreciation of Buddhism. Therefore, I say my daughter is a bodhisattva who has saved me."

What do you think? Is the daughter a bodhisattva? As far as the mother is concerned, she is. Perhaps she actually is a bodhisattva at this tenth level of practice who has taken the form of her daughter in this life. Would you ever be able to know it if she were? You are reading this book, perhaps even practicing Chan. Did anybody influence you in this regard? You may never be able to know for sure just who or what they are. Nevertheless, you should have deep gratitude for what you have been exposed to and what you have learned. Unfortunately, there are a lot of people who won't respect or listen to anyone whom they cannot certify to be the best, the truest master. Most of these people are incapable of learning anything from anyone, even when they are with a great master. Thus we should be grateful, and look upon anybody who helps us in our practice as someone of the tenth stage.

A disciple once asked master Nanquan Puyuan (748–835), "Where will you go after you die?"

He replied, "I am going to the foot of the hill to be reborn as an ox."

The disciple looked puzzled and said, "If you are going to become an ox (which is considered a rather lowly form of existence), can I follow you there?"

The master replied, "Possibly you could become an ox too, but if you do, you must come chewing a sprig of hay."[7] Nothing more was said after that, so it is up to you to contemplate what Nanquan is all about, and why he was going to be reborn as an ox.

Notes

Preface

1. Holmes Welch, *The Practice of Chinese Buddhism, 1900–1950* (Cambridge, Mass.: Harvard University Press, 1967); also idem, *The Buddhist Revival in China* (Cambridge, Mass.: Harvard University Press, 1968). For recent Buddhist developments in Taiwan, see Liying Kuo, "Aspects du bouddhisme contemporain a Taiwan" in *Renouveaux religieux en Aise*, edited by Catherine Clementin-Ojha (Études thematique, no. 6. Paris: Publications de L'École française d'Extrême-Orient, 1997), pp. 83–110; and Charles Brewer Jones, *Buddhism in Taiwan: Religion and the State, 1660–1990* (University of Hawaii Press, 1999).

2. *Jingde chuandeng lu,* in *Taishō shinshū daizōkyō,* edited by Takakusu Junjirō and Watanabe Kaikyoku (Tokyo: Taishō Issaikyō Kankōkai, 1924–1935). no. 2076, vol. 51.458b22–26. *Taishō shinshū daizōkyō* is hereafter abbreviated as "T."

3. *Zhenzhou Linji Huizhao chanshi yulu,* T. no. 1985, vol. 47.498a16–17.

4. On Suzuki's tour and comment, see Holmes Welch, *The Practice of Chinese Buddhism, 1900–1950* , p. 472.

5. These developments are discussed in detail by Holmes Welch, *The Buddhist Revival in China* (Cambridge, Mass.: Harvard University Press, 1968).

6. *Zhenzhou Linji Huizhao chanshi yulu,* T. 47.497c8–9, 499b27–c5, 500a27–c15.

7. *Jingde chuandeng lu,* T. 51.458b22–26; also, see Yanagida Seizan, ed., *Daruma no goroku. Zen no goroku I* (Tokyo: Chikuma shoten, 1969), pp. 31–32.

8. The chapter on "Principles of Harmonizing Body and Mind" is based on Sheng-yen's influential *Chan de tiyan* (Experiencing the Heart of Chan) (Taipei: Dongchu chubanshe, 1980); the chapter on "Buddhist Precepts and Meditative Development" is taken mainly from his *Jielu xue gangyao* (Essentials for the Study of the Precepts) (Taipei: Tianhua chuban, 1978). They are included here for the simple reason that they provide the most effective summation of important aspects in Sheng-yen's system of teaching—the former as a regular part of his intermediate course on Chan meditation, and the latter as preparatory instruction for bestowal of the Three Refuges, five precepts, and bodhisattva precepts. Finally, the subsection of Prerequisites for Chan Practice, entitled, "The Spirit of Chan Practice: Four Conditions Essential to the Practice of Chan," has been adapted from *Getting the Buddha Mind* (New York: Dharma Drum Publication, 1982), a collection of master Sheng-yen's dharma-talks edited by Ernest Heau.

Introduction

1. On the subject of Taixu and his reforms, see Holmes Welch's *Buddhist Revival in China* (Cambridge, Mass.: Harvard University Press, 1968), pp. 51–86. For the Tianning Monastery and its academy, see pp. 115–16.

2. The following account of master Sheng-yen's life is based variously on oral interview and published biographies and autobiographies. The latter include: Sheng-yen, *Guicheng* (Taipei: Dongchu chubanshe, 1968); Sheng-yen, *Sheng-yen fashi xuesi licheng* (Taipei: Zhengchong, 1993); Chen Huijian, *Renjian jiaoyu de Sheng-yen fa shi* (Taipei: Zhonghua foxue yanjiusuo fahui, 1990); Sheng-yen, *Getting the Buddha Mind*, ed. Ernest Heau (New York: Dharma Drum Publications, 1982).

3. Sheng-yen, *Getting the Buddha Mind*, pp. 1–2. Also see master Sheng-yen's short tract on *Guanshibyin pusa* (Bodhisattva Guanyin), Dongchu foxue xiao congkan no. 6 (Taipei: Dongchu chubanshe, 1992), pp. 1–4. Sheng-yen records that, when Langhui taught him this method, he related to him a story about Yongming Yanshou, one of the most renowned scholars and Chan masters of Song Dynasty China. Plagued by obstacles, Yanshou took up practice of the Lotus repentance rite, during which he dreamed that Guanyin poured healing elixir into his mouth. Instantly Yanshou's mind brightened; he acquired illimitable eloquence; and henceforth he was able to write his comprehensive syntheses of the Buddhist teachings.

4. *Guanshibyin pusa*, pp. 1–4.

5. For master Sheng-yen's views on funerary services of this sort, see his *Weishenmo zuo foshi* (Why Perform Buddhist Funerary Services?) (Dongchu foxue xiaokan 4, Taipei: Dongchu chubanshe, 1990). In the latter he states (p. 4), "Originally the vocation of the Buddhist renunciant was by no means confined to the role of delivering the dead; rather, the ultimate objective of the renunciant's salvific effort was the living, not the dead, even though Buddhist practitioners definitely regard with great importance practices that can assist salvation at the approach of death."

6. Sheng-yen, *Getting the Buddha Mind*, pp. 3–4.

7. Ibid., p. 4.

8. Ibid., with supplements from Chen Huijian, *Renjian jiaoyu de Sheng-yen fa shi* (Taipei: Zhonghua foxue yanjiusuo fahui, 1990), p. 27.

9. For details on Yang Renshan (or Yang Wenhui), see Welch, *The Buddhist Revival in China*, pp. 2–22.

10. Sheng-yen, *Getting the Buddha Mind*, pp. 7–8.

11. Ibid., pp. 8–9.

12. See Chen, *Renjian jiaoyu de Shengyan fashi*, pp. 24–25 and 29.

13. See Ven. Yin-shun (translated by Dr. Wing H. Yeung, M.C.), *The Way to Buddhahood: Instructions from a Modern Chinese Master* (Somerville, Mass.: Wisdom Books, 1998).

14. Dongchu was himself responsible for providing the copy of the Taishō Daizōkyō that was used for the Xinwenfeng chubanshe facsimile reproduction of the Dazang jing. In addition to authoring a two-volume history of Buddhism in modern China (*Zhongguo fojiao jindai shi*, Taipei: reprinted in 1974, Dongchu chubanshe, 1989), he also wrote a book-length historical study and survey of Japanese Buddhism, the first of its kind in Chinese.

15. Sheng-yen, *Getting the Buddha Mind*, p. 9.
16. See ibid., pp. 9–10.

Chapter 1

1. From the *Damo lun*, in Yanagida Seizan, ed., *Daruma no goroku*. Zen no goroku 1 (Tokyo: Chikuma shoten, 1969), p. 58.
2. Philip B. Yampolsky, *The Platform Sūtra of the Sixth Patriarch* (New York: Columbia University Press, 1967), pp. 137–38.
3. Burton Watson, trans., *The Zen Teachings of Master Lin-chi* (Boston: Shambala, 1993), p. 53.
4. The term Hīnayāna, or "Lesser Vehicle," is a pejorative designation developed in Mahāyāna circles, where it is used to qualify the Buddha's "earlier" teaching of the Four Noble Truths and arhatship as a doctrine that was preparatory and, hence, inferior to the Buddha's "true" teaching of the Mahāyāna path of the bodhisattva. As a term that is particular to Mahāyāna Buddhist doctrinal discourse, it should not be equated with the historical Theravādin tradition.
5. *Zhonglun* (*Mūlamadhyamaka-kārikā*), *Taishō shinshū daizōkyō* hereafter abbreviated as T., no. 1564, vol. 30.2b.
6. For a full translation see Burton Watson, trans., *The Vimalakirti Sūtra* (New York: Columbia University Press, 1996), pp. 104–11.
7. Watson, *The Zen Teachings of Master Lin-chi*, pp. 31 and 53.
8. Urs App, *Master Yunmen: From the Record of the Chan Teacher "Gate of the Clouds"* (New York: Kodansha International, 1994), p. 94.
9. See, for example, the discussion of the three samādhis and eighteen emptinesses in the *Da zhidu lun*, T. no. 1509, vol. 25.206a–213c and 285b–296b.
10. From *Jingde chuandeng lu*, T. 51.336a–337a.
11. Op. cit., p. 100.
12. Ibid., p. 76.

Chapter 3

1. Supplementary portions of this chapter are taken, *passim*, from Sheng-yen, *Jieluxue gangyao (Essentials in the Study of the Vinaya Precepts)* (Taipei: Tianhua chuban, 1978), e.g., pp. 1–2, 9–10, 256–62.
2. In the case of the eight *uposatha* precepts, precepts six and seven of the ten novice or *śrāmaṇera/śrāmaṇerikā* precepts (which prohibit wearing perfumes and personal adornments, respectively) are combined into the sixth precept. The tenth novitiate precept, which is not included in the list of eight *uposatha* precepts, is the injunction against carrying money. See Sheng-yen, *Jieluxue gangyao*, pp. 95–109.
3. Ibid., pp. 110–17.
4. Ibid., pp. 256–59.
5. Ibid., pp. 259–63 and 283–97. For the *Brahmajāla Sūtra* or *Fanwang jing*, see T. no. 1484, vol. 24; the *Youposhejie jing*, T. no. 1488, vol. 24.

Chapter 4

1. For a listing of the thirty-two marks, see Paul J. Griffiths, *On Being Buddha: The Classical Doctrine of Buddhahood* (Albany: State University of New York Press, 1994), pp. 97–101.

Chapter 5

1. See *Empty Cloud: The Autobiography of the Chinese Zen Master Hsü-yün*, translated by Charles Luk, with revisions by Richard Hunn (Longmead, England: Element Books, 1988), pp. 3–8.
2. *Zhonglun,* T 30.2b.

Chapter 6

1. See the discussion of intrinsic Buddha-nature in *Daban niepan jing,* fascicles 4–10 T. no. 374, vol. 12.385b–428b or T. no. 375, vol 12.625b–673b.
2. Philip B. Yampolsky, *The Platform Sutra of the Sixth Patriarch* (New York: Columbia University Press, 1967), p. 137; also, *Nanzong dunjiao liuzu Huineng dashi shifa tan jing,* T. no. 2007, vol. 48.338b29–c2.
3. On this question, see John McRae, *The Northern School and the Formation of Early Ch'an Buddhism,* Kuroda Institute Studies in East Asian Buddhism, 3 (Honolulu: University of Hawaii Press, 1986).
4. *Ruizhou Dongshan Liangjie chanshi yulu,* T. 48.522b4–9.
5. Yampolsky, *The Platform Sutra of the Sixth Patriarch,* p. 134 fn. 48; also see *Liuzu dashi fabao tanjing,* T. no. 2008, vol. 48.349b22–26.
6. *Jingde chuandeng lu,* T. 51.246a9–10.

Chapter 7

1. See *Linji Huizhao chanshi yulu,* T. no. 1985, vol. 47. For translations of the Record of Linji, see Ruth Fuller Sasaki, *The Record of Lin-chi* (Kyoto: The Institute for Zen Studies, 1975); and Burton Watson, *The Zen Teaching of Master Lin-chi* (Boston: Shambala, 1993).
2. Ruth Fuller Sasaki, *The Record of Lin-chi,* p. 25; *Linji Huizhao chanshi yulu,* T. 47.500b22–24.
3. Sasaki, *The Record of Lin-chi,* p. 20; T. 47.499c6–9.
4. Sasaki, *The Record of Lin-chi,* p. 25; T. 47.500b25–c1.
5. *Jingde chuandeng lu,* T. 51.219a22–b1.
6. Sasaki, *The Record of Lin-chi,* p. 47; T 47.50a19–21.
7. William F. Powell, *The Record of Tung-shan* (Honolulu: Kuroda Institute, 1986). p. 49.
8 *Jingde chuandeng lu,* T. 51.336a20–22.
9. See Yunqi Zhuhong (1535–1615), *Changuan cejin,* T. no. 2024, vol. 48.1104b123.

10. Zhuhong, *Changuan cejin*, T. 48.1103c17–18.

11. See C. C. Zhang, *The Practice of Zen* (New York: Harper & Row, 1959); also, K'uan-yu Lu (Charles Luk), *Practical Buddhism* (London: Rider, 1971).

12. For Xuyun's discussion of *huatou*, see K'uan-yu Lu (Charles Luk), *Chan and Zen Teaching*, First Series (London: Rider, 1960), p. 23.

Chapter 8

1. Yanagida Seizan, trans., *Daruma no goroku. Zen no goroku*, I (Tokyo: Chikuma shoten, 1969), p. 32.

2. Sengcan, *Xinxin ming*, T. no. 2010, vol. 48.376b5–6, 377a3–4.

3. Philip B. Yampolsky, *The Platform Sutra of the Sixth Patriarch*, p. 139.

4. *Zhiguan song*, in *Chanzong Yongjia ji*, T. no. 2013, vol. 48.389b28–29.

5. *Jingde chuandeng lu*, T. 51.321a18–19.

6. Ibid., T. 51.321a20–21

7. *Yunzhou Dongshan Wuben chanshi yulu*, T. no. 1986a, vol. 47.515b17–19.

8. *Ruizhou Dongshan Liangjie chanshi yulu*, T. no. 1986b, vol. 47.522b17.

9. *Fuzhou Caoshan Yuanzheng chanshi yulu*, T. no.1987a, vol. 47.529b25–c7; the exchange also appears in *Jingde chuangdeng lu*, T. 51.336c26–337a9.

10. *Jingde chuandeng lu*, T. 51.321a.

11. *Hongzhi chanshi guanglu*, T. no. 2001, vol. 48.100a–b and 98a–b. For the *Lancet of Seated Meditation*, see Carl Bielefeldt, *Dōgen's Manuals of Zen Meditation* (Berkeley: University of California Press, 1988), pp. 99–101.

12. *Hongzhi chanshi guanglu*, T. 48.78b7–9.

13. Ibid., T. 48.73c9–10.

14. Ibid., T. 48.73c5–13.

15. Ibid., T. 48.73c14–24.

16. Ibid., T 48.74a11–12.

17. Zhiyi, *Mohe zhiguan*, T. no. 1911, vol. 46.56b.

18. Yampolsky, *The Platform Sutra of the Sixth Patriarch*, p. 136; *Nanzong dunjiao liuzu Huineng dashi shifa tan jing*, T. 48.338b19–22.

19. *Chanzong Yongjia ji*, T. 48.389b21.

20. *Hongzhi chanshi guanglu*, T. 48.98b5.

21. *Mozhao ming*, in *Hongzhi chanshi guanglu*, T. 48.100a26–27.

Chapter 9

1. *Jingde chuandeng lu*, T. 51.240c18–23.

2. *Linji Huizhao chanshi yulu*, T. 47.505a–b.

3. Zhu Shi'en, *Jushi fendeng lu*, in *Xuzangjing* (Hong Kong: Hong Kong Buddhist Association, 1967), vol. 147, pp. 857–934.

4. The routines of meditation halls at Jinshan and other major Chinese Chan monasteries during the first half of the twentieth century are described by Holmes Welch in *The Practice of Chinese Buddhism*.

5. *Laiguo chanshi zixing lu* (Taipei: Tianhua chuban gongsi, 1981), p. 15.

Chapter 11

1. See Zhishao, *Rentian yanmu*, T. no. 2006, vol. 48.315c–316a.

2. Yanagida Seizan makes the case that Puming can be identified with Jiang Zhiqi (1031–1104), a certain quasi-monastic teacher who was familiar with Chan teaching, but who also showed strong Daoist leanings. See Ueda Shizuteru and Yanagida Seizan, *Jūgyūzu* (Tokyo: Chikuma shoten, 1982), pp. 251–262.

3. Ibid., pp. 247–257.

4. See, for example, D. T. Suzuki's *Manual of Zen Buddhism* (New York: Grove Press, 1960) and *Essays in Zen Buddhism*, First Series (New York: Grove Press, 1961), pp. 363–76; Paul Reps, *Zen Flesh Zen Bones* (Rutland: Tuttle, 1969); and Philip Kapleau, *Three Pillars of Zen*, revised and expanded edition (Garden City: Anchor Press, 1980).

5. See Yanagida Seizan, *Shinjinmei, Shōdōka, Jyūgyūzu, Zazengi*, Zen no goroku 16 (Tokyo: Chikuma shoten, 1974), pp. 205–24.

6. Philip B. Yampolsky, trans., *The Platform Sutra of the Sixth Patriarch* (New York: Columbia University Press, 1967), p. 180.

7. *Jingde chuandeng lu*, T. 51.259a28-b1.

Index

Abhidharma, 66
"abodes of Brahma," 80–81
Abodes of Mindful Observation. *See* Four
    Stations of Mindfulness
afflictions of the three poisons, x
Āgama sūtras, 9–10
Amitābha Buddha (*Amituo fo*), 8–9, 12, 75,
    76, 77–78, 79, 127
amituo fo, 75, 77
Ānanda, xix
ānāpānasmṛti, 45
Anhui, 3
apramāṇa-citta, 80–84
amṛta, 162
āsana, 34
aśubha-bhāvanā, 71–72
Avalokiteśvara (*Guanyin pusa*), 75–77, 80
Avataṃsaka Sūtra, 9–10, 48, 53. *See also*
    Huayan Sūtra, and doctrinal formula-
    tions

baguan zhai jie, 45, 56
Baizhang Huaihai, 117, 165, 173, 201
Bantetsugyu Rōshi, 11–12
Beitou, 7, 12
biguan, 9
Blue Cliff Record (Biyan lu), 123–24, 200
Bodhi, 180
Bodhidharma, xi–xii, xv, 18, 122, 170,
    189; Indian, 113–14; and "Mind
    Dharma," 114
bodhisattva precepts, 58–59
Brahmājāla Sūtra (Fanwan jing), 58–59
brāhmavihāra, 80–84
breath, meditation on, 67; concentration
    on the *dantian*, 70–71; counting the
    breath, 67–68; following the breath,
    68–70

breathing, forms of, 42–44
Buddha, viii, x–xi, 5, 8–10, 17, 19, 27, 29,
    35–36, 49, 53, 55–61, 63, 66–67,
    98, 100, 104, 108, 110, 112–13,
    119, 127, 163, 164, 166, 167, 177,
    181, 183, 187, 198, 203, 214, 218;
    merits of, 80; nature, ix, xii, xv, 59,
    76–77, 104, 109, 117, 124, 127,
    143, 166, 175–76, 206, 214; world,
    215. *See also* Amitābha Buddha;
    Buddha Mind; Buddhahood; con-
    templation, of Buddha's form;
    Śākyamuni Buddha
Buddha Mind, 49, 74, 76, 79, 80, 84, 110,
    113, 115
Buddhahood, 5–6, 30, 49, 55–58, 60,
    104, 108–10, 111, 145, 180–81,
    191, 203, 218
Buddhism, vii–ix, 2–3, 5, 8, 64, 94, 96,
    100, 108, 110, 122, 125, 165, 196,
    199, 218–19, 222; and compassion,
    103, 132; and doctrine, xii–xiii, 5,
    12, 17, 196, 197; in East Asia, ix–x,
    xiii; four cardinal evils, 55; monas-
    teries, 4, 37, 165 (*see also names of
    specific monasteries*); path of fulfillment,
    60, 71, 102, 107, 166; problem of
    affiliation, x; and reform, 7; retreats,
    173–74; and schools, xii, 11, 113,
    208; scriptures, 45, 115, 137; system,
    146; teachers, 45, 63, 67, 84, 122;
    and teaching, 70, 176; terminology,
    160; and tradition, ix, 17, 20–21,
    27–29, 35, 44, 49, 54, 62, 64, 85,
    102, 110, 111, 164, 208; in the
    United States, 195; values, 189; and
    virtues, 61; vocabulary, xix; and writ-
    ings, 85. *See also* Chan Buddhism;

Prajna (ENLIGHTENING)
'INSIGHT.'
(LIBERATING)

SHUNYATA < GROUNDLESSNESS
EMPTINESS.

Sila - Moral Purity.

Samadi - MEDITATIVE TRANQUILITY, CONCENTRATION.

DHYANA - CLASSES OF MEDITATIVE CONCENTRATION/ABORPTION

Prana - VITAL BREATH. VITAL ENERGY.

Printed in Great Britain
by Amazon.co.uk, Ltd.,
Marston Gate.